THE END OF THE CHINESE DREAM

THE END OF THE
CHINESE
DREAM

WHY CHINESE PEOPLE FEAR THE FUTURE

GERARD LEMOS

YALE UNIVERSITY PRESS
NEW HAVEN AND LONDON

For information about this and other Yale University Press publications, please contact:
U.S. Office: sales.press@yale.edu   www.yalebooks.com
Europe Office: sales @yaleup.co.uk   www.yalebooks.co.uk

Set in Minion Pro by IDSUK (DataConnection) Ltd
Printed in Great Britain by TJ International Ltd, Padstow, Cornwall

Library of Congress Cataloging-in-Publication Data

Lemos, Gerard.
    The end of the Chinese dream: why Chinese people fear the future/Gerard Lemos.
        p. cm.
        ISBN 978–0–300–16924–9 (hardback)
1. Chongqing (China)—Social conditions—21st century. 2. Chongqing (China)—
Social life and customs—21st century. 3. Social change—China—Chongqing.
4. Social stability—China—Chongqing. 5. National characteristics, Chinese. I. Title.
    DS796.C5925L46 2012
    951'.38—dc23

                                                                        2012000174

A catalogue record for this book is available from the British Library.

10 9 8 7 6 5 4 3 2 1

Contents

Illustrations

Acknowledgements

Many of the people to whom I owe an enormous debt of gratitude are of course Chinese and living in Chongqing and Beijing. Mentioning them by name would obviously be unwise. That they are not receiving the recognition they individually deserve in no way diminishes my debt to them or my appreciation of their assistance and advice.

David Foster, now Director of the Croucher Foundation in Hong Kong, made the Wish Tree possible and, during that time, we became good friends. I want to thank him and his wife Connie Lau Foster who were wonderful hosts, extremely skilful at opening Chinese doors and wise counsellors on the limits of the art of the possible. I spent many days and evenings with Simon Kirby in Shanghai and Beijing picking his brains for his encyclopaedic knowledge of China and in particular Chinese contemporary culture and twentieth-century Chinese history. Zhou Xun, from Hong Kong University's department of history also provided a wealth of knowledge from her oral history work: the insights from her collection of first-hand accounts of ordinary people's experiences from around China were invaluable. On our travels in Beijing and Xian, Martin Palmer gave me a wonderfully expert analysis of contemporary and ancient Daoism and its role in contemporary Chinese society. Thanks to all of them. I discussed the ideas I wanted to propound in the book over many long, congenial lunches with John Gray and I owe him many thanks for his penetrating insights and unflinching grip on what is going on not just in China, but throughout the world.

Bi Xiaolan worked closely with me on translating the Wish Tree responses, bringing clarity to the translations and insight into the Chinese way of thinking, at least as expressed in the responses. Francis Bacon accompanied me during much of the fieldwork in Chongqing and Beijing. He was a practical and good-humoured accomplice, managing all the logistics as well as some of the thorny politics. He also undertook much of the early in-depth and rather technical research on Chinese social policy. David Barrie and Kevin Ryan assisted with the Wish Tree and David Barrie and Sara Llewellin worked with me to deliver the training to community workers in Chongqing. Namrata Sandhu did a lot of detailed analytic work on the Wish Tree responses. Haran Sivapalan helped with my understanding of mental health in China. Tom Pile contributed his contemporary knowledge of life in Beijing together with thoughtful reflection on, and meticulous editing of, the manuscript. My great thanks to all of them.

My agent Arthur Goodhart, above and beyond the call of duty, put a huge amount of effort and experience into turning an idea into a book. I want to express my enormous thanks to him. I also want to thank Robert Baldock of Yale University Press who was an enthusiast for the book from the first time we met as well as making a host of wise and challenging suggestions for ways to improve it during the writing. Thanks also to Patricia Williams who was a kind and supportive reader who made lots of practical suggestions. Last but certainly not least, my heartfelt thanks to my partner Paul Crane. As well as providing boundless emotional and practical support while the book was being written, he also did extensive duty as reader, assiduous editor and index-maker.

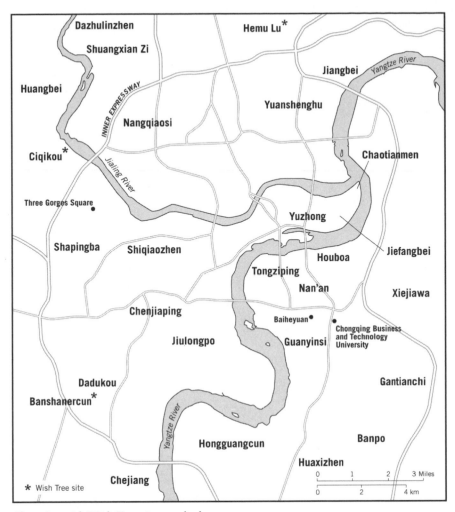

Chonqing with Wish Tree sites marked

Introduction

This book is about the experiences of ordinary Chinese people mostly living in Chongqing, an unglamorous industrial mega-city with an unforgiving climate. The book recounts how they feel about what is happening to them. In a country where officialdom is keen to control the impressions and information that foreigners receive, the book is also the tale of how I found out what thousands of ordinary Chinese people think about their lives and their futures and how that information was taken out of China. What people told me revealed the larger trends in contemporary China which are generally hidden from the view of foreigners, including the media. Drawing on what I found out, I explain the wider social forces at work in China and where they will lead.

After Reform and Opening in 1978 the Communist government was in a rush to burst the dams of sclerotic, state-controlled collectivism in farms and factories and to use global capital to release pent-up economic growth without diluting Party control. The hope was that the remarkable economic growth since the 1980s, new jobs and spreading prosperity could be harnessed to achieve social stability and cohesion after the unremitting turbulence of the Mao years. At the same time the ancient traditions of Confucianism could be revived in a twenty-first-century form to legitimate one-party rule but also to bind the old and new wounds of Chinese society. Prosperity, security and stability was the Chinese dream in the 1980s. Although political reform was indefinitely abandoned after the 1989 Tiananmen protests, since 2002 President Hu Jintao's policies, the 'harmonious society' and the 'scientific path to development' have been meant to ameliorate the insecurities that followed the seismic economic and social transformation.

Despite being endlessly invoked these policies have achieved little. Confucian sentiment is indeed once more making its mark on ordinary people but in terms of consolation, not cohesion, as part of a wider nostalgia. Inequality has grown exponentially. Social protection and family life have collapsed in the cities and the countryside, leaving people anxious and frightened. Hundreds of millions of people are displaced from rural areas to cities with an insecure job, or no work at all, not knowing their fate and fearing the worst. The government has smashed the old 'iron rice bowl' of jobs, healthcare and education. The state and its officials are all too often inefficient, corrupt and unreformed. Citizens can have no expectation of reliable, honest public administration. The absence of the rule of law gives people no right to redress for failures and misdemeanours. The leviathan of the Communist Party has taken control not just of politics, but of big business and the market. The Party won't spend enough money on rebuilding public services and social welfare, focusing instead on creating an under-used infrastructure, keeping the growth rate up and the exchange rate down, building up enormous foreign exchange reserves and shoring up a grossly extended and unsustainable banking system, kept afloat only by ordinary people's savings. Most people are left to fend for themselves, anxious and traumatised. Meanwhile the senior Party hierarchy and their families have become immensely rich plutocrats, turning public assets and revenues into private gain. The People's Republic of China is now run by the wealthy for the benefit of the wealthy. The short-lived Chinese dream of prosperity, stability and security for all has stalled and died.

I found out all this between 2006 and 2010 when I was a Visiting Professor at a university in Chongqing. Getting behind obviously misleading official propaganda and closely controlled encounters with 'the masses', I wanted to find out ordinary people's innermost thoughts, their wishes and dreams. So I built wish trees in down-to-earth communities in Chongqing and then in Beijing. Without restraint ex-farmers and ex-factory-workers told me what they thought and felt. It was a long way from the official mantra that China was becoming a 'moderately wealthy' country under the benevolent leadership of the Communist Party. The *laobaixing* (literally the 'old hundred names', but colloquially used to mean ordinary people) were volubly critical. People protest about what is happening to them and constantly resist. The lack of political freedom catches the eye of Western commentators but ordinary Chinese people know – and will tell those who ask – that their problems are much more complex and difficult to solve than that. Only a few can ever benefit from the new opportunities. Most are anxious and scared about what might happen to them without a job, healthcare, security or family support in old age and with no safety nets. They pray with a desperate devotion, reviving old mysticisms and cultivating new ones; they save as much as they can, but they can never save enough. Some numb the pain by taking their fears and frustrations out on themselves – even committing suicide. A long, dark shadow of fear and trauma has spread across Chinese society. Chinese people are deeply insecure about themselves and their future just when the rest of the world has become star-struck by the apparent prospect of China's imminent glory.

CHAPTER 1

Getting Nowhere in China

The form is familiar to every official foreign visitor to China. On arrival for a formal meeting the visitors are shown into a VIP suite. Huge identical armchairs are arranged around three sides of a square. At the centre sits the most senior Chinese official next to his illustrious foreign guest. A small coffee table and floral display separate them. The assembled officials and secretaries distribute themselves around the remaining armchairs in order of precedence. The host begins with a long, prepared speech. After his (it's rarely her) effusive welcome to the visitors his remarks may follow the expected lines, or he may just say what is uppermost in his mind. This first shot often lasts an unbroken twenty minutes. It has to be matched, sight unseen, by an equally long, formal, detailed and supposedly coherent response. The visitor must think on two mental levels simultaneously: absorbing the complicated opening gambit and preparing a sensible response. Concentration often fails, so the response turns out to be unpredictable, rambling and full of non-sequiturs. The host then responds to the confused visitor and so the meeting meanders into a bewildering and inconclusive spiral. No one else in the room joins the conversation unless invited; a rare outbreak of informality. Interpreters complicate the already problematic situation. A long speech in Chinese may be recounted in an alarmingly short translation, creating the obvious suspicion that much of the original statement has been ignored. Similarly, the carefully balanced and nuanced response often receives an inexact and incomplete translation. An army of anxious flunkeys fluster around distractingly, paying little attention to the proceedings. The unwary visitor concludes that most of these meetings are formal, formulaic and futile, and is left to wonder how anything ever gets decided.[1]

In January 2006 I visited China for the first time to meet academics and officials involved in social policy. I travelled to Beijing, Shanghai, Guangzhou, Shenzhen and Chongqing. The encounters with government officials and intellectuals followed this dispiriting formal format – except for one. In Chongqing in January 2006 I attended a seminar at a rapidly expanding university south of the city. This was an unusually free-form and animated academic seminar. Unlike the usual stiffness and structure the scene was recognisable from universities anywhere: a bare, scruffy meeting room; a wobbly projector; out of focus, incomprehensible graphs on a crooked screen and a group of casually dressed middle-aged men and women in a heated argument all claiming that the evidence, as well as history and philosophy were on their side. The meeting was obviously not stage-managed.

The animated debate was about whether the government was deliberately starving some parts of the countryside of investment, particularly funds for schools, to force the peasants to move to the city with or without official household registration papers (*hukou*). The free marketeers suggested that generous provision of public services and welfare in the countryside would simply encourage people to stay put whether or not they had a job or any prospect of getting one. Since there was already a massive labour surplus in the countryside, this was obviously a dead end for millions of people and a tremendous waste to the economy. To an economist generous welfare was, in other words, a moral hazard. One professor, herself the daughter of a farmer,[2] argued firmly in a loud, excited voice, the colour in her face rising, that central government had in effect decided to starve the countryside of funds for education and public services because they saw no point in educating peasants if they wouldn't be able to contribute to the economy. This was inhumane and despicable in her view, leaving the farmers with no reason to stay in the countryside and nowhere else to go. Another even more eminent professor, a thin man in his eighties sipping tea continuously from his own flask, argued that the authorities obviously did not want farmers to move to the city, because they authorised aggressive harassment and expulsion of street vendors and porters by much-loathed city enforcement authorities (*chengguan*). Most of the evicted street vendors were rural residents without household registration. With no proper papers from the authorities migrants cannot

get a job in the formal labour market or access to public services so
their presence in the cities is semi-illicit, making them a soft target for
official bullying and easy to remove. The two professors – somewhat ellip-
tically – were in dispute over one of China's biggest and most intractable
economic and social policy issues. Far more people live in the countryside
than farms can support, but there's nothing for them to do in the cities.
This was my first encounter in China which felt like an open debate with
few political holds barred, even with a foreigner present. It was most
refreshing.

The academics explained how responsibility for providing and paying
for education and welfare had shifted to local authorities. This had created
great inequalities. The government was also shifting the balance of obligations for education, health and pensions from the state and state-owned
enterprises to local government, companies and individuals. Millions who
were 'lay-offs' from state-owned enterprises could no longer rely on the
free education, healthcare, a job for life and the pension they were promised in the old days. With the European experience of closing loss-making
heavy industry in mind, the academics asked me what I thought the consequences of all this might be. Because I have no talent for inscrutability, my
scepticism about these welfare plans was evident. The proposed approach
of channelling welfare mostly through companies and employers would
leave those outside the formal labour market with minimal state handouts
administered by poorly funded local authorities. That would, I speculated,
incubate a host of other social problems which would soon become intractable. I explained that the European experience of social welfare, while
eradicating the harshest experiences of post-war deprivation, had in many
ways been discouraging. Regardless of how wealthy or relatively equal a
country or society becomes, and even during labour shortages, a residual
group seems to remain unemployed and dependent on welfare. This group
cannot or will not find paid work or become self-reliant.[3] Demand for
welfare grows inexorably. Eventually it becomes enormously expensive
and, in bad economic times, unaffordable. The clamour for cutting welfare
expenditure becomes persistent and impossible to ignore but the problems
don't go away.

Long-term unemployment is bad enough, but the social consequences
are even more serious and unpleasant. This excluded group rapidly grows

distant from the mainstream of society. Self-destructive behaviour becomes the norm, such as taking drugs and committing crimes for immediate gratification, or at least numb amnesia, at the expense of long-term self-interest. As successful people leave poor areas, the neighbourhood becomes a 'sink estate'; a no-go area for the talented and ambitious, compounding the exclusion of those that remain. These neighbourhoods have few economic opportunities and the heart is cut out of family and community life. The crime and violence that inexorably grow in such 'badlands' mostly consists of those left behind fighting among themselves. My own research had shown that policing and law enforcement rarely permanently eradicated this kind of crime and violence. At best symptoms were removed without treating causes. Many perpetrators of crime and violence had mental health problems or came from dysfunctional families in which parental control had collapsed. Many more serious criminals were tied into complex networks of drugs, gangs and prostitution. These underlying problems had also to be addressed along with the cultures and economic structures that had spawned them. Welfare wasn't enough.

Soon after the British general election in 1997, with the sociologist Michael Young I published a book called *The Communities We Have Lost and Can Regain*,[4] written in part to influence the incoming Labour government's plans. In the UK the industrial collapse of the 1980s had hollowed out labour markets and, inevitably, the communities that supported them. Once the factories and docks closed, the residents saw no future for themselves. They might previously have risen to the managerial ranks or, if they had a more belligerent bent, become union leaders or local politicians. Without these prospects the most resourceful and gifted had got up and gone. Left behind were those with little or no get up and go: the old, the infirm, the feckless – and the recently arrived immigrants.

Our book argued that much more was needed to understand the invisible social dynamics of these communities. Only then could their residual capabilities be rebuilt. The alternative was to demolish these estates and 'regenerate' the area with office blocks, shopping malls and art galleries. Communities would simply be scattered. Those with little enough would be left with nothing, seeking to make a new start somewhere else without friends or family nearby and without the education or skills to join the postmodern 'knowledge economy'. The ugly neighbourhoods might disappear, creating an illusion of progress, but the people who had lived there would be no better off and, worse still, might restart the cycle of deprivation and exclusion elsewhere, beset with the same problems of crime and violence. In social terms nothing useful would have been achieved.

In the past, I told the academics, I had arranged short exchange visits between people from the slums of the Philippines, India and South Africa and those who lived in poor neighbourhoods in the UK.[5] The dirt-poor people from the global south, who lived near rubbish tips, by railway lines and in shanty towns, all said they were shocked by the loneliness and listlessness of the lives of welfare-dependent people in the UK. Generous financial handouts were received, but life's richness was absent: no company, no sharing of food, no family reciprocity, no neighbourliness and, above all, no weddings. A slum dweller from the Philippines had asked me why weddings had been abolished in these communities. I explained they hadn't been abolished; it was simply that nobody bothered any more. She looked astonished and appalled. My Chinese listeners were appalled too. On the basis of European and American experience of welfare, I warned, China should be careful what it wished for. A little classical economics went a long way in social destruction. Following this extended exchange we all went out to lunch in a restaurant for the faculty on the campus. Toad and turtle, which are recalcitrant in their adhesion to chopsticks and were a new experience for me, were on the menu.

Our discussions continued throughout the afternoon. I was asked to tell them about some of my research experiences. Since I had painted a rather bleak picture of British cities before lunch I now pursued a slightly different tack. I told them about a place where the authorities imagined that the problems were much worse than they truly were. The Aylesbury estate in south-east London is one of the biggest municipal housing project in Europe with 3,000 homes and 10,000 residents. By the 1990s it had become a notorious 'ghetto'. Built in the 1960s, its rectangular concrete blocks with thousands of regimented windows and balconies looked out on a six-lane highway and a concrete flyover always busy with traffic that was often at a standstill. In the inhumanity of its scale and its utter disdain for the natural environment it would not have disgraced the more grandiose fantasies of megalomaniac Soviet urban planners. Inevitably the area boasted the full repertoire of contemporary social evils: crime, unemployment, drug dealing, ethnic tension, broken families and children with one parent or none. Opposite the offices of the Department of Health, the estate was in the direct line of vision of some of the most powerful politicians in the British government. It was a constant reproach to the powers that be. Successive governments had made plans to demolish and redevelop the estate. All had been thwarted by local resistance. Officials were baffled by the apparent perversity of the residents. After his election victory in 1997 Tony Blair made a speech on the estate about his new government's ambitious plans to tackle social exclusion and neighbourhood collapse. Such a well-known 'failure' of municipal housing and urban planning was the perfect backdrop, eloquently symbolising the problems that his fresh government was intent on eradicating. The plans he announced and the enormous expenditure that would accompany them were to be totemic of New Labour's social ambitions.

The local authority which owned the Aylesbury estate commissioned me to find out what people thought of living there; in particular, why they were so opposed to demolition, which seemed the obvious solution to the hideous ugliness and social breakdown. I decided to do a house-to-house survey, with local people helping as volunteer researchers. The survey explored how residents felt about the place and the people, asking seemingly banal questions; for example, did they know their neighbours? Did they take their neighbours' parcels in if they were delivered when the neighbours were out? Did they have relatives living on the estate? How many friends did they have locally? Who looked after their children if they were at work? And so on. I had honed these questions in many settings to test the strength of community feeling.

Contrary to the popular image of a terrifying, crime-ridden ghetto, the survey uncovered several vibrant communities on the estate. A long-standing community of white people had lived in south-east London all their lives and had strong historic ties to the now defunct docks in Rotherhithe and Bermondsey on the south side of the River Thames from where Britain had once dominated the world's trade. Their extended families went back generations in that area of working-class London. They were now old people living on pensions, but still bore the distinctive hallmarks of white working-class culture in the old docks. They were parochial, inward-looking, reliant on one another. They had a love of song and an attractive disdain for their lily-livered betters in Britain's seemingly ineradicable social hierarchy. In the 1970s the estate had become unpopular and 'hard to let'. Impoverished young artists, children of 1960s urban libertarian values, were given flats at cheap rents because no one else wanted them. Now middle-aged, many of them had become successful artists, as well as partners and parents. Middle age had tempered, but not destroyed, their alternative perspectives. They liked their flats, even if they were ugly from the outside. Inside, the rooms were big with plate-glass windows along one wall that allowed light to stream in; perfect as studios for painting and sculpture. In the 1980s and 1990s many immigrants had moved in, from West Africa mostly. Ambitious, God-fearing young couples with small children were studying hard for professional qualifications while working equally hard as taxi drivers or cleaners in hospitals. Their ambition was to get out of municipal housing, buy a house with a garden in a leafy suburb, start their own businesses and give their children a good enough education for them to join the professions. All the while they maintained strong links with their family back home, some of whom relied on their remittances. On a Sunday morning the local Methodist church was packed with smartly dressed, socially conservative black people. Without much money, their lives were hard but hopeful.

The well-known problems of drugs and crime were endemic on the estate but it turned out that most emanated from squatters and illegal occupiers living in specific blocks of flats. The troublemakers needed to be evicted en masse and fairly cheap and superficial improvements made to the lighting and appearance of public spaces, stairwells and walkways. I thought the estate, which was structurally sound, could easily and cheaply be turned into a very successful urban neighbourhood. It might be an eyesore to some, but those who lived there liked their lives and their communities. Some even liked the buildings. Opposition to demolition and upheaval was, as it turned out, all too easy to explain. I wrote a report detailing all this. The local authority debated the findings at length, seeking reasons to ignore the unwelcome conclusions. They hoped for a justification for demolition or, at least, some suggestions of ways to persuade local people that getting rid of the estate was the best bet. Undaunted, they ignored my conclusions and announced grandiose plans to demolish the estate at vast cost and over a twenty-year timescale. There was another obstacle. A majority of the residents had to approve these plans before they could go ahead. Unsurprisingly, the council lost the ballot by a huge majority and the great redevelopment plans were once more scuppered.

The leitmotif of this tale is that virtually all social policy, even if well intentioned, well designed and supported by unlimited resources, always elicits conflicting reactions and undesired, unintended consequences. The best laid plans are rarely a match for the power of social arguments and political pragmatism that will undoubtedly be ranged against them from competing directions. The result is rarely consensus; almost always compromise and muddle. Such is the lot of the social policy analyst. Economic and foreign policy are not, I had found, much different or better. These experiences had taught me the wisdom of focusing not just on devising policy, but on emphasising with equal force the means of effective implementation and, in particular, the skills and training of junior functionaries who were theoretically responsible for turning plans into reality.

My hosts took considerable comfort from the deficiencies of UK civil servants and policy-makers; academics are invariably consoled by the reassuring discovery that others also have their great insights cast aside by the foolish and cynical powers that be. That this was a global experience, not just a feature of Communist China, was heart-warming indeed. Our day was topped by a convivial dinner in the university faculty restaurant. As we sat down we were handed surgical gloves for handling the goose feet while sucking the juice out of the webbing. Every single item on the menu was from some bit of a goose. In conversation, the senior people in the research centre suggested I might be well placed to advise on some of the research and training activities they were undertaking for the municipality. I took this to be mere politeness but said I'd be happy to help, confidently expecting nothing to come of it.

When I got back to the UK the international office of the university contacted me and asked for my curriculum vitae, which I sent. A few months later they contacted me again, after some inevitable bureaucratic delays in getting the approval of the Ministry of Education in Beijing, to ask me to become a Visiting Professor. I agreed and plans were made for me to visit a few months later, in July 2006. On a boiling hot day in the middle of one of the worst droughts in Chongqing's history an impressive red certificate embossed in gold Chinese characters was presented to me at a good-natured reception with lots of inquisitive postgraduate students eager to try out their English on the exotic new foreign professor.

I wanted to undertake a research project to demonstrate qualitative research techniques, rarely used in China, to postgraduate social sciences students. One possibility was interviewing people who had lost their homes as a result of the building of the Three Gorges Dam. The gigantic dam was the cherished ambition of former Premier Li Peng (1987–98) and had previously had Mao's enthusiastic support. It was, by any standards, a remarkable engineering achievement but it had been beset by persistent controversy. The environmental consequences were untold and possibly disastrous. There had been irrepressible allegations of large-scale corruption and at a conservative estimate more than a million people had lost their homes and land; in many cases without, it was alleged, adequately or honestly distributed compensation. All research needs official permission, however, and foreigners undertaking unsupervised primary research was unheard of; out of the question, in fact. All social investigations involving foreign nationals must be conducted by organisations approved by the Division for the Administration of Non-Governmental and Foreign-Related Surveys. Their names are recorded and licences issued. The regulations of 2000 and 2001 say that groups or individuals from outside the People's Republic of China must ask Chinese organisations to conduct statistical research on their behalf.[6]

So surveys were off the agenda. However, permission was granted for me to visit communities to meet local officials and, I hoped, local residents. This was better than nothing. If all went well, it might be possible to be more ambitious. Everyone told me that whatever the rules said many things became possible in China once one had acquired *guanxi*,[7] contacts and relationships. I was to be accompanied by academic colleagues and an entourage of graduate students whose skills in qualitative research would theoretically be improved by observing my conduct of interviews. Some neighbourhoods we were to visit were in Chongqing and others were in the towns, cities and villages along the Yangtze River towards the Three Gorges Dam. In October 2006 I returned to Chongqing and went, with students and academics, to a village outside Wanzhou, a small fairly remote city on the

Yangtze. Large sections of the city had literally been moved up the high, steep river bank.[8] All such visits begin with a briefing from officials. Upcountry these are rather different to the VIP suites in ministries in Beijing. Here in the dusty, unused community meeting room portraits of Marx, Engels, Lenin, Stalin and Mao Zedong looked sternly down on those assembled. The most senior local official, a short, thin man with a harsh, suspicious expression, fired off a staccato and monotonous stream of policies and statistics about the help poor people were receiving. They had been given new land, re-trained and received financial compensation. If they remained destitute (to the sceptical satisfaction of the authorities) they received a small state cash handout, the so-called Minimum Living Standard, about *RMB*200 a month.[9] While all this was briskly read out in a bored tone some of the other officials feigned passing attention. Others walked over to the window and stared out with their hands behind their back, their faces blank. Several made calls on their cellphones. One slowly turned the pages of a newspaper. Indifference evidently was not thought bad manners. This briefing was long-winded, unilluminating and largely incomprehensible even after extended cross-examination. The suspicion formed in my mind that there might be something to hide which would prove frustratingly difficult to find out.

A short walkabout followed. We were instructed 'No photo!' – awakening further suspicious thoughts. The students happily ignored this sanction and snapped away on their cellphones, so I followed suit. The local officials exchanged nervous glances. Soon they told me to stop. I was not just an innocuous graduate student. The village had expanded, with new houses for people displaced by the rising Yangtze. These new houses had flat roofs and were covered with cheap, shiny, ceramic, white tiles. The staring but friendly local people lined the street. No foreigner had ever visited here before. We were invited into one of the farmers' houses. He had, naturally, been selected for this honour. Apparently he and his wife and child had lived further down the valley but had been displaced by rising waters. In the suspiciously large flat above an enormous garage cum grain store, the plastic wrapping had not been removed from the mattress. There were no sheets on the mattress or any evidence that anyone had ever slept in the bed. An enormous television and a stereo with huge speakers looked similarly virgin. It was clear that nobody lived in this flat. It was just a false propaganda showpiece, designed crudely to mislead. These timid people at least had the good grace to look nervous as if they were not really convincing themselves, let alone persuading the listener.

The couple who had been instructed to say they lived there confirmed that they still farmed a small plot of land. They were also attending the skills training centre in the village. All in all, they claimed implausibly, they were quite happy with how things had turned out. My incredulity was expressed in uncharacteristic silence. The training centre was up the road in a disused, unconverted factory building. The courses were managed by another local farmer, who looked a good deal more prosperous than the one living in the brand new flat. He was not a new arrival displaced from lower ground by the flood waters; he was a long-time resident of the village and lived in an old flat. As well as running the training centre he had farmland on the side of the valley below. He had bought more land from less industrious local farmers, expanding his own holding and wealth. He also ran the village grocery and his daughter worked in a factory in Guangzhou. His *guanxi* was obviously excellent if he had been given permission for such diverse entrepreneurial activity. All other spontaneous conversation with the local citizenry was politely but assiduously prevented by circling officials, as relentlessly attentive as well-trained and obsessive sheepdogs. Before long the official car with a special number plate and darkened windows whisked us away and transferred us to a private room in a restaurant. The local officials were relieved that the visit had passed off uneventfully and delighted that they could now join in an excellent meal along with plenty of alcohol at official expense; paid for in other words by taxes on the universally poor local people.[10]

I had encountered some commonly experienced trends in contemporary Chongqing intellectual life. A vibrant and surprisingly open academic and policy debate collides with a slow-moving, bureaucracy absorbed with its own vested interests and rivalries with little interest in social trends or the outcome of policy sent down from Beijing. Implementation is left to hard-hearted, corrupt Party officials, long devoid of ideological fervour. As the Chinese saying goes, heaven is high and the emperor is far away (*tian gao huang di yuan*). Leadership rivalry and sclerosis alongside corrupt administration are hardly new features of Chinese society: their roots extend deep into history, prefiguring the Communist takeover of 1949.

The new thing since the 1980s was the rapid and, as far as social cohesion and welfare protection are concerned, disorganised and destabilising pace of change.

More prosaically, the evidence of my own eyes was making me sceptical. Though I had received numerous official briefings and indeed met a few ordinary people, the encounters had always been so circumscribed I was sure I had not heard or seen anything approaching the truth. I felt, like so many foreigners before me, I was getting nowhere in China. I had heard so many rumours and so much gossip about official incompetence and corruption – some of it freely admitted by the authorities and reported in the newspapers – that I remained highly sceptical that the policies to support people through economic transformation were really working, whatever the official blandishments. Since nothing in human history approached the scale of transformation under way in China, the number of casualties and the depths of their travails must be enormous. I was also sure, on the other hand, that however seismic and problematic the upheaval had been, people would have proved resilient and resourceful, qualities the Chinese have many times had to draw on in the twentieth century and before. Getting permission to ask penetrating questions and creating an environment in which people could speak freely in response had so far defeated my professional ingenuity. If I wanted to know the thoughts and feelings of the *laobaixing* I would have to think of a more creative approach that would elicit large amounts of reliable information. The difficult conundrum was that it would also have to be an activity for which official permission would be given. But before embarking on the challenge of devising ways to excavate the truth about China's changing society from the thick and deliberately misleading strata of official propaganda, secrecy, denial, dishonesty and obfuscation I needed to get to know the city of Chongqing better, which is far off the foreigner's beaten track. The next chapter is about the city. I also needed to understand much more about the economic and social changes that had taken place since the 1980s. That is set out briefly in Chapter 3 as context for what ordinary people subsequently told me about their hopes and fears.

CHAPTER 2

Chongqing

Far inland 1,500 kilometres (around 900 miles) to the west of Shanghai at the confluence of the mighty, muddy Yangtze River and its greener tributary, the Jialing, stands Chongqing, a vast, explosively expanding, industrial metropolis in south-west China. Historically Chongqing was a strategically placed river port connecting outward-looking Shanghai to China's rural, authentic chilli-fuelled Wild West. The Nationalists established their wartime capital in Chongqing when the Japanese occupied Shanghai. For a while it was a cosmopolitan city, but nowadays, with the political centre of gravity back in Beijing and the business capital established in Shanghai, change comes later and slower to Chongqing. Nevertheless, the true hardy, resilient, unsentimental, stoical and superstitious Chinese character is to be found away from the coastal cities. Even with its authentic Chinese atmosphere, Chongqing feels like an open and dynamic place because of its long history of trade and exchange. Since 1998, having been designated China's fourth city (after Beijing, Shanghai and Tianjin) because of its relative proximity to the strategically important Three Gorges Dam, Chongqing has been given the brief of economic development for south-west China. It has expanded to become one of the world's mega-cities. Thirty-one million people, considerably more than the population of Sweden and the Netherlands put together, live within its municipal boundaries.

Deep in the rocky, wooded valleys of the two rivers the city is surrounded by mountains. Extreme natural humidity darkened and thickened by pollution creates the brown fog that blankets the city most of the year. Bright days are rare; the moon is hardly ever visible at night. Day after day the mountains are obscured from view. In winter the temperature stays well below freezing and cold, wet fog penetrates the bones. Summer temperatures rise far above 40 degrees Celsius. Summer heat and humidity bring discomfort, if anything, more extreme than the winter.

At the old centre of the city is the *Jiefangbei* (meaning liberation monument), an obelisk-shaped clock tower, a monument to the Communist Liberation in 1949. Early in the morning, rain or shine, the elderly still gather around the clock tower for *taiji*, the traditional, slow-moving, exercise ritual drawn from martial arts. But most of the rest of the area, which takes its name from the monument, has become futuristic and pulsating. The streets around the monument are pedestrianised. The pavement is made of ceramic tiles, grey-white and shiny; slippery when wet. At night huge neon advertising hoardings light up the street scene as if it is permanent daytime. Young police officers patrol on rollerblades or in electric golf carts. Chongqing's first Starbucks and Pizza Hut are in the square around *Jiefangbei*, as is a large but mostly deserted Emporio Armani.

Out of respect for China's 'liberation' by the Communists in 1949, planning rules used to prohibit buildings taller than the monument, but since the 1990s the area has been almost completely rebuilt in high-rise concrete, glass and steel. The few remaining old brick-built five- and six-storey blocks are being demolished and replaced with 20- or 30-storey skyscrapers. Many of the new buildings look good from the outside, better still from a distance and best of all when lit up at night by high-tech lights. By contrast, close up on a cloudy day shoddy building standards are all too visible. Interiors are poky and shabby. Light switches are crooked and paint applied too quickly, before the plaster dried, flakes off here and there. Small red pagoda-roofed temples with walls blackened by candle smoke and incense cling on, tucked between building sites and skyscrapers, like some revered whispers from the past.

The best views in Chongqing are from Chaotianmen, the peninsula at the confluence of the rivers and not far from the liberation monument. This was once the landing stage for the frantic comings and goings of river traffic, but river freight has been in decline, especially since the construction of the Three Gorges Dam between Chongqing and Shanghai. Now only the passenger ferries taking tourists to the Three Gorges gather at the jetties along with a few boats turned into multi-storey restaurants. Goods brought in by boat along the rivers used to be carried up by the street porters, the *bang bang* men with bouncing and bending bamboo poles on their shoulders. The goods arrive mainly by road now but the *bang bang* men and the wholesale market are still there.

The wholesale market at Chaotianmen is in a warren of harshly lit warehouses on both sides of a busy street, expanding higgledy-piggledy up steps leading off the main streets. Entire shops are given over to selling a single item: bras or wigs, socks or underwear. Hundreds of each item are displayed in closely packed rows. The modern retail experience of brands and design is absent. Prices are by negotiation. Russian and Chinese traders operating along the Mongolian border buy in bulk. The shopkeepers look aghast and angry if a customer wants to buy only a single T-shirt or one pair of trainers. Up the steps and off the main street the shops and stalls sell a profusion of bright red lanterns for New Year celebrations and packets of red envelopes (*hong bao*) for gifts of money to children and newly married couples. At the top of the steps food sellers serve bowls of noodles and dumplings out of steaming woks for a few *kuai*[1] from stalls in the street. The great Chongqing delicacy is *dandan mian*, fresh noodles still smelling of flour with chilli oil, chopped pork and spring onions, particularly warming for breakfast on a damp winter morning. Vegetables are sold down the shady side alleys. There is a huge underground refrigerated market for fish and meat. The physical structures may have been rebuilt piecemeal over the years, but the bustling, unsmiling commercial atmosphere of bargaining, selling and buying has not changed for centuries.

Everywhere in Chongqing the rush for the new is evident, but the old spirit of place and people remains tenacious – at least for the moment. Chaotianmen is not the only unchanging market in the city. Smaller markets are squeezed in between construction sites and new buildings all over the changing face of Chongqing. They have been at the centre of most neighbourhoods' way of life for centuries. Just off the main square of *Jiefangbei* down a narrow street behind the skyscrapers is a flower market. On both sides of the road are buckets of highly scented lilies and roses. When the water level abated the river plain used to be the perfect place to grow exotic flowers. They flourished in Chongqing's hot humid climate. Nowadays they are grown en masse in greenhouses.

A short way down the street an older world opens up. A complex network of narrow streets and steps spidering outwards in several directions forms a local food market. Outside one small shop living ducks are tightly packed in rows on metal shelves. Tied together by their feet, they cannot escape. Opening and shutting their beaks they gasp for air, water and freedom. In China, as in all hot countries, people like their food fresh, especially meat. Dead animals heat up – and go off – fast. Live animals have an inbuilt cooling system. Another bamboo cage contains chickens tightly packed; yet another one rabbits. One shop has live pigeons for sale. These, unlike the ducks, chickens and rabbits, may not be destined for the dining table. Many Chinese people are avid pigeon-fanciers. A home-made pigeon house is precariously balanced on the roof of many an old home, from where pigeons are released with tiny humming whistles attached to their tails. On large wet wooden boards live eels are pulled out of plastic water tanks, stretched out to prevent them wriggling and deftly slit and skinned from end to end in one rapid stroke of a sharp knife. The shopkeeper picks up large live toads by the midriff, squeezing to check their juiciness and making their tongues pop out, then places them in small, thin plastic bags. There they will shortly suffocate. They will be recently dead and still fresh when they reach the cooking pot. Housewives bustle from stall to stall, selecting the best produce, haggling now and then. Sacks of dark red Sichuan dried chillies (with their special lip-freezing properties) are stacked outside many shops. These are used lavishly to cook, among many other delicacies, *Mapo doufu*, a delicious combination of meat or fish and *doufu* (bean curd), cooked in oil suffused with chilli. Some fruit stalls have boxes of pomelos, a large citrus fruit bigger than a grapefruit. The ones at the top are half-peeled to show their ripeness and juiciness. At another stall a Uighur from Xinjiang in the far north-west of China is selling piles of shiny chestnuts. In among the food stalls are open-air dentists and barbers.

A few hundred metres in another direction from the liberation monument, across a busy roundabout, is a nondescript wide pavement. In the daytime a few people, apparently strangers, hang around talking, but it is not idle chat. They are buyers and sellers in a people market. The prospective employers might be looking for domestic help, someone to work in a restaurant kitchen or on a construction site. The unemployed are out-of-towners (*waidiren*) looking for a living; any living. The supplicants soon learn the rules: 'At the people market you only speak when spoken to and don't butt in and say you'll take a job when a boss is talking to someone else. That'd be like stealing someone's rice bowl. If you do, there'll be a fight for sure.'[2]

In the evening, if it's not raining, the people market is temporarily gone and the wide pavement is packed. Good-humouredly vying for space, rival groups of formation dancers bump into each other. Loudspeakers blast out competing soundtracks. One group is ballroom dancing, men twirling women as well as women dancing with women. Another group is line dancing American-style. Each good-natured group observes, emulates and follows their leader, though nobody seems to mind being out of step. On the edges of the pavement men have set up laptop computers on low upturned boxes. The light from the computer screens bathes a small group of shabbily dressed, squatting silent men in an eerie greenish glow. They are watching lists of stock market prices change or checking gambling websites. Here and there hawkers sell hot food or children's toys for next to nothing.

A flight of slippery, broken concrete steps descends steeply from this wide pavement to a rough, makeshift neighbourhood. Shibati (Eighteen Steps), where those pavement dancers live, is one of Chongqing's slums, tucked into a cleft in the cliff in the middle of a prosperous business district. Ramshackle wooden structures hold together awnings of bamboo reed panels and plastic or metal sheets which are joined and suspended at crazy angles. Beneath are shops, hairdressers, food stalls, video screening rooms and gambling dens, all brightly lit by harsh fluorescent tubes. Chickens scratch about on the pavements and in the shops' forecourts. As in the neighbourhood markets, in front of one shop rows of live ducks stare out at passers-by. The metal shelf they sit on is balanced on top of cages of large chickens, pigeons and rabbits all crammed together. The animal stenches clash and rise. Other shops make and sell snow-white steamed buns. Unleavened sesame bread is artfully stacked on another stall.

Small singing birds hang in bamboo cages outside shops. Behind curtains DVDs are screened on television sets. A small huddle, mostly men, have paid a few *kuai* to watch. These mini-cinemas display scruffy movie posters and compete raucously. The volume is turned up full to attract business and drown the others out. The score of a Kung Fu action movie noisily eclipses a romantic epic across the road. Everywhere, at low tables, in shops, in houses, at dining tables by windows, groups of four people are playing mah-jong or cards. A few intent observers watch over the players' shoulders. No money is visibly changing hands. Gambling on board games is illegal, but money must be involved behind the scenes, so intense is the concentration of the players and so great the traditional Chinese love of gambling.

At the bottom of the steps the street widens and wanders on downhill. The paving stones are broken and the road is potholed. Cars cannot access this neighbourhood because it is jammed into a fold between high buildings on the steep cliff above the river. Further down the street the buildings become even more broken down. There are no more shops, just people selling old cell phone chargers, or second-hand shoes and clothes spread out on ragged blankets. Behind are dark hovels with narrow entrances, low ceilings and tiny rooms. These are the dormitories where migrant workers live, many to a room, lonely and far from home.

In living memory the only way to cross the river was to be ferried by a boatman, but now new concrete bridges cross high above the river at each end of the long road. Across the river from Chaotianmen a hulking new opera house dominates the riverscape. In profile it looks like a monster ship at sail. Also across the river is Nanbin Lu (South Shore Road). Six lanes of traffic stream down both sides of Nanbin Lu, sometimes coming to an inexplicable and extended halt. Nanbin Lu used to be an ugly row of brick-built factories and smokestack chimneys. Towards the end of the road some factories are still there, now empty and dilapidated, waiting for the developers to demolish and rebuild them. Most of the factories have been replaced by new flashy glass and steel restaurants. They are enormous, brightly lit and many are expensive.

Diners are greeted by slim young women wearing high-collared, tight-fitting red silk *qipao*, slit on both sides up to the thigh. Inside the restaurants the diners eat at large linen-covered tables in one of several vast air-conditioned dining rooms. Off the corridors are numerous dining rooms fitted out for parties of all sizes. Behind these closed doors business dinners and banquets take place out of sight of prying eyes. Relationships are established; promises made; Party officials wooed; bribes agreed; deals done. On a dry, warm night the diners eat outside on long balconies looking out across the river. When night falls the buildings opposite light up. All the restaurants on Nanbin Lu seem to be full every night. Families and business parties make the atmosphere hum.

The famous Sichuan speciality hotpot is generally the favourite dish. A vat of chilli-infused oil bubbles and spits, heated by a gas brazier burning up through a hole in the centre of the table. Into the boiling oil the assembled party throw pieces of raw fish and meat, including various unappealing bits of offal, such as rabbits' ears, goose intestines, small catfish, sheets of ox tripe and throat cartilage.[3] After a few minutes, when the food is cooked and saturated with chilli oil, the diners can retrieve it with chopsticks. Either they place it daintily on their esteemed guest's plate or they devour it themselves, immediately and gleefully. The business parties are continually punctuated by toasts, to honour either the whole table or one individual. Everyone toasts one another, thanking people for a favour or wishing them good luck. The people in these restaurants are Chongqing's new aspiring middle classes. Neither rich nor any longer poor, they are in a hurry to embrace consumer lifestyles made possible by the new business opportunities. They are seeking to live the Chinese dream.

After a tasty meal and a convivial evening out with the family or business contacts, diners stroll along a newly built boardwalk by the river. Young lovers conduct their courting under the boardwalk, one of the few dark, discreet places in the noisy city centre. Children eat ice creams. Dog-walkers take a leisurely evening stroll. On the river, flat commercial barges without lights carrying building materials cast barely perceptible shadows as they slide silently past the pleasure boats. Towards the end of the road a small cable car takes people high above the Jialing River back to *Jiefangbei* from Nanbin Lu. The wire stretches high above the river and the small red car swings gently as it crosses its counterpart halfway across. It dates from the Mao era when the boatmen who used to ferry people back and forth were too slow and old-fashioned and concrete bridges still too expensive. To find a high enough landing stage the cable had to be stretched inland, so that the car could deposit its passengers. In the final few moments the car passes between blocks of flats at eye level on both sides. Inside, under bright light bulbs small children are still at their desks doing their homework late into the night. In the same room their parents are already in bed fast asleep.

All this happens within a short distance of *Jiefangbei* and is typical of the varieties of Chinese modernity: skyscrapers and motorways with noodle stalls and housing estates in between. In the midst of showy new money slums like Shibati are tucked away, visible only to the knowing or the curious. The old and the new jostle together. As far as buildings are concerned, the new is winning, but, in terms of the people, the most striking impression is gross inequality, evident everywhere. The rising tide of economic growth has not raised all boats. The rich and the poor (mostly migrants to the city) live cheek by jowl; so do the past and the future. The present seems all too transient, disappearing before your very eyes.

The new sprawling Chongqing is not laid out traditionally with a centre from which the city radiates outwards; the landscape is too mountainous for that. Several city 'centres' are strung around the mountains, connected by motorways, flyovers, tunnels and monorails. New leafy, low-rise suburbs and gated estates fill the gaps. In places mountains have simply been removed, like a rotten tooth, to ease the smooth and rapid passage of a motorway or a flyover. Each new zone has its own central business district, a moving kaleidoscope of rapidly changing buildings and streetscapes as old buildings are torn down and new high-rise office blocks and flats replace them. Many half-built structures remain unfinished, stalled by the financial overreach of an indebted speculative property developer.

Across the Yangtze to the north of *Jiefangbei* is the most prosperous district of Chongqing, Jiang Bei (North River). On these streets are car dealerships for BMWs and Lamborghinis, shopping malls and upmarket blocks of flats. This is where the professional upper middle classes now live. Young married couples live in newly built (and mostly heavily mortgaged) flats in high-rise blocks, protected by gates and a security guard. Typically the flat is compact but comfortable with a single bedroom, a big television in a small sitting room and a dining area off the kitchen. During the day the *aiyi* (meaning aunt, but also the common form of address for a maid), invariably a migrant from the countryside recruited in the people market, cleans the flat, washes clothes and prepares the evening meal. Chinese employers require 'presenteeism', being in the office until late, so few young professionals get home early enough to cook their own evening meals.

Higher up the pecking order from the young professional middle classes, the entrepreneurial and business elite live in large brick houses locked in gated communities in suburbs wedged into the interstices between the new central business districts and multi-lane highways. They too are protected by security guards and tall electric gates, and are made instantly leafy by fully grown trees replanted from the countryside. They are never far from a golf course. Some new developments are even built on the course. The ban on golf was only lifted in 1984. Due to its popularity among the rich and powerful 400 new courses opened between 2004 and 2009 despite a moratorium on their construction after concerns about the sequestration of agricultural land and water.[4] For developers, golf facilities are a way of selling the million-dollar homes that surround them.

By comparison with the northern suburbs of Jiang Bei the south of the city is relatively underdeveloped. The Japanese-built monorail that runs east–west to the outlying parts of Chongqing still has an incomplete southern extension. Here, ordinary people's lives are conducted in less modern, more downmarket settings. Ex-factory-workers still live in the old five- or six-storey brick tenements. In the community square in the middle of the blocks of flats old people exercise on simple, brightly painted fitness equipment. Some are enthusiastic, almost frantic, pushing and pulling bars and pedals. Others are more desultory. Most people are either playing mah-jong or Chinese chess or watching others play. Some have their dogs tucked under their arms. Other dogs are on leads. Though dogs are clearly the objects of strong emotional attachments (a child substitute, some have argued)[5], they are also cooked and eaten in winter for their heat-giving properties (not the pets, of course). Rumours of rabies outbreaks, however, can still lead to impromptu vigilante groups beating local dogs to death with sticks and stones, sometimes in the presence of their owners.

At the end of the square is the recently built community centre. A clinic has been opened on the ground floor. Upstairs, computers look new and unused (unlike the overcrowded commercial internet cafes). In the narrow room next door is the library with its small, neat collection of books, similarly pristine and neglected. On the first floor there is a community hall with a stage. One warm afternoon a group of elderly ladies were learning to read music and play electronic keyboards.

Just ten minutes from these old factory communities in the south of the city is the countryside, where families still live on smallholdings. Houses are set above soaked rice paddies. When I drove out to this area I saw peasants in wide-brimmed straw hats and blue denim tunics, legs akimbo, bent over small luminescent green rice shoots. Next to the paddies a row of fruit trees protected the crops from the wind. In front of the houses on a concrete terrace, a threshing floor, lay long shafts of harvested cereal. A young man sat on a low stool stripping the ears off the stalks in a deft sweep of one hand, the other hand holding the tall, thin shafts firm between his knees.

In these few districts in and around Chongqing are etched the main contours of the society that has emerged all over China since Deng Xiaoping's 1980s reforms. The super-elite are hidden away in leafy, gated communities near golf courses. The upwardly mobile young professional middle classes have moved to city centre high-rise flats, near to restaurants and shopping malls. The unemployed factory workers still live in their run-down tenements with nothing to do, but with their old way of life surprisingly intact. The impoverished migrant workers from out of town are hidden in slums, eking out a precarious living and, last not but least, hundreds of millions live in the countryside; some thriving, many subsisting, a good many struggling.

In 1998 Chongqing and its immediate rural hinterland were carved out of Sichuan province and made a stand-alone metropolitan administrative area, reporting directly to the national government in Beijing. The administration is led by a powerful Mayor and an even more powerful Communist Party Secretary. As well as creating a strategic regional centre for the enormous effort involved in building and maintaining the Three Gorges Dam, Beijing's intention was to use Chongqing's traditional role as an entrepôt along the arterial axis of the Yangtze River as a foundation for turning the city into a financial and business centre. The new municipality was set aggressive targets for economic growth for the backward south-west of China. These are supposed to be met by raising rural productivity in the city's hinterland, as well as by large-scale but controlled migration to the expanded city and by modernising and consolidating traditional industries such as the production of cars and motorcycles. In theory this will create jobs and economic development for the whole Sichuan region which has so far not kept pace with its pushy coastal counterparts. Some economists say the west of China is the next, last and perhaps most promising economic frontier. Fortunes, it is said, will be made as the rural Wild West is opened up to industry and commerce.[6] Success so far has been mixed.

The central government in Beijing also gave Chongqing licence to find solutions to some of China's most knotty problems: political participation and social welfare. Powerful universities have rapidly expanded, attracting Chinese academics with national and international reputations and drawing on foreign 'experts' like me. There has been a range of experiments in new approaches to public scrutiny of official decision-making. Citizens can publicly question heads of local government offices about their decisions. More radically, all significant local government rulings were subject to public hearings – in person, on television and on the internet. By 2007 the authorities in Chongqing had organised more than 600 public hearings on a range of thorny issues: compensation for farmers whose land had been taken; minimum wage provisions; prices of utilities and public services, including water, electricity, natural gas, road and bridge tolls, education, public health, public transport, sewage and refuse disposal.[7] Follow-up action was taken on a few issues. Public hearings on the price of the monorail led to fares for a single journey being reduced from *RMB*15 to just two *renminbi*. A blanket ban on fireworks imposed during the spring festival after an accident caused nasty injuries was lifted due to public pressure. But these experiments and minor decisions would hardly merit the description transparency, much less democracy.

A different light was cast on these well-laid plans for smooth and rapid economic and political transformation in 2009. In reality, it turned out, substantial hitches had cropped up. The recently appointed Party Secretary for Chongqing, Bo Xilai, initiated the biggest anti-corruption purge China has ever seen. Bo Xilai is high profile. A member of the national Politburo in Beijing, he had been Minister for Commerce before coming to Chongqing. He has long been tipped for the top.[8] His anti-corruption investigation in Chongqing netted 9,000 suspects, including 50 public officials, and exposed organised crime, prostitution, drug trafficking, illegal mining and many cases of citizens being arbitrarily and unlawfully dispossessed of their land, sometimes violently.[9] Party officials and particularly the police seemed to be heavily implicated. The Chief of Police was removed and the army was brought in to clean up the police force. Local people flocked to the courts in their hundreds to watch the trials. 'Scientific development', it seemed, had created many opportunities for rent-seeking, bribery and protection rackets.

Bo Xilai's subsequent moves were less obviously populist and more ideological. In speeches and campaigns he espoused slogans and icons of the Mao era rarely mentioned by other leaders these days. Operas from the Cultural Revolution were once more performed in public in Chongqing and smaller towns and cities. Some 13 million cellphone users in Chongqing received 'red text messages', featuring sayings from Mao's *Little Red Book*.[10] A 20-metre-high statue of Mao on a 14-metre pedestal was erected on a university campus in 2008. The statue can be seen from miles away. In 2011 Bo initiated a 'Red Songs Campaign' demanding that staff in municipal district offices, government departments, commercial operations, universities and schools, state radio and TV stations should sing the so-called 'red songs', which according to Bo would help to 'reinvigorate the city with the Marxist ideals of his father's comrade-in-arms Mao Zedong'.

He also introduced high-profile social welfare initiatives. The Communist authorities (and some of their predecessors) have always sought to control the destabilising movement of rural people to the city by implementing a household registration (*hukou*) system. Without this registration you cannot get a job (in the formal labour market at least) or access to public services like education and health. Being a 'city dweller' with official registration papers is therefore a highly valued asset. In cities like Beijing and Shanghai *hukou* has practically become a currency and is actively traded in a lively grey market at inflated prices. Migrants to the cities without household registration are consigned permanently to a life on the social and economic margins. The national leadership has always been stubbornly reluctant to relax household registration, knowing that it is a powerful tool of social control, but Bo stepped out of line. *Hukou* was made available for rural migrants to the city, though with unattractive caveats like losing access to their land in the countryside after three years.

As demand for food soars in China, along with food prices, the pressure to increase output is intense in official minds. Land lying fallow in the countryside owned by migrants to the city, in the view of economists, is a serious impediment to agricultural efficiency. Jobs in the city, however, are still hard to come by for migrant workers with limited education and skills. The available jobs are insecure and people could be dismissed in an instant. So migrants feared they might have to return to the countryside and were reluctant to surrender their land. They have good grounds for their fears: the economic downturn of 2007 resulted in more than 20 million people having to return to the countryside. Chongqing's target was to turn 10 million farmers into urban residents by 2020. According to the *People's Daily*, by the end of August 2010 only 44,700 households had taken up the offer.[11]

Bo's other high-profile welfare initiative was building social housing for subsidised rental and subsequent sale to migrant workers and others on low incomes. Recognising that the new low-cost housing was unlikely to cater for all those priced out of China's runaway property market, and perhaps with an eye to publicity, the first tranche of housing was allocated by lottery. The first winner, in March 2010, was Tong Xiaoqing, aged 61. She is a retired worker from a state-owned factory who lost her husband and two children to illness or accidents by 2005. In order to pay the medical bills she had to sell her flat that same year. Since then she has lived alone in shabby apartments, moving four times when she could not afford rent rises. Her minimal pension would never cover the rent on a decent flat in the private market.[12]

Xi Jinping, Hu Jintao's potential successor, visited Chongqing in December 2010 and gave Bo's policies a ringing endorsement, in stark contrast to the silence that has emanated from President Hu Jintao and Premier Wen Jiabao. Xi said Bo's efforts to promote Maoist thinking had 'gone deeply into the hearts of the people and are worthy of praise'. Similarly, the social housing policy was 'a virtuous policy'.[13] But it seems this counted for nothing. Bo was dismissed in March 2012, his ultimate political destination unknown.

When it comes to Communist Party heritage, other than being direct descendants of Mao or Deng Xiaoping, they don't come more impressive than Bo Xilai. Bo Yibo, his revered father, had an impeccable Communist pedigree. He joined the Party aged 17 in 1925. He was captured by Chiang Kaishek's Guomindang and, under orders from the Party, signed an anti-Communist confession. He was on the Long March in 1934–35. After

1949 he rose through government and Party ranks to become Finance Minister and Vice-Premier. He was purged during the Cultural Revolution following a large 'struggle' rally targeting him at the massive Beijing Workers' Stadium. He was tortured by the Red Guards and imprisoned in some of the worst conditions for 15 years. During that time his wife was beaten to death. He was purged again by the Gang of Four during their brief spell in control after Mao died. Rehabilitated once more, he was one of the Communist Party 'eight immortals', a group of powerful veteran leaders around Deng Xiaoping. He argued for a crackdown on the Tiananmen demonstrators. Bo Yibo, like Deng, stands for Communist authoritarianism combined with economic rationalism. That makes him a powerful symbol of the trajectory of leadership thought and policy between 1949 and 1989. With the exception of Bo Xilai, the remainder of his six children live abroad; a common trend among the families of top leaders.

Bo Xilai's son, Bo Guagua, is set to join this illustrious family history, though his ambitions and experiences are more attuned to twenty-first-century definitions of success. He attended Harrow in the UK, a leading private school near London whose illustrious alumni include Winston Churchill. After Harrow, Bo Guagua went on to Balliol College, Oxford, another famed, elite educational institution, to study Philosophy, Politics and Economics, and from there to the Kennedy School of Government at Harvard. Bo Guagua has evidently relished his time away from China and has taken on the habits of Western youth, making him the Western style of party animal, rather than the Communist variant. While at Oxford photos of him appeared on the internet, showing him enjoying the high life at parties, shirtless and the worse for wear, festooned with attractive Western girls. These pictures provoked extensive online envy and criticism. Some asked how a mere Party functionary could afford such expensive foreign education, not to mention the accompanying pleasures.[14]

These three generations of the Bo family represent all the important trends in the lives of senior figures in the Communist Party. A history of Party loyalty and power brought down by repeated exclusion and denigration under Mao; a pragmatic authoritarianism under Deng and, in Bo Xilai's case, attempts to stay ahead of the game in both economic and social policy during the more recent low-key and secretive leadership transitions;

playing a political game of snakes and ladders. Bo Guagua is being educated for a career as the model high-flying global cosmopolitan.

Just as his family history contains all the threads of Chinese political life over more than 60 years Bo Xilai's activities in Chongqing are emblematic of the contemporary dramas in Chinese political life: the leaders' continuing belief in the value of Communist propaganda in a consumer society; the lack of progress on greater equity in general and social welfare in particular; ideological disputes within the Party; jockeying for power between leadership factions. Bo's 'princeling' status makes him and his downfall especially symbolic and significant.

CHAPTER 3

Chaos, Reform and Inequality

In 1974 a new well was being dug in the village of Xiyang in Shaanxi province, a few hours away from Xian. While digging their new well farmers uncovered broken pottery, a common occurrence where so many tributaries of Chinese history converge. Soon the magnitude of their discovery was revealed: a buried terracotta army, built by the first emperor Qin. The enormous site is still not fully excavated after more than thirty years. In the three 'pits' thousands of life-size statues of soldiers and horses stand in serried ranks of four stretching back in long columns almost as far as the eye can see. The soldiers' many expressions and postures give the army a lifelike quality.

From Changan in AD 221 the first emperor Qin created the empire later known as China. Changan, now known as Xian, was an imperial capital until the end of the Tang dynasty in AD 907. The city was the eastern terminus of the Silk Route, long controlled by China and a conduit for wealth and knowledge, as well as China's continuing encounter with Islam, a heritage visibly represented by the Great Mosque. Uniquely for a mosque it is a series of pavilions in traditional Chinese architectural style with pagoda roofs; a great Islamic place of worship also incontrovertibly Chinese.

The emperor Qin may have been a successful warrior and empire builder, but he knew his methods were not popular. The newly created bureaucracy came to regard him as a merciless tyrant.[1] The emperor needed constant military protection from his enemies and similar protection for the afterlife; his nemesis might still await. Almost immediately upon his accession he commissioned the building of his mausoleum complete with terracotta army. Building continued for his entire reign.

At the time the tomb was discovered China was convulsed by the turmoil of the Cultural Revolution. The Great Leap Forward had comprehensively failed to turn it into a modern industrial economy. Mao believed China's old-fashioned, superstitious culture had made the country supine. That was at the heart of historic failures since the humiliating Treaty of Nanjing in 1842 and China's subsequent dismembering and exploitation by foreign concessions. The backward attitudes of the masses had withstood constant propaganda and indoctrination and remained a seemingly insuperable impediment to creating a Communist utopia. Mao especially abhorred Confucian beliefs. From the countryside himself, he was highly critical of the hold of traditional family-based ways of agricultural production. As well as old attitudes, middle-class businesses must also be broken up if Marxist-Leninist state-controlled economic structures, refined by Mao Zedong thought, were to gain permanent traction in a backward, overwhelmingly rural society.

The Communist Party was also in poor shape by the 1970s. Mao was continually preoccupied by disputes and rivalries among the leadership. He had many scores to settle. In the early 1960s he knew that Liu Shaoqi, the President of China and the second most powerful man in the Party, Premier Zhou Enlai and Deng Xiaoping had no appetite for another convulsive upheaval. In the cities, towns and in the countryside away from these internecine struggles the Party was brought down by seemingly ineradicable corruption. In 1964 Mao showed his disgust with characteristically earthy brio. 'You can buy a Party Secretary for a few packs of cigarettes, not to mention marrying a daughter to him.'[2]

From 1966 Mao encouraged Red Guards, originally students from Tsinghua University quickly joined by many others, to overturn the old order. Worthless traditional book learning should be replaced by revolutionary struggle, violent if necessary.

> The thought, culture and customs which brought China to where we found her must disappear and the thought, customs and culture of proletarian China, which does not yet exist, must appear ... Thoughts, culture, customs must be born of struggle and the struggle must continue for as long as there is still danger of a return to the past.[3]

The enthusiasm of Red Guards was genuine enough. At the age of 12 Jung Chang, author of *Wild Swans* asked her father for 'a name with a military ring to it'. He suggested Jung, which means martial affairs, as a substitute for her childhood name Erhong, the rather more lyrical 'Second Swan'. Two years later at 14 she joined the Red Guards 'thrilled by my red armband'.[4] The Cultural Revolution, to begin with, was a youth movement. The Red Guards set off on their angry, destructive and often violent expeditions, across cities or on long train journeys, with much merriment, singing revolutionary songs and fired up by the rectitude of their youthful ardour. They were escaping dreary, regimented life in traditional universities. In their own minds their actions need not be justified by a coherent political programme. Stronger passions gave them their rationale: to remove reactionary obstacles to a radically brighter, but poorly defined future.

The influential 'New Left' thinker Wang Hui takes a more balanced, less condemnatory view of the origins of the Cultural Revolution than that of other historians. The Communist Party was becoming embedded in the state bureaucracy, he argues. This left ordinary people who had been fired up by revolutionary ideals feeling like outsiders:

> The political debates in the early stages of the Cultural Revolution included currents that hoped to smash the absolute authority of the Party and the state, in order to further the goal of progress towards genuine popular sovereignty . . . Efforts at social remobilisation and stimulation of political life outside the Party–state context were crucial characteristics of this early period. Due to the forceful reassertion of the Party–state system, most of these innovations were short-lived.[5]

From these unclear but idealistic beginnings things soon descended into chaos. In the pursuit of contradiction and upheaval leading to political renewal, senior people in business, bureaucracies and universities were denounced, tortured and banished. Academics were displaced. They were humiliated and tortured by Red Guards. Libraries were destroyed and books burnt. Many temples and ancient monuments were ruined in the Cultural Revolution. Zhou Enlai drew up a secret list of buildings, and monuments, including the Forbidden City, that had to be preserved from the mob. People suspected of lacking revolutionary ardour were imprisoned and tortured in so-called 'struggle' sessions by, for example, being forced to stand in the aeroplane position: bent forward, head bowed and arms stretched out behind, while a crowd of onlookers were goaded into shouting criticisms and denunciations, interspersed with ringing declarations of passion for the revolution and Mao Zedong thought. Although these 'struggle sessions' might end in people baying for the unfortunate victim's blood in an orgy of emotion, some of this ardent denunciation was fake and theatrical. Cheng Nien the wealthy and cultivated widow of a Shell executive, and herself an employee of the company and therefore suspected of being a British spy, was denounced in 'struggle sessions'. As she was taken back to prison afterwards, she heard the formerly shrill, shouting crowd calmly and casually discussing the weather and whether to stop for a bowl of noodles as they made their way out. Victims were imprisoned until they confessed to their 'crimes', wrote a self-criticism and denounced friends and members of their family. Cheng Nien remained in prison for more than six years. Meanwhile her daughter was also 'struggled' against, for refusing to denounce her mother. She was murdered for this. Cheng Nien came to believe that she herself was spared death only by the intercession of senior leaders like Zhou Enlai.[6]

Even Soong Qingling, the widow of Sun Yatsen and a female icon in Chinese contemporary history, was targeted by Red Guards until Zhou Enlai and Mao both stepped in to protect her. They could not however stop Mao's wife Jiang Qing from storming into Soong Qingling's elegant house by the lake in Beijing and trying to cut off her long hair, always worn in a classic bun. To Jiang Qing, in her grey Mao suit and with her short hair tidily under a peaked cap with a red star on the front, the older woman's elegance was evidence of bourgeois and counter-revolutionary tendencies. But the older woman's implacable dignity and resolve prevailed and Jiang Qing was forced to back off. Soong Qingling's hair remained untouched.[7]

Schoolchildren and students suddenly disappeared with no notice to their family, packed off to be re-educated in the countryside by peasants. Often the peasants resented them when they got there. They were more hungry mouths to feed and had neither skills nor the stamina to do anything useful. Sometimes they were violently attacked by the peasants who had troubles enough of their own.[8] Many remained in the countryside for years, without permission to return to the cities. By the time they returned they were strangers to their own family and their education was irrecoverably ruined. Yan Xuetong, now a leading thinker about international relations and a scholar of pre-Qin thought, was sent at the age of 16 to a construction corps in the far north of China:

> In May, water in Helongjiang still turns to ice. When we pulled the sowing machine, we were not allowed to wear boots. We walked barefoot over the ice. Our legs were covered in cuts. We carried sacks of seed that could weigh up to 80 kilogrammes. We carried them along the raised pathways around the paddy fields. These were not level; make a slight misstep and you fall into the water. You just thought of climbing out and going on. When you struggled to the end and lay down, your eyes could only see black and you just could not get up. . . . [We] saw people being beaten to death, so you became somewhat immune to it.[9]

Xi Jinping, China's top leader from 2012 was, by his own account, locked up 'three or four' times. In Shaanxi, he had to attend daily 'struggle sessions', and was forced to read out denunciations of his father Xi Zhongxun. He is reported to have run away from his assigned farm in August 1969 but was arrested and sent back the following year. He suffered a year of primitive, cruel treatment before redeeming himself by carrying shoulder poles of twin 110-pound buckets for several miles in the mountains, reportedly without tiring. He was also apparently big and strong enough to beat the local farmers in wrestling matches.[10]

As in the famines caused by the Great Leap Forward, the greatest human degradation caused by the Cultural Revolution was cannibalism. In the town of Wuxuan a geography teacher, Wu Shufang, was beaten to death. One of the other teachers started to cut off sections of her corpse:

> After he had cut out the heart and the liver, along with the flesh from the victim's thigh, the crowd took off. They carried some of the hunks of the flesh away in plastic bags . . . Wu Shufang was cooked in three places. One was the school kitchen . . . When the flesh was cooked, seven or eight students consumed it together.[11]

Many people went mad, reduced to a broken physical and mental shell. Some committed suicide, unable to take it any longer. These uncontrolled forces turned to chaos and had to be restrained. As early as 1968 the Red Guards collapsed into factionalism. With intellectuals banished and bureaucrats and civil servants denounced and expelled, the military 'was the last major Chinese institution whose command structure remained standing . . . military personnel ran the gutted government ministries, tended fields and administered factories'.[12] Not for the last time the Communist Party was forced to turn to the People's Liberation Army to maintain a semblance of order.

One of Mao's motives in unleashing the Cultural Revolution was to undermine both President Liu Shaoqi (until he was denounced and placed under house arrest where he died amid strong rumours of officially ordered medical neglect) and also Premier Zhou Enlai. Along with Deng Xiaoping, these more pragmatic Party leaders had eroded Mao's absolute power and he greatly resented it. Lin Biao, Mao's most recently anointed heir apparent, had collected Mao's most important sayings into the famous *Little Red Book* in a famously sycophantic act of deference. It did him no good in the end. By 1972 Lin Biao had in turn become an object of suspicion. Along with his son, he was said to be planning to assassinate Mao. The plot became known to Zhou Enlai and, during an apparent attempt at escape to the Soviet Union, Lin Biao's aeroplane crashed over Mongolia seemingly because of a lack of fuel.

The subsequently released papers about Lin Biao's supposed plot compared Mao at length to the unpopular first emperor, Qin, drawing attention to their shared tyrannical tendencies. Allegedly, slogans for an anti-Mao campaign had been drafted, including 'Down with the contemporary First Emperor'. One concession was made to Mao's achievement in uniting China after a long war, an achievement he shared with the Emperor Qin: 'Of course we do not deny [Mao's] historical role in unifying China. Precisely because of this, in the history of our revolution, we have given him the trust he deserves.'[13] But this trust, according to the conspirators, had been misplaced: 'He is not a true Marxist-Leninist but the biggest feudal tyrant in Chinese history who, under the guise of Marxism-Leninism, follows the doctrines of Confucius and Mencius,[14] and implements the laws of the First Emperor.'

Mao had compared himself to the first emperor, to highlight both his achievements and his willingness to be ruthless. In his 1936 poem 'Snow', Mao was already predicting that his achievements would outstrip even those of the greatest of the previous holders of the mandate of heaven. China is,

A land so rich in beauty/has made countless heroes bow in homage. / But the First Emperor, Han Wudi, Tang Taizong, Song Taizu and Genghis Khan/All are past and gone!/For truly great men/Look to this age alone.[15]

In 1958 after a campaign to silence intellectuals the previous year, Mao compared himself to the first emperor: 'he buried 460 scholars alive; we have buried [46,000] scholars . . . we have surpassed the [first emperor] a hundredfold.'[16]

With a few intermissions leadership in China seems never to have lost the characteristics it had under the first emperor: a distrust of what the people might do with freedom, never-ending factional fighting in the leadership and a bureaucracy whose corruption and venality comprehensively undermines even the most visionary and altruistic ambitions of its leaders. The only fall-back has apparently been authoritarianism.

After a long struggle with cancer, during which he too was often denied medical treatment by Mao, Zhou Enlai died in 1976. Shortly before his death, in one of his final public acts, emaciated and terminally ill, Zhou exhorted the country to follow the 'great . . . important . . . and . . . far-reaching' events of the Cultural Revolution and the anti-Confucius campaign by striving to achieve 'comprehensive modernisation' in four key sectors, 'agriculture, industry, national defence and science and technology'.[17] He was seeking to set a different course for China's future while not reviling its recent past, displaying all the diplomatic skills for which Zhou was globally renowned.

Zhou's death provoked a great outpouring of public grief. On the eve of the *Qingming* festival, Chinese culture's day of the dead, thousands of people spontaneously gathered around the Monument to the People's Heroes in Tiananmen Square to mourn. They laid wreaths, banners, poems, placards and flowers at the foot of the monument, eulogising Zhou and criticising the Gang of Four, the hardline group led by Jiang Qing who intended to take over the leadership and the country after the ailing Mao's imminent death. The next day more than a million people from all parts of society passed peacefully through the square. But when the mourners returned the following morning, 5 April, the memorial tributes were gone, removed during the night by the authorities for fear of the strength of public feelings that were building up. Most of the crowd dispersed disconsolately but peacefully. The remaining mourners were arrested after disturbances and imprisoned. They were not to be released until Deng Xiaoping took power several years later, keen to distance himself from the Cultural Revolution and its excesses.

A few months later, in September 1976, Mao also died. The superstitious believed that the massive Tangshan earthquake in July 1976 presaged the end of the dynasty. [18] Hua Guofeng, a weak and compromising leader took over and a couple of years of chaos followed while the Gang of Four ran amok and attempted to seize power. Open conflict prevailed in the leadership. Deng Xiaoping, closely associated with Zhou, was banished, stripped of his power and position, as he had been during the Cultural Revolution. Following a bitter struggle the Gang of Four were eventually arrested and imprisoned. After that things calmed down.

Remission from the continuous upheaval since the early 1960s meant people had high hopes of Deng Xiaoping and his policy of Reform and Opening initiated soon afterwards in 1978. A new Chinese dream of a future of prosperity and social calm began to take shape. In the early 1980s Shenzhen, Shuhai and Shantou in Guangdong province and Xiamen in Fujian province were all made Special Enterprise Zones (SEZs) and encouraged to attract foreign investment and engage in foreign trade. The proximity of the new SEZs to Hong Kong and Taiwan gave them easy access to capital and management expertise, harnessing diaspora investment. Between 1979 and 1992, US$116.4 billion was pledged for investment in China; 71.7 per cent of that came from Hong Kong and Taiwan; only 7 per cent from the US and 5.8 per cent from Japan. Investments from European countries were even smaller.[19] Shenzhen was transformed in 25 years from a fishing village into a city of 11 million people and rising. Skilled workers were readily drawn to the new urban mega-manufacturing zones, however arduous and uncongenial the working and living conditions. Infrastructure development was sponsored by local government, using freely available credit. Beijing took an uncharacteristically laid-back view of regulation on prices, production targets, taxes, duties and employment laws in the SEZs. All this came together to create a spectacular manufacturing and export boom. As a result throughout the 1980s further SEZs were created, including the whole of Hainan Island, off China's south coast, now a resort renowned for licentious living.

Deng Xiaoping, still fresh from his battles with the Gang of Four, knew that their way of thinking had not been eradicated by their imprisonment. Factions in the leadership were opposed to his reforms and were still keen to continue with a hardline Marxist-Leninist approach to the economy. Deng's position as Supreme Leader was not yet secure enough for national experiments, even if his innate pragmatism had allowed them. SEZs gave policy-makers the opportunity to experiment with and test reform policies without risking large-scale and unpredictable national consequences. The liberals among the Chinese leadership were emboldened by these early successes to advocate Reform and Opening more fervently, without which China's economic transition might have been politically impossible and therefore stillborn.[20]

Reform in the countryside was to produce just as dramatic effects. In 1978 Deng Xiaoping introduced the household responsibility system. This put an end to the collective farms and gave farmers the right to use a plot of land for 15 years and to sell any excess agricultural production on the open market. Once the traditional family organisation of farms had been reinstated, productivity increased dramatically. In 1984, under the new title of Town and Village Enterprises (TVEs), reformed small businesses began to concentrate on labour-intensive industrial production, instead of collective farming, since rural workers were plentiful and cheap. Freed from the diktats of a command economy they produced goods in response to unmet consumer demand. Since local government essentially owned the TVEs taxes were low, credit was cheap and contracts were readily forthcoming. Their success was extraordinary. Although Chinese government figures may have exaggerated the achievements of TVEs,[21] the annual rate of growth of these industries from the mid-1980s to mid-1990s was estimated at about 25 per cent.[22] The exact figures may be disputed but the ubiquitous presence of busy TVEs is evident to any traveller in the Chinese countryside.

Starting from such a low base, China's progress in agriculture since Deng's Reform and Opening is amazing by any historical or geographical standards. Between 1979 and 1984 the Chinese population grew annually by 1.3 per cent. Agricultural production, on the other hand, grew by as much as 11.8 per cent a year. Rural incomes have increased by more than 15 per cent a year. In agricultural Guangdong, a real success story, incomes doubled between 1978 and 1984 – and doubled again in the following six years. Across China the number of abjectly poor people has fallen from 33 per cent of the population in the 1980s to 12 per cent by the millennium. During the same period the proportion of the population working in agriculture has fallen from 80 per cent to 50 per cent. The proportion of people facing hunger has fallen by three-quarters and Chinese children are getting taller and heavier. In the 1960s Chinese people on average consumed about 1,600 calories a day. By 1998 that had risen to nearly 3,000 calories per day, in line with international norms.[23]

These reforms as well as raising rural incomes also created a massive surplus of labour in the countryside. Some of those who did not find a place in the new rural small business environment migrated to the city. The work they found was unappealing: physically arduous labour on building sites, long hours in restaurants and noodle bars, or carrying heavy loads.[24] Urban employers could dispense with their services at a moment's notice and economic downturns sent millions of migrants back home, but life in the country was not secure, easy or pleasant either. Even these insecure jobs were preferable to backbreaking toil or listless inactivity in the countryside.

By the 1990s many rural people, particularly young women, were travelling far from home and finding employment in factories in the cities. 'Factory girls' lived a strange life cut off from their families, living in a dormitory, working all hours and answering to an overseer. They didn't earn much but it was more than they could dream of in the countryside. If they lost their job, other opportunities might materialise through connections and conscientiousness. They could get a more congenial job outside the factories, like selling real estate on commission. They had little enough in the city, but their thrift was admirable and the money they set aside and sent home further increased rural incomes. They started a new life and also began to feel that life's possibilities might have opened up for them too.[25] Not everyone made it in the city, however. Prostitution soon became rife. Many of the sex workers were sacked factory employees struggling to make a living and support a family back home.

All these changes were made in the name of economic development. In pursuit of the same goal, however, something much less liberating, more intrusive and coercive was simultaneously introduced. In 1979 the one-child policy comprehensively destroyed the traditions and dynamics of families and communities. Local officials could interfere in personal deci-sions with impunity. Once the policy took hold, boys were much preferred and the abortion or abandonment of girl children, a phenomenon previ-ously associated only with the remote countryside, became much more common. Children over and above the quota were hidden, only let out from home after dark, or sent away to the countryside to grow up in another family. Parents became over-protective and neurotic about their only child, obsessed by education and future success. A generation of spoilt single children grew up living lives full of pressure and fear about what would happen to them alone in the world and single-handedly carrying all the burdens of family obligation. Old people, used to relying on a large family for care in old age, were left isolated, unsupported and guiltily reluc-tant to ask for help from their overstretched, pressurised child.

Not all these radical economic and social changes were welcome and, notwithstanding their reputation for stoicism, Chinese people have always protested, even in the darkest years of the famine.[26] Many did not unequiv-ocally welcome the new dispensations under Reform and Opening. Protests started as early as 1978–79. Behind a scruffy hedge and under a row of leafless sycamore trees at the intersection of two of Beijing's busiest streets – the Avenue of Eternal Peace and Xidan – a Democracy Wall flourished. In the autumn of 1978 *dazibao,* big character posters, began to appear. The comments on the posters quickly became increasingly critical of the lead-ership and the elite. Demands for human rights and democracy started to appear before long.

> Citizens of China do not want a paper constitution. We don't want hunger. We don't want to suffer anymore. We want human rights and democracy.[27]

All those years of propaganda under Mao had left their mark and they were now being turned on the Communist Party. Many protests were couched in Marxist-Leninist language and sentiment:

> To make people think that democracy and human rights are only slogans of the Western bourgeoisie and the Eastern proletariat needs only dictatorship . . . is something that cannot be tolerated anymore.[28]

The artist Ai Weiwei, then little known, was one of the Democracy Wall activists.

> We all knew about our parents' fight for a new China, a modern China with a democracy and a science. And then suddenly they had a chance in the late 1970s and early 1980s to rethink that part of history. We started to realise that the lack of freedom and freedom of expression is what caused China's tragedy. So this group of young people started to write poetry and to make magazines, adopting a democratic way of thinking. We started to act really self-consciously and with a self-awareness to try to achieve this – to fight for personal freedom. . . . There was a wall. We called it 'the Democratic Wall'.[29]

In his reference to democracy and science Ai invokes the spirit of the New Culture Movement and the May the Fourth Movement (named after the date of student demonstrations in Beijing in 1919), guiding lights for the Democracy Wall protestors. Even before the collapse of the Qing dynasty in 1911 an intellectual movement was growing which advocated learning from the West. This New Culture Movement stood for a comprehensive modernisation of Chinese life, including more freedom for women and an end to patriarchy; an acceptance of other cultures rather than the continual assertion of the superiority of ancient texts, especially Confucius; greater democracy and, generally, a social and political orientation away from the past and towards the future. In 1919 after the fall of the Qing dynasty and the humiliating sidelining of China's demands in the Treaty of Versailles which ended the First World War, the intellectuals of the May the Fourth Movement felt China was being held back by tradition and should learn from the West's progress, the essence of which they, like others before them, saw as science and democracy.[30] They argued that China's rigid traditional education and examination system needed to be radically reformed. International influences should be introduced. The economy should be industrialised. The atrophied post-Imperial political system needed wholesale reform. For a short period their views prevailed, but the descent into warlordism and the outbreak of civil war and then world war meant that their views never took irreversible hold.

Lu Xun, 'the most brilliant writer of the May Fourth Movement',[31] with the unflinching eye of a novelist unencumbered by the need to conceive a programme for government, describes in his short stories how the vastness, complexity and backwardness of rural China was always likely to overwhelm simplistic utopian modernisation schemes. While deploring the conditions in which poor people were forced to live, he retained a healthy scepticism towards modernising projects which seemed, too often, to unleash intolerance and brutality without doing much to meet their stated goals of improving the lot of the poor.

By the end of 1978 the Democracy Wall was attracting thousands of people every day to see the characters written up the night before and to join in heated debates, or listen to impassioned impromptu speeches. Deng Xiaoping, still consolidating his leadership after his battle with the Gang of Four, initially welcomed the Democracy Wall, telling Robert Novak, an American reporter, with typical bluntness, 'Democracy Wall is good.' The *People's Daily*, the voice of Chinese officialdom said, 'Let the people say what they wish, the heavens will not fall.'[32]

Such an open attitude was not to last long. Criticism soon went beyond negative commentaries on the Cultural Revolution and Mao's legacy to attack the current leadership. A few weeks after his return from his triumphant, Stetson-wearing trip to the USA on 16 March 1979 Deng announced that the Democracy Wall protesters had gone too far. They were accused of using the issue of democracy to fan old resentments against the Party about the Cultural Revolution, forming secret cabals with agents from Taiwan and having unauthorised relationships with foreigners. Deng went on to outline a new orthodoxy, the Four Cardinal Principles: to uphold socialism, the dictatorship of the proletariat, the leadership of the Communist Party of China and Marxism-Leninism-Mao-Zedong thought. The old drama was back to haunt the new emperor. Deng came to believe, like all his reforming predecessors, that the only way to modernise China was with authoritarianism close at hand. Perhaps he had never had much doubt about that.

Despite the crushing of the Democracy Wall, the 1980s were undoubtedly the most liberal period of the Communist era. The madness of the Cultural Revolution had ended. There was greater freedom of the press. A degree of religious freedom was restored. Economic benefits were being gained by hundreds of millions of people. Emboldened by the new spirit of optimism, in December 1986 student demonstrators taking advantage of the more relaxed political atmosphere began to agitate for more rapid reform. They were inspired by Fang Lizhi, a physicist from University of Science and Technology of China who made critical speeches saying policy reform was proceeding too slowly.[33] University life was also still humdrum and regimented and that too was a source of student protest. Compulsory calisthenics were no longer to the taste of students, nor was a prohibition on dancing at rock concerts. Students called for campus elections, the chance to study abroad and greater availability of Western pop culture. The suspicions of conservative Party elders were confirmed. Reform was leading to an unwelcome loosening of political control of society. Hu Yaobang, a leading advocate of reform, was blamed for the protests and forced to resign as General Secretary of the Communist Party in January 1987. Premier Zhao Ziyang, another reformer, became General Secretary and as a counterweight the staunch conservative, Li Peng, was made Premier – thereby institutionalising the certainty of leadership conflict. Although a marginal figure by April 1989, Hu Yaobang was still allowed to attend Politburo meetings. In the middle of an otherwise inconsequential discussion on 8 April Hu Yaobang suffered a heart attack and was taken to a nearby hospital. But he never recovered, and died on 15 April.

At the first meeting to plan the obituary and funeral chaired by Zhao Ziyang concerns were raised by Zhao himself about the possibilities of unrest and protest surrounding the funeral; he was remembering, no doubt, public mourning after the death of Zhou Enlai. This exchange is reported in the *Tiananmen Papers*, the leaked but extensive and authoritative accounts of Party dealings during that period:

Zhao Ziyang: Comrade Qiao Shi, please keep a close watch on how Comrade Yaobang's death might impact society.

Qiao Shi: At the moment society's in pretty good shape. Things are fairly stable. There are no signs of any large or organised disturbances. Personnel at all levels of the security and legal systems will keep close tabs on responses in society to Comrade Yaobang's death.

Yao Yilin: Consumer prices are rising fast. And the gap between rich and poor is getting bigger. We'd better watch that some people don't use the mourning for Comrade Yaobang as an excuse to make their complaints.

Zhao Ziyang: We should keep a close eye on the universities, especially ones like Peking University. College students are always the most sensitive.

Li Tieying: Things are good at the universities. It's not very likely that there'll be any trouble.[34]

Even at this early stage the leaders had an acute sense of the sources of dissent – inflation, inequality and student unrest – but they could only think of security responses for dealing with protests. Discussion of the protests' legitimacy or the need to respond positively and make concessions came weeks later; too late as it turned out. The grievances expressed in the early protests in slogans, speeches and characters written on the walls centred on political issues: freedom of the press, leadership accountability, the release of political prisoners and corruption by leaders and their children.[35] Even as early as 1989, the issue of 'the princelings' – the children of Party leaders who seem to monopolise power while amassing untold wealth – was provoking people's anger. A member of the Politburo Standing Committee, the highest power in the Party where all authority comes together, Tian Jiyun, gave this revealing assessment of the protesters' motives and their implications.

A lot of stories circulate these days about cabals of the 'princes', the 'secretaries' and 'sons-in-law' and it makes people sick. The Party's fallen very low; if we can't get the Party in order we'll never get rid of corruption and turmoil will always be with us.[36]

Although ordinary people had reasons to be optimistic, they also had criticisms. Indeed their greater sense of possibility coupled with the more liberal atmosphere gave them the confidence to speak out for a better future. Before long the protests spread from Beijing to other university campuses around the country. By 20 April 1989, a little more than two weeks after protests began in the capital the leaders were encased, out of touch as ever in their former Imperial compound in Zhongnanhai. They were receiving reports from university authorities, sometimes at hourly intervals, about student protests on campuses, including those in major cities like Xian, Nanjing and Wuhan. A wider and growing set of demands was reported: the failure to promote younger officials, and old leaders still exercising too much power. Intellectuals particularly resented the stripping of powers from their champion Hu Yaobang and were concerned that the Party had failed to stop the decline in social mores and social order. A narrow student political protest within a fortnight had spread and drawn in students around the country, as well as intellectuals. The list of demands was rapidly turning into a general critique of the economic and social policies of the Communist Party, as well as an ever more strident critique of the leaders themselves and their families. Meanwhile the senior leaders were as ever in a stalemated conflict. They had not even got as far as deciding how to commemorate the death of Hu Yaobang.

Zhao Ziyang felt throughout that the students were patriots, not seditious revolutionaries to be suppressed as a political threat. He felt many of their criticisms were genuine, certainly heartfelt, should be listened to and that the students could be reasoned with. He recorded views secretly and they were published posthumously.

At a Politburo Standing Committee meeting I said that we should not forbid the activities of the students who were merely holding their own commemorations while the Central Committee was holding memorial services. There was no reason why we should reserve for ourselves exclusive rights to commemorate Hu, while forbidding the students to do so. I suggested we punished according to law only those who engaged in the five types of behaviour: beating, smashing, looting, burning, or trespassing. In all other normal circumstances, there should be an attempt to reduce tensions.[37]

While Zhao Ziyang was away on a long-planned trip to North Korea, the hardline faction led by Li Peng prepared to publish a critical editorial in the *People's Daily* condemning the protests and accusing the protesters of being rioters, but first they needed the agreement of Deng Xiaoping. Li Peng and others visited him on 25 April. In the *Tiananmen Papers* Deng is reported to have said,

> A tiny minority is exploiting the students; they want to confuse the people and bring the country into chaos. This is a well-planned plot whose real aim is to reject the Chinese Communist Party and the socialist system at the most fundamental level. We must explain to the whole Party and nation that we are facing a most serious political struggle. We've got to be explicit and clear in opposing this turmoil.[38]

The 26 April editorial in the *People's Daily* contained almost exactly these words. It was as incendiary as anticipated. The editorial was broadcast on the campus of Peking University on the evening of 25 April and led immediately to further demonstrations in Beijing and many other cities too, including Shanghai, Hangzhou, Nanjing and Xian. On 28 April, with Zhao Ziyang still in North Korea, the *People's Daily* published another editorial pursuing the often to be repeated allegation that the students were being misled:

> All innocent and well-meaning young students should understand that in any large mass event dragons mingle with the fish. People with hidden intentions are just waiting for you to get too excited and for your actions to go too far so they can exploit you for their own profit.[39]

The protesters in Tiananmen Square were all too well aware of the historical significance of May the fourth and commemorated the anniversary. By 6 May they were planning a hunger strike. The leadership, including the elders, an officially retired group led by Deng Xiaoping, were particularly anxious about how all this would appear to the world media, which would be closely watching the impending visit to China of Gorbachev, the Soviet President.

On 14 May some of China's leading intellectuals appealed to the leadership to negotiate. Three days later a million people, now including many ordinary factory workers and local citizens, as well as students and the original protesters, demonstrated in Beijing. The situation was clearly now out of the authorities' control and by 19 May Deng and the elders had decided to reject Zhao Ziyang's suggestions of conciliatory negotiations. Zhao was summarily removed from power and lived out the rest of his days under house arrest. Martial law was declared in Beijing on 21 May. The protesters were unbowed. In defiance art students from Beijing's Central School of Fine Arts built a Goddess of Democracy, a statue inspired by New York's Statue of Liberty – an inflammatory gesture in itself, confirming to the hardliners that the protesters were under the influence of seditious foreigners. She was erected on 29 May. There was a standoff in the square between the protesters and authorities. By 4 June the moment had come for the army to move in and clear Tiananmen Square. The world watched as a thin man with a carrier bag refused to give way to a tank. Later, once he was out of the way, the tanks rolled in and hundreds of people died.[40]

After the demonstrators had been dispersed amid much bloodshed and killing, the army did not return immediately to barracks. For several days in effect they 'terrorised' Beijing, restoring order, cleaning up.[41] Under martial law troops began a political offensive, interrogating residents and 're-educating' the population about the need for 'stability'. Military personnel occupied various civilian institutions, in particular educational and research institutions whose members were active in the demonstrations: the Chinese Academy of Social Sciences, the Commission and Institute of Economic Reform of the State Council, Beijing University, Beijing Normal University, Beijing Aeronautics Institute and the China Politics and Law Institute, which were labelled the 'six disaster zones' by the military authorities. Soon after the uprising Deng Xiaoping praised the army for being the 'Great Steel Wall' of the Chinese Communist Party. The army's 'heroic deeds' were applauded and 'counter-revolutionary elements' who 'sought to overturn the state power' were denounced. But the Great Steel Wall had some weak links and the People's Liberation Army (PLA) needed to remove disloyal elements from its own ranks. There were courts martial and disciplinary action against hundreds of officers. Soon afterwards there were also wide-spread personnel changes in the senior reaches of the armed forces. Officers who had distinguished themselves at Tiananmen or were proven to be ideologically sound were promoted. The message was strongly reinforced throughout the army for several years; discipline should prevail in the ranks. Although the Party had been rescued by the army the Party was absolutely in control and seditious allegedly Western influences promoting democracy should be resisted by any means necessary.

Western media reported that students and intellectuals had taken to Tiananmen Square to campaign for freedom and democracy, but there was much more to the 1989 protests than that. One Tiananmen demonstrator, Wang Hui, now an academic and one of China's leading intellectuals, took the view in a 1997 essay that many of the demonstrators in Beijing and elsewhere were factory workers, not just students. The students undoubtedly sought democracy and freedom, but this was, in his view, not some international movement for democracy like those in Eastern Europe in 1989, nor was it a 1968-style youth uprising pursuing vaguely defined but deeply sought individual freedoms. The concerns of the ordinary factory workers and other demonstrators were price stability, social security, protection from the icy blasts of an unfettered market economy and an end to corruption and crony capitalism.[42] This analysis is confirmed by reports sent by provincial parties to Beijing. In Xian, for example, crowds of more than 10,000 people – comprising workers, officials and other local residents – gathered every day. Their discussions included subjects such as inflation, salaries and housing problems.[43]

Wang Hui also notes that aspects of reform created the anger that led to the Tiananmen protests taking hold and spreading. As reform unfolded clashes of interest appeared between departments, levels of government and between localities and the centre. In the cities urban workers, who had been lionised during the Mao years, were discovering the limits of the benefits of reform and facing up to what they would lose. These groups of people retained a generally supportive view of reform but started to doubt the benefits to them personally; their scepticism has grown subsequently. The division between the city and the countryside was also growing. The vast surpluses of workers in the countryside were prevented from coming to the city, at least legally, by the household registration system. The Chinese dream was stalling, not only as a result of political repression. All this constituted 'a crisis of legitimacy'. From intellectuals to factory workers and peasants people did not question the need for reform, but the distribution of benefits. They began to ask in whose interests the state and the Party were acting. They also began to doubt the equity and the efficacy of the authorities administering the reform. 'If one links the 1989 social movement to the historical conditions from which it came, it is possible to see clearly why demands for democratic freedoms were connected to demands for social equality.'[44]

The events of the Tiananmen suppression paralysed the leadership once more. The putative national leader Jiang Zemin, drafted in from Shanghai suddenly and unexpectedly, could not find his own course or a strong support base. He was so new to the top echelons that he could scarcely find his way around the leadership compound in Zhongnanhai. Other voices were arguing forcibly for the need to slow down reform and reassert social and political control, at the expense, if necessary, of economic development. Deng Xiaoping's Southern Tour in 1992 was designed to remind Jiang and the new leadership that the Deng-approved combination of market reform and state authoritarianism commanded great support among the people. The enthusiastic public reaction as an elderly Deng travelled around the go-go cities of Guangdong sent a powerful message to Beijing. The new leaders tampered with his legacy at their peril. The implied warning from Deng and his allies of popular retribution against any backtracking into hardline Marxist economics has been heeded, both by Jiang and his successor Hu Jintao.

Following the suppression of the Tiananmen demonstrations, and Deng's choreographed reminders and warnings, economic reforms were redoubled. Currency policy was set to promote exports. The improvement in export conditions that this brought about gave rise to opportunities for consolidation among companies and state-owned enterprises. Prices were aligned between the market and state-controlled firms. Whole new areas like Pudong across the water from Shanghai's famous Bund were opened for development. Millions of peasants left the countryside in search of factory work. These steps were all moving economic policy towards market mechanisms, but it was marketisaton that had in part been responsible for discontent and protests. So in suppressing protests the licence to move forward with market reforms was, according to Wang Hui, won through violence. The underlying discontent and the unwanted consequences – 'corruption, privatisation, the influence of special interest groups in public policy making, overheated development (in Shanghai, Hainan and other places) and the resulting financial crises, problems in the social welfare system, ecological crises and many other social problems' – remained without effective responses or resolution.[45] 'As a set of political arrangements, the formation of market society has not only failed to eradicate those very historical conditions targeted by the 1989 social movement but has in fact legalised those arrangements.'[46]

In the early 1990s, with the commitment to reform reasserted, the loss-making state-owned enterprises were under renewed scrutiny for their poor productivity and profitability. They soon started to close. Public expenditure through factory units was slashed in an effort to make those enterprises profitable. During the 1990s the government laid off 50 million workers in state enterprises and redeployed another 18 million to jobs that lacked the benefits of their old jobs.[47] The 'three irons' were removed from these people. The 'iron chair' of a job for life was whipped away. The 'iron rice bowl' of employment and the 'iron wage' of a guaranteed income and pension went the same way. Workers at centrally controlled urban state-owned enterprises dropped from 76 million to 28 million in the ten years from 1993. The immediate effect for most people was an acute and absolute loss of security. For the first time they faced the prospect of unemployment, no healthcare and no pension. Children's education would henceforth have to be paid for. Minimal social security payments for the unemployed were available only to the tiny few who were utterly destitute, and getting the money involved a humiliating encounter with generally uncaring local officials; perhaps even the payment of a bribe. The price of food rose rapidly as state subsidies were removed, though there was plenty more food available as the farms were decollectivised and became more efficient. With more money around and unheard-of inequalities appearing everywhere, corruption and bribery became rife. Not just in big government contracts, but in small day-to-day ways, people found themselves being bullied and having to pay bribes to get any one of the host of permissions and licences needed to conduct ordinary life. The grievances recorded in responses to the wish tree in the following chapters took root in this period. Optimism began to dissipate.

Against the backdrop of this boiling ocean of competing and contradictory social and economic currents and counter-currents the 'fourth generation' of leaders under President Hu Jintao took over as General Secretary of the Chinese Communist Party in 2002 in the first relatively smooth leadership transition of the Communist era; a surprise in itself to many. Hu's previous career had been undistinguished and characterised principally by loyalty to the Party and to his superiors. He had made little or no impact in the provinces of Gansu, Guizhou and Tibet where he had been Party Secretary, although he had declared martial law in Tibet to suppress demonstrations. His affability, contact-building and consensus-seeking skills were however second to none. He had also benefited from the patronage of Party elder Song Ping. He had worked with Song in Gansu, and Song subsequently rose to lead the exceedingly powerful Organisation Department, which has inordinate influence over appointments even at the most senior level.[48]

Reflecting his long-standing preference for avoiding intellectual conflicts, the approach which Hu developed, first stated a year after he took office, was for the Party to strive for the goal of building a 'socialist harmonious society'. In 2005 in a speech to the Central Party School, an influential ideological arena, Hu set out his vision; more a wish list than a coherent political philosophy:

> The socialist harmonious society we want to build should be a society featuring democracy, the rule of law, fairness, justice, sincerity, trustworthiness, amity, full vitality, stability, orderliness, and harmony between mankind and nature.[49]

The new Premier Wen Jiabao was no less committed to this pragmatic world-view. He was a skilled economic manager who had thrived under the reforming Premier Zhu Rongji during the Jiang Zemin era from 1989 to 2002. Wen had been at Zhao Ziyang's side when he tried 'too late' to negotiate with protesters in Tiananmen Square in 1989. But once Zhao fell Wen was also despatched, so he was not implicated in the subsequent crackdown. After becoming Premier he cultivated his image as 'Grandpa Wen' relatively untainted by brutal displays of force. Despite his commitment to market economics, Wen had also been a long-time advocate of a more equitable distribution of the benefits of reform, including social welfare. His motives were not entirely born of compassion. He could see the risks to society and, implicitly, the Party. Speaking in 2004 Wen stressed the risks of 'polarisation of the rich and poor, increased unemployment, expansion of

urban–rural and regional disparities, intensification of social contradictions and deterioration of the ecological environment . . . then social unrest
and retrogression will be unavoidable'.[50]

This set of ideas collected under the rubric of the harmonious society
draws heavily on Confucianism, so reviled by Mao, but reinterpreted by
more recent Communist leaders to bolster their own shaky legitimacy.
Confucius's vision of political leadership was of highly moral leaders with
irrefutable integrity observing rites and rituals which by their wisdom and
reliability would bring order and harmony to society. In such a society
ethical behaviour would flourish throughout the population and leaders
would never need to resort to violence to establish authoritarian social
order, which Confucius regarded as a threadbare facsimile of the sort of
harmony he had in mind.[51]

> If for one day one can overcome oneself and return to rites then all under
> heaven will accept one's benevolent authority.[52]

Gone were the calls for struggle and continuous revolution. Instead the
goal was to build a society that was 'moderately well off' (*xiaokang*), an
aspiration first asserted under Deng's leadership in the 1980s. Confucian
thought was back on the syllabus in schools and his legacy was celebrated
in popular culture, most notably in front of a global audience during the
opening ceremony for the 2008 Beijing Olympics which featured a huge
contingent of performers dressed as traditional Confucian scholars.
Confucius was also enlisted in China's public diplomacy. The government
launched more than 300 Confucius Institutes around the world to promote
Chinese language and culture. This 'neo-Confucianism' reached its high
water mark in January 2011 when, without announcement or official
celebration, a statue of Confucius was erected on the corner of a street just
off Tiananmen Square. If a statue could move, Confucius could have
turned his head to contemplate the Mao mausoleum. If Mao was to rise
from the dead, he could turn angrily to see his old *bête noire* Confucius.
The only other statues in Tiananmen Square are of anonymous people's
heroes. Even Sun Yatsen, the father of modern China, only merits a large
and removable hoarding from time to time, so a large, bronze statue of
Confucius, the old villain of Communist orthodoxy, was an audacious

move – which proved too bold. Just as the statue had arrived without fanfare, equally suddenly it disappeared a few months later, in April 2011.[53] Despite much internet speculation no explanation was given for its removal, as none had been given for its arrival.

The Central Committee of the Chinese Communist Party passed a resolution in October 2006 that addressed 'the major issues concerning the building of a socialist harmonious society' – committing the state to achieve social harmony by 2020. Perhaps the most notable target in the Party's resolution was that the 'widening of the gap between urban and rural development and development between different regions [will] gradually [be] reversed'. GDP per capita increased sevenfold between 1991 and 2006 and the proportion of people living under the poverty line (measured as *RMB*850 per person per year in 2002) fell from 30 per cent to 12 per cent between 1991 and 2001.[54] But at the same time income inequality between cities and the countryside increased year on year. In 1991 rural incomes were about 58 per cent as large as urban ones; in 2006 just 30 per cent.[55] The inequality between provinces has also increased: in 1991 the standard deviation of regional GDPs was *RMB*459; in 2001 it was *RMB*2763.[56]

A second 'contradiction' in the leadership's sights was the level of perceived procedural injustice. This was most keenly felt in the compensation which landowners received when their land was bought or expropriated under compulsory purchase. A survey of over 1,500 villages in 2005 found that farmers who received a lump-sum payment got, on average, *RMB*8,000 per *mu*[57] (Since the average farmer holds about 5 *mu* of arable land, this represents approximately four years' urban salary.[58]) Understandably, two-thirds of farmers who received compensation in cases of land acquisition and were forced to move to the city were disappointed with their treatment. More seriously still, a lack of due process prevented farmers from voicing their opinions: most were not notified of land expropriations in advance or consulted on the level of compensation. To make matters even worse, affected farmers seldom had access to independent courts for an unbiased ruling when the expropriating agency (typically the Ministry of Land and Resources) failed to address their concerns. Farmers have inevitably and understandably protested about their treatment. In the first nine months of 2006 alone, the state reported a total of 17,900 cases of 'massive rural incidents' in which 385,000 farmers took part.[59] Although news of them is routinely suppressed, many were certainly violent confrontations – some involving fatal shootings by the police or security forces.[60]

At the same time as the country's institutions failed to protect the poor and marginalised, they continued to benefit the rich and well-connected – by offering opportunities for corruption and graft. Plenty of opportunities arose, for example, for exploiting the difference between low planned prices and high market ones and rent-seeking with regard to the allocation of trade certificates and export permits. Inconsistently enforced tax, banking and finance regulations also create possibilities for graft. As a result many people felt there was an unfair bias. The law did not adequately protect them from a government eager to seize personal assets, yet it too readily shielded dishonest officials from prosecution or penalty.

The third major target for the Communist Party in building a harmonious society was exerting a greater degree of control over 'the ideological and moral qualities, scientific and cultural qualities . . . of the whole nation'. As more people live longer, the attitudinal differences between older and younger generations have become more stark. People who have witnessed war, revolutions and famines now live alongside a generation which knows only cell phones and internet gaming. Wealthy entrepreneurs and business people find themselves struggling against the hang-ups of socialist mindsets in every direction. The Party fears that as people are exposed to new ideas, either through travel or the internet, and as Maoist orthodoxy fades further into the past, they will begin to find more points of disagreement with one another and greater cause to seek special consideration from the state. Ultimately the concern is that such discord and friction between sections of society might eventually lead to challenges to one-party rule and calls for increased democratic participation. These fears are coming to pass.

Allied to Hu Jintao's concept of the harmonious society is his notion of scientific development. If a harmonious society is the chosen destination, Hu's doctrine of Scientific Development sought to explain how the country will get there. As its title suggested, the doctrine partly implied a range of economic development plans, such as growth by industrialisation and through investment in scientific research. To that extent 'scientific development' challenged a free market free-for-all. But the phrase also carried a more important connotation: that the path of the country's development should be determined using scientific principles – as opposed to Mao's irrational, inconsistent populism, vividly remembered but never discussed.

The origins of this idea are not new; Lenin himself wrote about taking a 'scientific' approach to socialist development and intellectual modernisers since the Qing dynasty have invoked science.[61] But since the death of Mao science has taken an even greater role in public affairs. Many of the Party leaders have backgrounds in the physical sciences.[62] President Hu himself was originally trained as a hydraulic engineer. Every Chinese schoolchild knows of China's proud ancient scientific traditions as represented by the 'four great inventions': paper, printing, the compass and gunpowder. Children are taught the philosophy of Sir Francis Bacon at school. Knowledge, they learn, is power and the way to achieve knowledge and thereby power is through the application of inductive rather than intuitive reasoning.[63] By contrast, few of the leaders are trained in the social sciences, which were suspended for over 30 years until the early 1980s. This perhaps explains why the leaders are perplexed by unpredicted turns of events in society. A positivist consensus, markedly different to Maoism, has emerged under Hu. Society is a mechanical system, the laws of which can be precisely determined and its attributes can be quantifiably measured. Ideas for public reform can be accurately hypothesised and tested; if they are successful here then they can be quickly expanded and implemented here, there and everywhere. The unyielding principles of science have been established at the heart of government in part as a way of departing from the superstition of the Great Leader's personality cult. All Mao's talk about contradictions and conflict is silently but comprehensively dumped, though not yet quite forgotten.

The doctrine of Scientific Development stresses the importance of objective decision-making. The rhetoric gives the impression that a single correct answer for each policy question can be found and that the government's sole task is to discover it. This line of thinking is seductive, but deceptive. In reality, policy decisions always contain some element of balancing the interests of different groups of citizens while not losing sight of practical effectiveness or 'do-ability'. Even under authoritarian regimes, genuine objectivity can never be pursued in practice. That implies that everyone sees the world in the same way, has consistent and identical interests, and never changes their mind. Hardest of all, the convinced have to cajole or coerce the sceptical and the indifferent. In the end it only encourages a monistic fiction that stifles disagreement and suppresses dissent without eradicating it – which, of course, may be attractive to the leadership from some points of view. The goal of consensual, orderly, linear, economic and social progress, to the dismay of scientific planners, remains illusory, not just in China, but everywhere.

By December 2005 Hu had developed the 'scientific development' concept to take in an enormous wish list of policy priorities stretching far beyond a narrow focus on economic growth. This included agriculture, energy, sustainable use of resources, competitiveness, innovation, improving administration, transparency, e-government, transforming state-owned enterprises, human capital, migration, ethnic minorities, education, social welfare, public health and safety and on and on. The speech he gave at the Central Party School was a tour de force of diagnosis and analysis showing that Party thinkers had certainly embraced Deng's nostrum to 'seek truth from facts'. But many of these problems did not have simple or ready answers, and some were extremely difficult: what is to be done with 700 million poor and under-employed peasants? How many jobs can be rapidly and realistically created? Sometimes potential solutions bumped into competing priorities. For example, rapid economic growth is simply not compatible with environmental sustainability. Policy solutions also collided with unshakeable Party doctrines. Transparency and administrative reform were set against the Party's opaque and sometimes inexplicable decision-making processes.[64] In a contest the Party was always going to win and scientific development was bound to lose.

China's political and social history since 1978 is too easily and simplistically characterised as rapid economic development and a stalled process of political reform with authoritarian crackdowns when necessary. The true picture is more complex. The leitmotif of the Reform era has indeed been rapid economic development, but this has always been attended by public protest and often stalled by leadership division. The underlying problems that create public discontent remain but the optimism of the 1980s – the years of the Chinese dream – has faded.

Inequality is still extremely high. Price inflation, especially in relation to food, is still unconquered. Jobs are still hard to find, even for the ever-increasing number of graduates. Even for those with jobs promotion seems too often to be blocked by the grip of immovable senior cadres and their henchmen. The media, and particularly the internet, are still heavily controlled. Leadership accountability and the behaviour of the children of Party leaders has not improved; quite the opposite. There is still no rule of law. Many political prisoners have disappeared, their fates unknown. Liu Xiaobo, who was awarded the Nobel Peace Prize in 2010, is only the most high profile of those. After an initial period of relative tolerance, religious observance is once more tightly controlled, especially Falun Gong. The rural–urban divide is as great as ever. Many millions of people are trapped in the countryside with no work and unable to move to the city because of the restrictions on household registration. Migrants to the city are harassed by law enforcers and denied public services. Insecure factory workers are exploited. Public services have to be paid for by the citizens and many can't afford them. All of these problems have been the subject of protests in the past and they may be *casus belli* again in the future. Faced with that situation the leaders will no doubt once more be argumentative and respond in a slow, confused but ultimately authoritarian way. The underlying dynamics and tensions in Chinese society put in place by Reform have neither changed nor been resolved. The constant and widespread protests may yet coalesce again into a bigger national uprising. A beguilingly, but relatively, quiet period under the Hu-Wen leadership should not be mistaken for a decisive and irreversible shift to the much-longed-for harmonious society.

CHAPTER 4

The Wish Tree

Back in the UK during the winter of 2006 I set about learning Mandarin and reading up on China's recent much-debated and contested history. I noted the urge to rejoin the mainstream of economic progress and modernity, but also that determined authoritarianism was facing multifarious spirited resistance. I began to think about potential participatory methods that would elicit thoughts and feelings about social and economic transformation from large numbers of Chinese people without falling foul of the authorities whose permission would undoubtedly be needed and no doubt hard to get. My mind went back to the wish trees I had seen around China. In traditional Tibetan Buddhist belief the wind carries prayers, including wishes on trees, from earth to heaven. Also found in Daoist tradition, attaching a wish to a tree is popular during lunar New Year festivities. Similar traditions and beliefs prevail in Japan and Korea as well as China.

Chinese people are universally superstitious. The right time and temperature to drink water is governed by all sorts of handed-down beliefs. If children get sick, peasants still believe that changing their name will help them to recover. Mothers with newborn babies are told not to take showers because it creates too much wind. Numbers have a special significance. The number four is unlucky, because the word when spoken sounds similar to the word for death. The number eight is lucky so the Beijing Olympics began at 8 p.m. on the eighth day of August (the eighth month) 2008. Astrology and the *I Ching*[1] are universal obsessions. This commitment to a vast ever-evolving range of mysterious beliefs stems from the open-ended ethos of Chinese spirituality. In the absence of an authoritative scripture, a single supreme deity or a hierarchical human religious authority like the Pope, beliefs from many traditions can be absorbed or new ones simply invented. Heresy or apostasy are alien concepts to the Chinese spiritual tradition. Appealing to universal notions of good fortune, so integral to the traditional Chinese way of thinking, seemed to me more fertile territory than traditional surveys that would only elicit circumscribed, self-censored answers, even in the unlikely event that permission was granted to conduct them.

The Jinyun (Red Cloud) mountains are roughly 100 kilometres north of Chongqing. In this group of nine mountains the Lion Peak is the most popular with visitors. There has been a Buddhist temple with mythical origins on that mountainside since AD 423, during the Southern Dynasties. The temple is a centre of study and teaching. At the highest point on Lion Peak is a viewing platform and just beyond the platform is a wish tree. People have written their wishes and tied them to a small weight with a red ribbon, which they have thrown on to the branch of the tree from the viewing platform nearby. Hundreds of wishes have been suspended from the branches, their messages carried up by the wind every time it blew. Like wishes, they were just out of reach. Snagged on the branch, they were believed to be more likely to come true.

I had also seen wish trees in two important and recently restored Confucius temples in Beijing and Shanghai. In the Confucius Temple in Beijing carved stone *bixi* (mythical tortoise-dragons) hold up pillars in pavilions between ponds converging on the main hall. On the lawns are ancient, gnarled, semi-fossilised cypress trees. In a specially built storehouse forests of stone steles, each the height of a human being, are stacked in dark, forbidding rows. All Confucius's teachings are carved on them in perfect lines of characters. Next door is the Imperial College where the emperor used to come to expound Confucian classics to audiences of thousands of scholars kneeling in silent, uniform rows. At the entrance contemporary students buy a thin wooden tablet, a little larger than a business card, with a red good luck knot tied at the bottom. Once they have written their wishes on it they walk through the pavilions and hang it along with hundreds of others on railings in the temple grounds.

The Confucius Temple in Shanghai, restored in 1999, is a tranquil oasis in the middle of the hectic city. It is a group of pagodas with curling roofs. In between the pagodas are still, reflective green fishponds full of large koi and goldfish that glint when they near the surface and the sun catches their scales. Twisted, ancient trees with deeply ridged bark and rugged rocks are arranged among the buildings and ponds. The rocks have been drawn from the bottom of a river and strategically placed to look like distant mountains. In traditional Chinese gardens short perspectives, enclosed by walls and buildings, evoke an unseen natural landscape. European gardens by contrast merge the man-made garden into the bigger vista beyond, creating a long, naturalistic perspective.

On their way into the temple, hundreds of students and their parents buy a wish card in the shop by the entrance. It's made of parchment-like waxed paper. On one side of the card is a picture of Confucius. They write their wish on the other side. Usually, though not exclusively, they wish for success in exams, prosperity in later life and safety and security (*ping an*) for their nearest and dearest. The card is then tied to the branch of a tree with a red ribbon, alongside many others. Cards are crammed tightly against each other along the long branches of many trees in the temple courtyard. On a sunny day the sunlight dapples through the leaves on to the cards, picking out someone's wish and casting it in high relief against the others in the shadows. The earnest hopes, yearning and personal disclosures of struggles or problems are always touching, sometimes moving. Never is there a hint of the irony or cynicism that Western students might express, just heartfelt sincerity.

On my third visit to China, in October 2006, I visited an old warehouse building in Shenzhen which had been turned into artists' studios. In one of these a Korean artist showed me how she had made wish cards and handed them to passers-by outside the Shenzhen Art Museum. She had lived in Shenzhen for a few months and the city seemed full of homesick people longing for something else, somewhere else. So she had decided to erect a wish tree outside the city's museum as an artistic expression of the longing that she sensed so many people felt, such a stark contrast to the showy, shiny economic dynamism that the city purported to represent. She asked them to write their wishes on the cards and tie them to an artificial tree she had made and erected outside the museum. This, she said, was an artistic installation that reflected her perceptions of Shenzhen. Everyone in Shenzhen came from somewhere else. Before it became a SEZ in 1979 it had just been a fishing village. Now she saw a city of millions of lonely, bewildered strangers.

I asked her if she had sought official permission to erect her wish tree outside the museum or if anyone had tried to stop her. She said it had not occurred to her that permission might be needed. Once she got started the police had come over and asked her what she was doing. She told them she was making a work of art outside the museum, an uncontroversial location. As she was on her own and didn't seem to be attracting a big crowd they wandered off, apparently unconcerned. She was left undisturbed for the rest of the afternoon. She had taken photographs and videos of the people who had filled in wish cards and put them on her tree. She planned to include them, the tree and the wishes in an artwork about the city. Many, as she had suspected, wished to return home, the shiny appeal of wealth and success tarnished by the harsh experiences of trying to achieve them.[2]

I had met a senior official in the Chongqing Civil Affairs Bureau in October 2006, an old-fashioned, ex-military man previously in charge of 'moral education' in the People's Liberation Army based in Chongqing. He was formal, but also direct, with a way of speaking that amused my Chinese friends. They reported that it was a passable imitation of Chairman Mao's declamatory bark. After the endless formalities, the conversation took a less scripted turn. He was not just being polite to a well-connected foreigner. He told me he was frustrated by the inability of local 'street-level' officials to contain and resolve local disputes. Some of these made it all the way to Beijing and left him and his department embarrassed and subject to criticism. In Chongqing alone there were 16,000 of these front-line officials. He said that I struck him as a practical person. In his view foreigners and people from universities were usually vague and indecisive. He wanted to know if there was anything I could do to help with the problems he had outlined. He seemed surprisingly well-disposed.

From the UK, after some reflection, I contacted the officials in Chongqing and proposed something along the lines of the wish trees. The reply came back early in 2007. Following my meeting with the senior officials in the Civil Affairs Bureau the municipality would like the university, with my help, to train local officials in techniques for involving local people in decision-making. This was in line with Chongqing's mandate to innovate in participation and the often frustrated wish of senior officials that their staff on the ground should manage tensions better.

Three neighbourhoods in the city, each with its own character and history, were selected to participate. All three had undergone a seismic economic shock. In one, farmers had lost their land for development and been rehoused on a new estate. In the second a huge tyre factory had closed and in the third a traditional neighbourhood had lost its chinaware factory and was being turned into a tourist destination. These were three microcosms of China's economic and social transformation: the involuntary displacement of farmers from their own land; the closure of loss-making, state-owned enterprises and the attempt by municipal authorities to attract new revenues from service activities like tourism. Ground-level officials in these particular neighbourhoods had, in the judgement of the Civil Affairs Bureau, shown skill and innovation in meeting the challenges of upheaval unlike many others. Change had been managed and achieved apparently without uproar; they were therefore good showcases for the harmonious society. The officials from the Chongqing municipality hoped to show the best face of their administration and its achievements as well as wanting their staff to learn from Western experience. These neighbourhoods were to be the laboratory for the Wish Tree.

In the UK at the beginning of 2007, as I seemed to have the official go-ahead, I asked a graphic artist to make a design for the tree and the leaf cards. The designer created a wish tree that was a stylised tree with many branches and no leaves, the better for affixing wishes written on leaves (Figure 1). It was designed on a computer so that the PDF image could be emailed to China where it could be blown up and the Wish Tree constructed

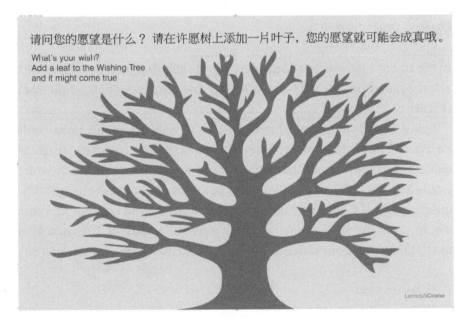

Figure 1. Design for the Wish Tree

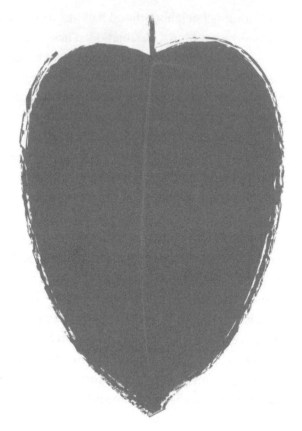

Figure 2. Design for Wish Tree 'leaf'

to the size of a large advertising hoarding. He also designed a postcard with a leaf printed on one side and space for the four questions on the back (Figure 2).

Space was obviously at a premium and so only a few questions could be asked. They had to be expressed in simple, non-bureaucratic language and strike to the heart of the economic and social changes in a way which would elicit people's true feelings and opinions about those changes. The questions should obviously not make the authorities so nervous that they would abort the whole venture. These were the questions I devised after much thought. No one raised any objections, so they were agreed (Figure 3).

- Who are you?
- What event changed your life?

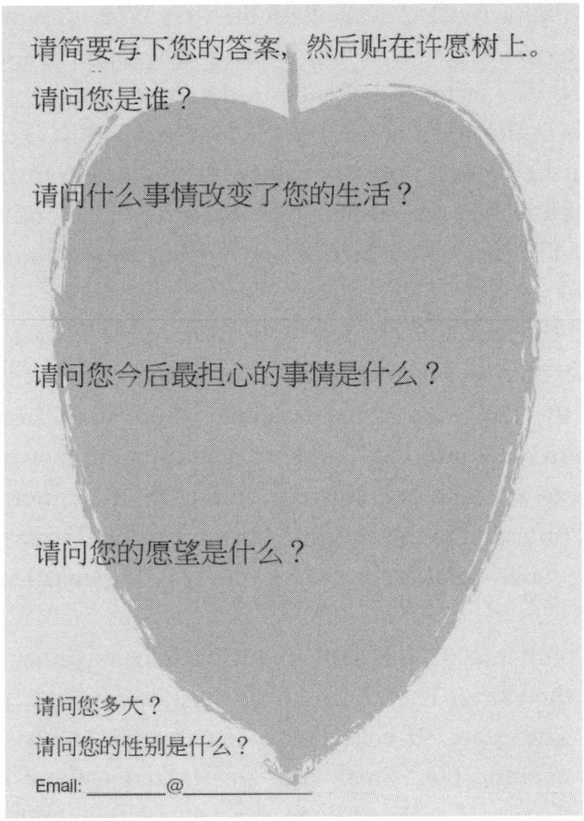

Figure 3. Wish Tree leaf response card

- What is your biggest worry?
- What do you wish for?

I could see that conducting the Wish Tree activity was going to make my next visit to China a rather different kind of trip; not the usual round of official meetings and frequent meals interspersed with lively academic debates. Everybody involved was in unknown territory. Chinese authorities and academics did not engage in these kinds of participatory activities and I had never done anything like this in China. I was now embarked on fieldwork requiring complex logistics. I decided, in these circumstances, to enlist the assistance of a researcher as there would be a good deal to do on the ground – not all of it predictable.

Soon after we arrived in May 2007 the first Wish Tree was erected at Hemu Lu (Harmony Road), a new housing development for people who were until recently farmers in Renhe in the Yubei district of Chongqing. The district is in the north of the city, the area being most extensively redeveloped with the highest property values and the best transport links. No surprise therefore that the farmers have been relocated and the farmland redeveloped. The fields were turned into a modern neighbourhood as the city expanded.

All around the new housing development were green wasteland and low hills. Officials had told us that the local residents were farmers who had migrated to the city. I asked the residents where their farms had been, expecting them to mention somewhere distant. Instead they pointed across a single field to the land just adjacent. In fact the city migrated to them; they had not migrated to the city. In return for the land they received a flat in one of the newly built blocks and a one-off compensation payment of RMB21,000.

Hemu Lu, built in 2001, was like a municipal housing project recognisable anywhere in the world. The design of the neighbourhood is repetitive and institutional. The estate is a collection of four- or five-storey blocks clad in white, shiny ceramic tiles. Small flats are stacked without originality or imagination on top of each other. In the ground floor units a few small grocery stores sell large sacks of rice, fresh vegetables and chillies. The windows are covered with bars. Running alongside the apartment blocks is a large concrete and treeless open space for community activities with brightly painted low-tech exercise equipment, as well as a seesaw and swings.

The Wish Tree was erected in this community square. The size of a large advertising hoarding on a wooden frame, it dominated one side of the square. The residents, by their own account, had little education, led simple lives and never had great expectations of getting rich. Most were now unemployed and re-employment chances were poor to negligible. Without land and with poor job prospects, they most were going to be living on the Minimum Living Standard (MLS), a stipend from the municipal authorities of just over RMB200 a month, with few opportunities to improve their livelihood. If they were old, they had to rely on state pensions paid at a lower rate because rural dwellers, according to government rules, are paid a smaller pension than urban factory workers. The only prospect of improving their material lot, for many of them, was through their child's dutiful fulfilment of their filial obligations, at least for those who had children with jobs outside the city and who sent money home.

Recognising that those who remained in Hemu Lu were likely to be old, poor and with little to do, the community leaders concentrated on organising activities for older people, for which they received an award from the government in 2005. Hemu Lu was recognised as a 'moral civilisation excellence window' under the official theme of Harmonious Neighbourhood, Harmonious Community. The problem for the cheerful local officials, who seemed to have a good relationship with the residents, was that leisure activities were really all they had in their gift and they were a poor substitute for land and livelihood.

The day the Wish Tree was erected was rainy. The bad weather did not put people off. A steady flow grew into a group of several hundred people. Half a dozen postgraduate students from the university, both male and female, enthusiastically handed out the leaf cards. People went into the community centre to fill in the card out of the rain. Sitting around tables in the library young adults helped older people with bad eyesight or those who couldn't read and write. It was a school day, so the children were at school. Many young adults had moved away for work or housing. Some sat thoughtfully on their own filling in the cards. Once satisfied with their answers they took the card and stuck it to a branch of the tree. Before long the branches were covered with cards (Figure 4). Latecomers had to search for spaces for their card. All went smoothly, without fuss in a low-key, good-natured way. This went on for several hours, people coming and going, standing around chatting, curious as well as talkative. The local official, a woman in her mid-thirties, looked on, smiling with benign satisfaction.

After a few hours people started to drift away and the numbers hanging around dwindled. I and my researcher sat down with the student volunteers and asked them to translate some of the cards. We were flushed with our success. Without encountering official opposition, we had managed to work our way into a remote community, which no foreigners had visited before, much less worked in; a place far from flashy Shanghai and grand Beijing, far even from Chongqing's city centre. We had managed to collect the views of several hundred poor people who had gone through an

Figure 4. Respondents sticking 'leaves' to the Wish Tree

unwanted and irreversible transformation. Apparently without censorship, constraint or restraint they told us what they thought. Did people feel that the drastic changes they were going through were all for the good after the benighted Mao era? Or were they more critical? My previous travels to remote places, like Wanzhou, with jumpy officials had suggested to me that there was much to hide. Were ordinary people concerned or unhappy, stoical or angry and, if so, about what?

The cards gave us a fascinating insight into people's lives and concerns, far more interesting, honest and revealing than anything I had heard or read before. After looking at a few dozen cards and noting the translations, we knew we had elicited a lot of good-quality information. People were telling us about the consequences of losing their farms. The biggest problem was losing their livelihood with their land. Their prospects for future employment were poor. Minimal government welfare payments were unacceptably low, they told us. Some people were deemed ineligible for even these minimal payments. Since their employment prospects were also negligible, this seemed unfair and they were even more unhappy.

Some had also struggled to overcome bureaucratic hurdles in getting a new flat and they were the most unhappy. Outright criticisms of the government were rare, but unhappiness about the effects of government policy was all too evident even in a preliminary scan of a selection of cards.

As there weren't many people about and the rain was unrelenting I suggested to the student volunteers that they start taking the cards down and storing them. They put the cards in boxes. All the materials were packed into the car, including the boxes of cards. The official, who had been co-operative and smiling throughout, looked a bit surprised and nervous that we were taking the cards away, but did not try to intervene or stop us. But she said she had to report this unexpected turn of events to her seniors at the municipal offices. When they were told we had taken the cards away without any official vetting, the more senior officials were predictably alarmed. They did not, however, run the risk of provoking an immediate confrontation by asking for them to be given back straight away. That might lead to a loss of face all round and I, like every foreigner who works in China, had been endlessly warned about the Chinese cultural tradition that made loss of face practically the most heinous thing imaginable. Instead we were told that some of the more senior office-based officials would be attending the Wish Tree event themselves in Ciqikou the next day to keep an eye on us and on the proceedings. No one said that in future the cards should not be taken away by us and, in the absence of that explicit prohibition, my intention was that the next day we would take the cards away again – though I feared that might prove difficult.

The next day the Wish Tree was erected in Ciqikou, a town in the northeast corner of Chongqing's Shapingba district. It overlooks the last stretch of the Jialing River before being subsumed by its larger cousin, the Yangtze, at Chaotianmen. During a civil war in the sixth century a temple had been built here, initially to safeguard local fishermen from the dangers of the river. Over time pilgrims flocked to pray within its walls. The town of Baiyachang (as Ciqikou was then known) prospered until the early Qing dynasty (seventeenth century). After a series of wars the Qing emperors encouraged inward migration to Sichuan hoping to dilute the rebellious spirit of the locals (a policy that has more recently been pursued in Tibet and Xinjiang). Legend has it that three brothers from a family that had made chinaware for generations travelled from Fujian province. One of the brothers specialised in making affordable porcelain bowls and he established a new business. Gradually the town became famous for china products. Eventually the area came to be known as Ciqikou, meaning china port.

During the Second World War the Nationalist government temporarily moved to Chongqing, a part of the country that was thought less accessible for Japanese bombers (though Chongqing was eventually extensively bombed by the Japanese). Politicians, academics and artists followed and turned Ciqikou into an intellectual hub. This illustrious history and its propitious *feng shui* have saved Ciqikou from destructive redevelopment. City administrators sought to preserve the area's layout, buildings and general feel by making it a tourist attraction. It was awarded the status of Chongqing Traditional Cultural and Historic District by the State Council in 1998. Protective measures, including limits on the size of people's houses, seek to preserve the traditional buildings and promote tourism. The Chinese have not adopted the Italian style of restoration, which largely ignores the building's original appearance and takes the condition of the building at the moment restoration begins as a starting point. What is preserved is already in general decay but will not decay further. Instead, the buildings in the tourist parts of Ciqikou are heavily restored to their perceived original state, rendering them inauthentic and plastic to eyes trained in European notions of the picturesque.[3] All signs of romantic decay and genteel distress have been removed. Most of the restored, rebuilt shops are painted bright red and sell life's inessentials: kites, hard sweets made with ginger, toys and silk clothes. One shop is even a mini silk factory, where staff stretch and pull at skeins of silk so that tourists can appreciate these ancient skills. About 5,000 (mainly Chinese) tourists visit the teahouses, handicraft workshops and food shops every day.

For a sense of old Chongqing, Ciqikou is the place to go, but not to the tourist area. The Wish Tree was erected in Maanshan village, above the rebuilt Ciqikou town. Maanshan has about 1,500 residents; many are elderly. Most worked in the chinaware factory until it closed. Now they rely on traditional crafts (such as embroidery or paper-cutting) or giving folk music performances for tourists in the town down below. As I walked through the village I witnessed their unchanged lifestyle. Outside a small one-storey, two-room house two elderly sisters washed their pots silently in a stone sink. Washing dishes and clothes as well as cooking are done outside on the front veranda in the traditional way. Since most domestic activity takes place outside, so does the socialising. Interiors are dark and functional. The houses on both sides of the narrow street were so close together that raised voices would be heard in every house. The windows on the street were protected by bars, not by expensive glass.

Up another level above these houses, the steps were broader and better looked after. They led to the courtyard of the ancient temple where coils of burning incense hung down. Thin blue plumes of smoke curled and floated up. Above them caged birds hung from the branches of trees. One of them, a super-clever black mynah bird within minutes started to mimic with eerie accuracy the unusual laugh of a foreigner. Listening to the cheerful birdsong seems bucolic but most of it is recorded, piped out of speakers to encourage and supplement the real birds.

Up still more steps you reach the highest level, the community square. The Wish Tree was erected here on a low stage under a yellowing portrait of Chairman Mao. Pagoda-style roofs with pointed and upturned corners on red pillars are set over open courtyards. Large Sichuan opera masks, brightly painted in blue, red and yellow with vivid curling black stripes, decorated the terrace, the paint chipped and faded by the constant damp. Under the canopies many groups of four older people sat round square tables playing mah-jong intently. The tiles were turned face down and a swirl of eight hands shuffled them around the tabletop making a clacking rhythm. Once a new set of tiles had been selected each player in turn slammed down their piece. Those not playing mah-jong were sitting on bamboo chairs chatting. Some women were knitting extremely fast. Two middle-aged women laughingly bounced each other up and down on the children's seesaw.

The male community worker in Ciqikou was jolly and friendly, older than his female counterpart in Hemu Lu, perhaps in his fifties. Evidently much respected and liked, he exuded bonhomie and self-confidence. He had arranged for posters to be put up inviting people to the Wish Tree in Maanshan. The town square was full and busy. I got the proceedings started with a short speech delivered, to universal astonishment, in Mandarin. As at Hemu Lu, people took cards from the students, thought carefully about their responses and then put them on the tree. The players returned to their mah-jong and the music was turned on for an impromptu ballroom dancing session. Middle-aged women once more seemed the most enthusiastic.

After the frisson of tension about the cards in Hemu Lu I wondered whether there would be an argument or if we would be prevented from taking the cards away, particularly as the more senior officials were present the entire time. Hundreds of people had participated in Ciqikou and we knew from Hemu Lu that interesting material was being elicited. I feared that the cards would simply be taken away by officials, never to be seen again. After all this effort I would never know what people had said. To head off this possible frustration, my researcher started work with the students from the university to translate what people had written as the cards were still being collected. That way at least we would have some translations noted down even if we didn't get to keep all the cards. But it was over-optimistic to hope that the translations could keep pace with the completion of the cards. With apprehension, I would have to ask if we could take the untranslated cards away. To my surprise and delight, without hesitation the good-natured community worker said, 'mei wenti', 'no problem'. We could return them when we had finished with them. He clearly didn't have much to be concerned about. I was finding out that when dealing with Chinese officialdom, what-ever the rules say, what actually happens in any situation is random and unpredictable. Local officials deploy much discretion in the application of rules, keeping as some say 'one eye open, one eye closed'. The watchful municipal officials raised no objections, no doubt drawing confidence from the local official's nonchalance. Relieved, I hoped the potential objections to us collecting and translating the responses had faded away once and for all. But I was wrong. The next day in Banshanercun brought trouble.

Banshanercun is in the Jiulongpo district of Chongqing. Built in the Bauhaus style at the height of Mao's era of Soviet-inspired industrialisation, it looks like a typical *danwei. Danweis*, along with the communes in the countryside, were the building blocks of the entire Communist system. Every working man and woman was registered to one whether that was a city ward, factory, rural production brigade, hospital, school or office. The Party leaders of each *danwei* had immense power over the local residents. In return the workers were promised cradle-to-grave security. That was the Communist social contract. Banshanercun is a large community stretching along winding roads and bounded by a four-lane main road at one end.

The area is dominated by a long, low, brick-built factory. The factory has a one-sided pitched roof and small windows turned black by pollution. This had been the tyre factory where 3,000 people once worked. The community, according to officials, had 6,800 residents. At least one member of most families would have been working in the tyre factory. All around it are grimy blocks of flats. A big walled concrete public space has a large school next to it and a small hospital beyond.

The tyre factory was a major supplier to Chongqing's car and motorcycle industry which manufactured cars for the whole of China but it was old-fashioned, unmechanised and unprofitable. It was closed as part of the restructuring of state-owned enterprises. In its heyday the tyres made in the factory would have automatically been bought by state-owned car manufacturers. Questions of demand and supply, price or profit, quality or cost simply would not have arisen. The only relevant metric by which to judge the factory's performance would be whether it met a target set as part of a complex five-year plan. Such was the planned economy, complete with enormous incentives to exaggerate economic success.

Nearby a high-tech factory manufacturing brake linings was built and opened. The new factory only employs 1,000 people so two-thirds of the workers in the old tyre factory did not get jobs. The authorities in Banshanercun have also built some new spaces for business, though they are not big enough to attract anything substantial or employ many people. The community leaders try to work in partnership with the local residents' committees who have a say in the organisation of the 'social security service station'. They have sought to pioneer 'people-oriented governance', dispute resolution and 'constructing harmony'. New facilities have been developed and activities arranged for the residents with time on their hands, like a tea garden and a small, under-used reading room. Microeconomic activities have been encouraged, such as small convenience stores, which are 'exploring ways of strengthening the community role in the market economy'.[4] The community leaders have also tried to improve public services, with birth control clinics, community medical services, 'civil reconciliation' and, interestingly, more security guards. All this wholesome and well-meaning activity by local officials, though hardly likely to replace the benefits of guaranteed lifetime employment, was evidence once more of the commitment to building a harmonious society manifested at the neighbourhood level. These positive activities were also, of course, why this community was chosen for the Wish Tree: to put the best official face forward.

The Wish Tree was erected in Banshanercun on a rare sunny morning. The sky was brighter, the atmosphere clearer than it had been in Hemu Lu or Ciqikou. Much less smog than usual hovered over the whole of Chongqing. That morning the square was lively and busy, crowded with smiling people of all ages. Neatly uniformed children from the school next to the square were gathered expectantly in tidy lines. Some wore the red scarves of Young Pioneers, the Communist youth leadership movement akin to the Boy Scouts. They jostled one another, the teachers frowning and telling them to stay in line. Middle-aged women in matching bright green trouser suits with yellow belts and sashes stood in long rows smiling, holding drums and drumsticks. They were a marching band and on cue they began to play and dance in formation.

The welcoming scene was much more formal and celebratory than those at Hemu Lu or Ciqikou. A senior official from the municipality gave a speech from the stage. I responded, expressing thanks. Everyone clapped; some cheered. Banshanercun was displaying its formal, structured *danwei* culture. Everyone in the neighbourhood worked together at the factory, unlike in the more mixed economy and community of Ciqikou. These factories were seen as the vanguard of Mao's revolution. The workers in them would have received a great deal of political education. Collective social activity outside the factory would have been encouraged, along with group calisthenics and the singing of Maoist anthems. *Esprit de corps* and the feeling of being among the superior castes building China's glorious future would have taken instrumental form in more generous welfare payments and pensions. Even if the over-the-top rhetoric wasn't really credible the lucky workers were well aware that they were better off than many others because they worked in a factory with all its structures and hierachies.

That morning older residents sat on walls around the square chatting, smoking and smiling at the children; men mostly with men, women with women. Some of the middle-aged women not in the bands sat smiling and knitting, their fingers flying, the knitting needles a blur as they chatted. If they saw someone they knew they walked across the square to talk to them, never missing a beat with the needles, knitting as they walked, their bag of

wool in a carrier bag over their arm. Again, the student volunteers circulated among the local residents giving out Wish Tree cards. Everyone
started filling these in, helping each other, checking what friends and relatives were writing. Some took the card away to think about their answers
and fill it in privately. They were evidently taking their responses seriously.
Once the cards were completed, people pinned them on the tree. The children went first, pushing and shoving to get their leaf on exactly the branch
they had selected. Then adults stuck their leaves on. Next came the women
in green from the marching band and then the older people, moving slowly
and making sure superstitiously that their leaf was placed next to their
sister's or friend's. The tree was soon covered with leaves and waves of
leaves had to be removed to make room for new ones. With all the music,
clapping and noise even those who had not heard about the Wish Tree
came down to the square to find out what was going on. Most of them
joined in, taking a leaf card, making a wish and placing it on a branch. A
few old men looked on in a bad-tempered way wondering what all this
noise was about and refusing to join in.

One old lady, short, stout and in a brown dress, came hurrying down
into the square after everyone else. 'Where,' she demanded, 'are the officials? I want to talk to them.' She was evidently trying to look and remain
calm. The municipal officials were pointed out to her. The old lady walked
straight up to the smart woman who was a senior municipal official, inter-
rupting her conversation. In a loud voice, the old lady started recounting
her grievances. The students, sniggering at the embarrassing scene, over-
heard and translated for me. The old lady said her small pension was not
being paid. Her husband was dead and her daughter worked far away so
she had no money to live on.

Obviously at a loss for words the official just gave the old lady a fixed,
enigmatic smile, making her even angrier. She started to shout and point.
An old man from the local community, seeing that none of the officials
knew what to do, tried to intervene. He took her by the arm and tried to
lead her away as she carried on shouting. She resisted, punched the old
man in the chest and shook him off. He backed away. The female official
tried to calm the old lady down, touching her arm and speaking softly.
Suddenly the old lady started crying and someone brought her a plastic
stool to sit on. She collapsed, crumpled and shrunken, and dabbed her eyes

with her handkerchief as the tears kept rolling. She cried loudly and without restraint. The officials continued to look anxious – but also a little relieved. The emotional temperature seemed to have peaked.

As the official moved quietly away from the old lady, who was now distracted by her own tears and upset, I went over to talk to her. Through the interpreter she said, 'My husband is dead. He was a Communist. He fought for liberation in 1949. We are the workers. We are the people. They must serve the people. My daughter is far away in Guangdong. I am sick.' She rubbed her stomach. 'I've had this lump for a long time. I think it's cancer. I can't afford to go to the doctor and I haven't told my daughter. I don't want to ruin her life. Anyway,' she concluded quietly with a fatalistic shrug, 'I'm old and I've had a good life.' Suddenly all the fight seemed to have gone out of her.

Over by the Wish Tree officials with worried expressions, including the woman whom the old lady had complained to, were taking the cards off the tree one by one, turning them over and reading what people had written. The incident with the old lady had evidently amplified their anxieties. They were too busy digesting what was written on the cards to notice me photographing them. Inevitably I wondered if the incident, along with whatever criticisms had been written, would mean that the officials would ensure that the cards were taken away without our seeing them. Once more I was close to finding out what ordinary Chinese people thought only, it seemed, to have the results of all this effort whipped away at the last hurdle. Throughout I had been at pains to stress that the Wish Tree was a participatory activity designed to help street-level officials to understand, prevent and resolve local disputes and problems. But it was precisely the local disputes and problems that they wished to conceal from international eyes. Wen Jiabao could talk in general terms about social tensions, but as far as municipal officials were concerned the revelation in detail of specific local problems was far more trouble than it was worth. Of course, it wasn't only us from whom they wanted to hide any problems; it was also their superiors.

Chinese bureaucracy is an elaborate chess-like game of bluff in which junior officials seek to conceal exactly what senior officials know they need to know. In an effort to get past lies and denials from the lower ranks many official meetings all the way up to the Politburo and the State Council are given over to listening to third party reports from all over the country. These are often collected privately and reported by journalists from the

Xinhua News Agency, which doubles as a channel for collecting internal security information as well as an official news and propaganda agency. This often reveals what local Party secretaries have sought to conceal.[5]

While the local people were still placing their wish cards on the tree the officials told us it was time to go for a meeting followed by lunch. I feared that once we were out of the way the cards might be removed never to be seen again. The tension heightened. Quickly I told my British researcher to stay behind and see if he could collect the cards or at least translate some of them. Since the senior officials were taking me away, he would only have to ward off more junior officials. Nonetheless I didn't especially fancy his chances. He would have to play dumb but tough, not a persona that comes easily to young social scientists. I went off to the meeting, looking longingly over my shoulder at the cards on the tree and feeling depressed.

The pre-lunch meeting promised to be long. We embarked on a desultory but tense and meaningless conversation about social welfare arrangements in the community. The meeting wore wearily on. After what seemed a long time the British researcher came into the room carrying a large cardboard box containing Wish Tree cards. He had asked the officials if he could have a look at them, spent some time taking notes of translations with the help of the student volunteers, and then simply picked up the box of untranslated cards and walked away with it to join the meeting. This insouciant act of bravery or foolhardiness had happened too quickly for anyone to gather their wits and stop him. He came into the room, greeted those assembled and sat down with the box on his lap, smiling nervously. The fate of the cards could not be ignored much longer.

The droning discourse about welfare statistics continued for a while longer, but in an increasingly halting fashion. Everyone's mind was now evidently elsewhere. After a short silence, the most senior official took a deep breath and said politely she did not have permission for cards to be removed and they must be taken back to the municipal offices. I remained silent for a while, playing for time. Then I said that this had not been explained to us in advance, obviously a fairly feeble riposte. After another pause I went on to say that we would need to analyse what the cards said in order to give feedback on local people's views at the training for street-level officials after the Wish Tree events. What was the point of participation and consultation if the responses were never analysed or discussed?

While they could see that argument was rational, it could also be interpreted as disingenuous. We were now in a classic Chinese situation I had many times been warned about. A way of saving face all round had to be found, but no one seemed to be backing down, nor was anyone pressing any advantage. Stalemate beckoned. There was a long, nervous silence. The officials looked troubled and uncertain, not wanting to reject my suggestion in case I 'changed face' and lost my temper. However, they could be in serious trouble if they simply let a foreigner walk away with the unchecked, unedited opinions of hundreds of people, especially if, as seemed likely judging by events with the old lady earlier, these opinions turned out to be critical. The silence continued while everyone tried to think of a compromise and kept one attentive eye on the box of cards, still on the vigilant researcher's lap.

Eventually I broke the silence and made a tentative suggestion. Perhaps we could have a look at the cards overnight and extract some interesting quotes to report back to the senior officials in the Civil Affairs Bureau. We could also use this material in the training. I thought that reminding them I had senior support might strengthen my hand. First, they might not wish to incur the wrath of their seniors and second, the senior officials would want to know what was on the cards anyway. I was not optimistic that this tactic would make any difference but anything was worth a try. I went on to say that we would return the cards the next day. Another long silence ensued. The officials racked their brains in vain for a face-saving objection. I then took a spontaneous chance, got up from my seat and said, 'That's agreed. Thank you very much. We will return the cards to you tomorrow.' I certainly had not won them over with eloquence or skilful deployment of argument. I had suddenly and simply exploited the advantage of surprise. We went outside, put the box of cards in the car, locked it firmly and suggested to the officials that it was time for lunch. They simply couldn't think of anything else to say or do so they lamely agreed and led us off to lunch which was, unsurprisingly, a disconsolate affair with a nominal, minimal display of toasting. I was nervous. They were fed up. We finally escaped with the cards and took them back to the office to be photocopied along with the others we had collected from all three locations. We photocopied cards late into the night, hoping that the photocopiers, renowned for having inconvenient minds of their own, would not break down. We returned the originals to the officials the next day in the same box.

As the officials had feared, the responses in Banshanercun did indeed contain many references to a single important local criticism. As well as losing their jobs after the factory had closed, the workers had lost access to free healthcare at the local clinic and small hospital. The medical facilities were still there but they were now in private hands. As a result medical consultations cost money. *RMB*800 was the health access fee, an initial payment for medical consultation. Since many of the factory workers were now living on the Minimum Living Standard of about *RMB*200 a month, this single fee was simply unaffordable. As far as access to medical care was concerned, for practical purposes there was none.

I went to the Civil Affairs Bureau in Chongqing a few days later to meet the senior officials who had given permission for the Wish Tree. This meeting with the ex-military official was much less formal and more businesslike, as we had met before. By then I had some preliminary data analysis, collated late into the night, about the issues that had been raised by respondents to the Wish Tree. I showed the assembled group of officials photographs of the activity, read out some quotes and set out tables of the initial, incomplete results. The senior official watched and listened intently without interruption as I talked in a slow, measured way for nearly half an hour about people's concerns. I talked about the breakdown of healthcare, in particular people's anxieties and complaints about the privatisation of the hospital in Banshanercun, the costs of education and worries about widespread persistent long-term unemployment. At that early stage this was as far as I had got in understanding the responses.

The senior official was clearly surprised by how much I had managed to find out in a few days, especially by using such a whimsical method as the Wish Tree. To begin with he did not know quite how to react, but as time went on, the thought obviously grew on him that both the method and the information collected could be useful. 'Good,' he said when I finished, 'I want to know how the training goes. This will be good for everybody. We will know what is going on in these places. We may be able to avoid these problems in the future.' My fear that he would ask how we had come to read and analyse the cards was unfounded. If he thought about it, he said nothing. He went on to say, perhaps seeing an opportunity for himself, 'I'm sure the Ministry of Civil Affairs in Beijing would like to hear about this.' This, judging by the tone in which it was delivered, was an opportunity, not a threat. Palpable relief was felt all round, especially by the officials that had been present in Banshanercun who had lost the battle for the Wish Tree cards. Honours were even.

Back in the UK the responses on the 1,427 cards were translated and analysed thematically. In Ciqikou 624 people participated, in Banshanercun 490 and in Hemu Lu 311. In total, 596 women participated, 372 men, and 459 whose gender was not known (Table 1). A substantial mixed random sample of local residents had given their views about their concerns and priorities without control or interference. We also had responses from all age groups from children of six years old to people aged over 80 (Table 2). The respondents, although not selected or representative, were also a good mix of ages and genders.

I tagged every topic mentioned by all the respondents for themes, and these are listed in Table 3.

So the responses to the Wish Tree had told a new story, different from the official propaganda of rapid, transformational progress on the 'scientific path to development' and the growth of 'a harmonious society.' Nor did the responses to the Wish Tree reflect the critiques of Western commentators: the absence of human rights and democracy. Instead the story was much more interesting, nuanced and personal. Many people welcomed the economic reforms after 1978. New opportunities had opened up and the evidence of prosperity for some could be seen all around in the city. A Chinese dream had emerged of security, prosperity and stability and

Table 1. Gender of Wish Tree participants

	Men	Women	Not known	Total
Hemu Lu	92	147	72	311
Ciqikou	176	231	217	624
Banshanercun	104	218	170	492
Total	372	596	459	1,427

Table 2. Age of Wish Tree participants

	0–19	20–39	40–59	Over 60	Unknown
Hemu Lu	13	86	87	66	59
Ciqikou	13	94	225	36	256
Banshanercun	203	31	42	113	104
Total	229	211	354	215	419

Table 3. Main topics mentioned by Wish Tree respondents

Subject	Number of respondents mentioning this subject	Percentage of total responses (n = 1427)
Health, sickness and healthcare	590	41.3
Family	469	32.8
Financial insecurity and unemployment	456	31.9
Politics	411	28.8
Ambition and social mobility	326	22.8
Communities, places and the environment	272	19
Education	195	13.7
Old age	181	12.7
Migration and land seizure	91	6.4

this optimistic prospectus was reflected in the responses to the Wish Tree. A tidal wave of entrepreneurship had gathered pace since the planned economy was largely replaced by a much more free market. However, not everyone could be an entrepreneur and some who tried their hand at business would fail. Many had come to feel they were in a poor position to exploit the new opportunities. Alongside the opportunities the changes had created a wrenching discontinuity which bred disquiet in itself. It wasn't just that many, perhaps most, people watched China's much talked about economic growth passively from the sidelines without any beneficial prospects for themselves. Worse than that, far from gaining, many had lost out. They were now worse off. Farmers had lost their land and livelihood. Factory workers had lost their jobs and their security. And the world that replaced the old certainties was one in which family life was horribly officially constrained. The new opportunities were literally a chance in a million and mostly for future generations, leaving many in the current generation to face an insecure, impoverished and dependent old age. Deng Xiaoping's new China had created a dream in the 1980s, but a dream for others. For most people, the dream, so quick to take shape, had just as swiftly died. The next chapter sets out, from the responses to the Wish Tree, what that Chinese dream might have looked and felt like.

CHAPTER 5

The Chinese Dream

Under Mao the height of ambition was a bicycle, a radio, a (notoriously unreliable) watch and a sewing machine. When a couple got married these four symbols of optimistic progress were their dowry. In Deng's time these were replaced by the 'eight bigs': colour television, refrigerator, stereo, camera, motorcycle, furniture, washing machine and an electric fan. Wags added that a man who wanted a wife also needed the 'three highs': a high salary; a higher education and a height of over 5 feet 6 inches.[1] By 2010, China's *Human Development Report* notes that people's aspirations were for 'three big things: an education, a house and a car'.[2] They also noted that, 'social security is in urgent need of reform' and that 'finding jobs, accessing medical services and attending school' have become the 'three big mountains' for Chinese people.[3] This combination of prosperity and security is the contemporary Chinese dream. The old monochrome, egalitarian urban society is disappearing and seems superficially to have been replaced by social and material aspirations, entrepreneurial dash and jobs in modern offices. But the most striking evidence of economic transformation is the rapid appearance of gross and unsettling inequality.

The World Bank reported that China's Gini coefficient, which measures deviation from perfect equality, had increased from 0.32 to 0.45, putting China on a par with the United States – the most unequal society in the developed world.[4] The extremes of inequality are just as stark within China. Shanghai, predictably, scores highest in China on the UN's Human Development Index. The level of human development in Beijing or Shanghai is roughly at the same level as that of the Czech Republic or Portugal. In Guizhou and Tibet, levels of human development are more akin to the Democratic Republic of Congo or Namibia, some of the poorest places in the world.[5]

Three aspects of extreme inequality have opened up in China. First, inequality between eastern cities and the rest of the country. Between 1993 and 2004, per capita GDP increased 2.7 times (in real terms) – but growth has not been even throughout the country. Average per capita GDP is much higher in eastern coastal provinces than central or western ones – and the gap widened in the 1990s. In 2009, the per capita GDP of Shanghai was RMB73,124. In Guizhou it was just 12 per cent of that, at RMB8,824.[6] Incomes have risen overall but per capita GDP in the poorer provinces declined from 68 per cent of the national average in 1988 to 60 per cent in 2004. Second, a huge gap between rich and poor opened up in the cities. A new rich emerged in the eastern cities and raced ahead. The urban rich were two and a half times better off than the poor in 1988. By 2000 they were five and a half times richer. Third, even though farmers in the countryside became better off in the early years of reform, the cities got richer quicker and the ancient, enduring gap between the cities and the countryside once more widened. These forces are cumulative, not parallel – so the worst off, as always, are the peasants who live on China's western periphery.

Ordinary people were obviously aware of these growing inequalities in their answers to the Wish Tree questions. This respondent, for example, linked inequality to social instability: 'The gap between the poor and the rich is too big and this affects stability.'[7] Another person was concerned about widely different income levels. While welcoming economic changes, they hankered for greater equality:

The policy of the Communist Party and the Reform and Opening Policy [changed my life]. We hope to lower the medical care fee because the living standard is not high and the salary is low. [I wish] for the people in China to all have the same salary.

Another participant understandably sees the standards in Beijing and Shanghai as aspirational for Chongqing people: 'Salary is too low to meet the living expenses. I ask for the same standard of income as in Beijing and Shanghai. Medical expenses are too high. We can't afford to get sick.'

Civil servants have the most secure employment conditions, reflecting their long-standing elite status. This respondent wants to reduce disparities between civil servants and employees in state-owned enterprises:

> I've been working for 34 years. I wish to get my salary raised to the same level as in Beijing and Shanghai. The salary in state-owned enterprise should be the same as those who work in government.

Concerns about inequality also arose from differences in access to public services between city dwellers and rural dwellers. Those classifications mean different entitlements to subsidies for medical care, among other services. The trouble is that millions of so-called rural residents are living in cities alongside 'city dwellers'. The latter can access services and subsidies from which people from the countryside are excluded.

> [I am] a retired worker. [I wish] there was no inequality between the urban areas and the suburbs in obtaining medical care. *(Man, 70)*

> Retirement [changed my life. My greatest worry is] getting ill when I am old. [I wish for] no inequality between the rural and urban areas for the medical card. *(Man, 66)*

However, paradoxically, increasing inequality can also be seen as the dawn of opportunity. Not everyone is left behind and loses out. Only a few can be really big winners, and people know this is an implausible prospect for them as individuals but some opportunities might come their way at some time, perhaps even enough to transform their lives. In 1985, 99.3 per cent of the population were relatively poor, with less than *RMB*25,000 to spend a year. That proportion has come down to 77.3 per cent. Going from being very poor to being extremely rich is rare but becoming a little better off is a realistic possibility.[8] As a survey conducted in 2004 by American and Chinese sociologists found: '63.1 per cent said they expected their families to be doing better or much better economically in five years and 61.1 per cent expressed agreement with the statement hard work is always rewarded'.[9] These optimistic views harking back to the 1980s dream of prosperity, security and stability were, however, heavily tempered by personal insecurity and worries about social stability in other replies recorded in the same poll.

The responses on the Wish Tree also reveal these paradoxes; mixed feelings of social and personal aspiration alongside growing anxiety. Many welcomed the rising economic tide even though they may not have benefited much personally, like this retired factory worker:

I'm a retired worker from the Chongqing general tyre factory. Our country is becoming strong and prosperous because of Reform and Opening policy – people's lives have been greatly improved. *(68)*

Some also gave credit to the Communist Party for beneficial changes in their life: 'The good policy of the Chinese Communist Party [changed my life] – life is becoming better' *(58)*.

One in six of the Wish Tree respondents specifically mentioned Deng Xiaoping's Reform and Opening from the late 1970s onwards. All supported reform but acknowledging its benefits did not extend to uncritical praise for all the government's policies. Even though people could see things needed to change they were most dissatisfied with the distribution of benefits: 'The Reform and Opening [changed my life]. Medical expenses and health access fee are too high [so] we can't afford to go to hospital. [I wish] to live a better-off life.'

One person specifically praised the Party leadership, while at the same time worrying about unemployment, health insurance and health costs, including the health access fee. They also hoped that social turbulence would be eschewed:

The care of the Chinese Communist Party, the Secretary-General Hu Jintao, Premier Wen Jiabao and the Chongqing municipal govern- ment [changed my life]. I'm worried medicine costs are too expensive and about the health access fee. [I wish] the policy is stable and increases harmony.

Praise is even given by this respondent to the Party for their minimal social welfare payment, but she is also worried about life's other difficulties:

Because of the concerns of the Party we got the Minimum Living Standard. When I am sick I can't afford to go to hospital. My children are getting older and don't have a job and haven't settled down. They are living with me and I also need to pay their expenses. The pension is very low and our medical insurance is only *RMB*23 a month. [I wish] to raise the pension and cancel health access fee. *(Woman, 67)*

If they are to aspire to a secure and comfortable life, people know they need more help from the government. This woman mentioned Hu Jintao's doctrine of the harmonious society while still expressing other concerns:

[I am] a resident of the Banshanercun community. Under the leadership of the Chinese Communist Party we have built a harmonious society which has changed my life. I wish to increase the low-income people's salary, cancel the health access fee and decrease the fee for a physical health check. *(Woman, 66)*

The following man even mentioned Chongqing's status as a municipality reporting directly to Beijing since 1998 as a factor that changed his life. Presumably he has in mind the accelerated economic growth and redevelopment of the city that has taken place since then: 'Reform and Opening. Chongqing's 10 years of being a municipality [changed my life]. [I wish] to live a better-off life' *(Man, 69)*.

Young adults, particularly those with a good education, are best placed to take the opportunities that economic development has brought. This student came as close as possible to the archetype of the aspirational, well-educated young person seeking success in the market society. His parents were successful in business. He had done well in education and, at the age of 23, he is planning an orderly future. In a society with more young men than women he betrays a little insecurity about finding a girlfriend. He has even thought of a way round the one-child policy without breaking the rules:

'[I am] a postgraduate student from the University of Chongqing. My parents' success in business [changed my life]. Because of this I can live a well-off life and receive a good education.' [My greatest worry is] 1. Health of my parents, 2. Economic development of my home town,

3. Public transportation and public security, 4. Development of my country. [I wish for] 1. Good health for my parents and friends. 2. Prosperity of my country. 3. To find an ideal job and to realise my value. 4. To find a good girlfriend. 5. To have twins.

Few people have this young man's conventional values and bland self-confidence. He lived in Ciqikou, the most traditional and mixed community with a sprinkling of better-off people. Many respondents to the Wish Tree aspired to middle-class professions. The most frequently mentioned was going into business. In the early days of Reform starting a business was thought rather vulgar.[10] Comfortable civil servants and people with good Party connections were shocked to see street vendors, noodle bars, light industrial factories, small shops and all manner of tiny businesses springing up, some literally on their doorsteps. Some of the socially inferior people newly engaged in previously denounced commercial activities quickly overtook the staid government-employed elite in wealth and status, much to the latter's dismay. Some overcame their disdain, suppressed their sense of superiority and 'jumped into the sea' of entrepreneurship – xia hai. Far higher earnings can be achieved by starting a business, but only if bigger personal financial risks are taken. Rags to riches stories appear in the newspapers but most new entrepreneurs don't become millionaires or anything close to it. Most seriously rich business people come from well-connected families; these are the new princelings whose parents are senior Communist Party figures. But even small-scale entrepreneurs have opportunities and welcome greater control over their destiny. This woman has lost her small business and she feels her independence has gone with it: 'Not having my own noodle stall [changed my life]. I can't be independent. My greatest worry is] health. [I wish] that my daughter has a happy life' (Woman, 49).

People take risks and work hard to start businesses because autonomy is an attractive prospect in such a controlled society. This person, also from Ciqikou where small businesses still thrive, sees commerce as a route to autonomy and peace of mind; although it's almost impossible without urban household registration:

I came from Maanshan to live in this big city. I miss the fresh air and tranquillity there. But I also enjoy the urban life. I'm still a guest of this city. I wish my child would one day be a resident and make contributions to the city. [I wish] to have my own small business and to live a peaceful life.

Others too welcomed the business-friendly environment: 'Having set up my own business changed my life. I'm worrying the policies may get changed in the future. [I wish] to expand my business.' Another person still had a china-ware business, the traditional industry of Ciqikou: 'Having set up my own business [changed my life]. [I wish for] the booming of the china industry' *(48)*. One respondent wanted to set up his own business as a hedge against the risk of losing his job: '[I am] a driver. [My greatest worry is] being out of employment. [I wish] to be a big boss in my own business' *(Man, 20)*.

Starting a business is a way out of the problem of losing your job, bringing independence and thereby, hopefully, security: '[I am] out of employment. [My greatest worry is] no security for the future. [I wish] to have my own shop' *(Man, 42)*. Age was no bar to ambition: 'I wish to become a big boss' *(Man, 62)*. At the other end of the age range, even children wanted to be entrepreneurs especially if, like this boy, their family didn't have much money: 'Being poor [changed my life. My greatest worry is] poor results at school. [I wish] to be a boss of a company' *(Boy, 11)*.

This woman's quote encapsulates a widespread change of attitude in favour of private sector employment and against the limitations of the old state-owned enterprises:

I work for a private enterprise. Walking out of the stated-owned enterprise [changed my life. My greatest worry is] no money. [I wish] to have loads of money *(Woman, 24)*

Nowadays there are also high-status and well-paid opportunities in foreign companies, offering the prospect of high pay for the most talented and high-flying, women as well as men.[11]

I'm a sales manager. I joined Coca-Cola Chongqing branch in 2002. I worked hard and got promoted. Being honest and hard-working changed my life. [My worries are] getting ill; social security. [I wish] to help people with difficulties. *(Man, 28)*

Many people, however, are less convinced about the benefits of entrepreneurial opportunities. Given the chance, they wanted a secure government job, which is still a passport to status and financial security, including
a pension of more than 80 per cent of final salary without any personal
financial risks. Government jobs can also offer considerable job satisfaction. Academics told me civil servants have genuine influence and opportunities for creative policy-making because Hu Jintao's 'scientific path
to development' has inculcated a more empirical, less ideological administrative ethos. Recruitment to even the most junior government jobs,
because of the terms and security they offer, is hugely over-subscribed.
In 2010 in Jinan, Shandong province the local authority advertised five
jobs for sewage porters (*tiao fen*), the most humble job imaginable –
carrying away human waste in two containers suspended on a bamboo
pole across the shoulders. Nearly 400 people applied and, after a rigorous
process of 'selection, observation and training', four graduates and one
diploma student each got a five-year contract.[12] Even carrying sewage
is a graduate opportunity if it comes with government terms and
conditions.

Stakhanovite effort at school, excellent performance in examinations
and a university education may still not be enough to get a secure government job. One postgraduate student told me in a disappointed tone that,
despite her good grades at university, she lacked the family connections to
get a government job. Less than 2 per cent of people who take the civil
service examination can expect a place.[13] This child seemed to know that
public jobs were attractive, especially for those from poor backgrounds:
'My family is poor. [I wish] to be a public official' *(Boy, 8.5).*

Becoming a teacher was the next most common ambition after being an
entrepreneur. This schoolgirl was a Young Pioneer, so presumably obedient
and well-behaved. She wanted to be a teacher: 'My greatest worry is I
couldn't enter a good university. My wish is to become a teacher and to
serve people.'

Being a doctor has similar attractions of security, permanence and
professional status as well as the added satisfaction of social usefulness. For
example:

Helping others to get rid of bad habits [changed my life. My greatest worries are] failing to enter medical school and not being able to serve people and the air pollution. [I wish] to become a doctor and to serve people. *(Girl, 11)*

Study [changed my life. My greatest worry is I'm] unable to find a good job. [I wish] to become an outstanding lawyer or doctor.

Only six years old, this girl apparently already knew she wanted to be a doctor: '[I'm] a student. Good results at school [changed my life.] I wish to be a doctor when I grow up.' Another young student also wanted to help people in a different way: 'Learning psychology [changed my life. My greatest worry is] I will fail to cure the mentally ill.'

This girl's dream was to be an air stewardess; a highly sought after and competitive role in modern China with superficial and misleading claims to glamour: '[I am] a student. My dream [changed my life. My greatest worry is] whether I can realise my dream when I grow up. [I wish] to be a stewardess.' *(Girl, 8)*. While this boy wanted to be a senior police officer in an elite, action-oriented force: '[I wish] to be a flying squad team leader.' *(Boy, 11)* Other professions mentioned included pilot, lawyer, tour guide, manager, sales manager, archivist, insurance salesman, engineer, architectural technician, white-collar worker and accountant.

Of the 58 people who mentioned wanting more money, 20 mentioned getting rich, making 'big money' or having 'a lot of money'. For example:

Losing my job changed my life. [My greatest worry is there is] no guarantee when I fall ill. I wish to have a lot of money, probably a million. *(Woman, 46)*

Losing my job [changed my life. My greatest worry is] no money. I wish I can make big money. *(Man, 21)*

Most people know they cannot achieve wealth beyond the dreams of avarice, but one remote possibility of achieving great wealth is winning the lottery, the only legal form of gambling in China: 'I hope to win the lottery – then I would change a lot of things'. *(Woman, 42)*. Five million

RMB is the most commonly advertised prize in the lottery, and winning the lottery is a way of coping with other misfortunes: 'Losing my job [changed my life. My greatest worry is] no money. I wish to win a lottery of five million.' (*Man, 48*)

Winning the lottery, although extremely unlikely, makes you rich without risks. The stock market is perceived to be another relatively easy way of becoming rich, but with the considerable risk of losing as well as winning. Trading stocks and shares has become a widespread obsession. People check stock prices all the time at home, on laptops, at centres for buying and selling shares all over the cities, on their phones, on street corners. For example:

> [I'm] a local resident. Getting re-employed [changed my life. My greatest worry is] I couldn't afford my medical expenses. [I wish] to make money probably through the stock market. *(Man, 52)*

This child seems knowledgeable beyond her years about financial markets: 'I'm worrying the stock my mum bought won't rise. I wish one day I can realise my five dreams.' *(Girl, 10)*.

Much share buying and selling in contemporary China is little more than ill-informed speculation. Stock markets like so much else in Chinese life display extraordinary and generally unexplained volatility, across the board and in the value of individual company shares. Taking a long-term view simply opens up greater unpredictability. The markets are dominated by short-term investors hunting for a rapid, preferably instant return. This obsession with the stock market may have some of its cultural and psychological roots in gambling, a tendency so strong in Chinese society that rooting it out has thwarted even draconian legal measures. But amateurs playing the stock market are also evidence of the amount of cash in the Chinese economy that cannot find a professionally managed investment home producing a decent return. Interest rates on bank deposits and bonds are kept artificially low to facilitate the relatively cheap financing of state-owned enterprises and other government cash calls. Rates, in other words, are set for borrowers not lenders. The restricted return may not even beat inflation. The only investments likely to make a real return for Chinese domestic savers are property and the stock market. Of these alternatives the stock market offers greater flexibility and immediacy. A smart amateur investor pretty quickly works out how to stop losses and the benefits of hedging even relatively small stakes. During the 2007 bull market the overall profits to earnings ratio went from a multiple of 15 to 50. The upside by comparison with all other investments was enormous. In a society with so much excess liquidity and constant inflationary pressures the amateur speculators turn out to be pretty smart, though considerable downside risks await the unwary.[14]

The wish for wealth stretches across the generations. Several children had it in mind to become rich:

> Family income [changed my life. [I wish] to become a trillionaire. *(Boy, 12)*

> [I wish] to become rich when I grow up. *(Boy)*

These two women wanted wealth for their children. The first senses opportunity; the second insecurity:

> Economic development of society [changed my life]. I wish my children would be rich. *(Woman, 70)*

> There's no security for the future. [I wish] that my child would become rich. *(Woman, 52)*

Children are the only generation susceptible to wildly fanciful professional ambitions. All big ambitions expressed in responses to the Wish Tree came from those too young to know better. For example:

> [I wish] none of my family would become criminals. I want to become a world famous supermodel when I grow up. I want to make a fortune when I grow up and all my wishes would come true.

> [I'm] James Bond 007. Nuclear weapons [changed my life. My greatest worry is] a nuclear bomb exploding in China. [I wish] to become China's Bill Gates. *(Boy, 12)*

> [I wish] to be a football player. *(Boy, 12)*

This child expressed a rather more high-minded ambition:

[I wish] to be a great inventor.

Accompanying changing attitudes to employers and professional ambitions are new lifestyles. Nowadays, with a well-paid and reasonably secure job, the priority has become owning a home. This is widely popular, bringing status and a tradable asset that would, the respondents hoped, appreciate in value, though widespread speculation in property means a crash is also more than likely at some time. A retired woman stressed the significance of getting a flat and saw it as a direct result of post-Mao policies:

Deng Xiaoping's policy is very good. Reform and Opening gave me a good house. The road's become wider and every year life is rich. [My greatest worry is] whether I can get a medical guarantee when I'm older and I worry my health is not good. I wish the policy could apply to everyone and future generations can live a better life. *(Woman, 62)*

In the old days tiny, shabby and uncomfortable flats were allocated by bureaucrats. Party officials told people when to get married, when to move and where. Modern home ownership, by contrast, means choice, freedom and privacy, as well as a potential return on investment. Owning a flat creates a personalised space to express individual identity. Mementoes, gifts from family and souvenirs from travels can be displayed. Nicely decorated flats also impress friends and family. Soft toys, free gifts with large household purchases, are piled on a bed or sofa making the place cosy. Opportunities and social mobility, however, contain risks, as these respondents note:

My job [changed my life. My greatest worry is] losing my job. [I wish] to have my own house. *(28)*

My choice of career [changed my life.] There is a way for everything. There is no need to get worried. [I wish] to have my most satisfying property (with a public swimming pool) in the area. *(Woman, 33)*

Owning a flat is a status symbol; a visible signifier of social arrival, a decisive break from the strictures of the past. Many people, particularly young professionals, buy flats with large, unaffordable mortgages. Friends told me how unmanageable debt leads to marital conflict. If the debt overwhelms the couple, they lose their home and have to move in with one of their parents, there to encounter intergenerational conflict to add to marital tension. Not everyone, however, is just seeking a speculative quick win from the property market. Wanting a new house can also be born of anxiety about the security and permanence of current living arrangements:

[I am] a job hunter waiting for redeployment. The Minimum Living Standard [changed my life. My greatest worry is] having no house to live in. [I wish] to have my own house. *(Man, 50)*

Being out of employment [changed my life]. I wish to cut down the education fee and have a house of my own. *(Man, 35)*

[Being laid off] changed my life. My greatest worry is] whether my daughter can have a job after her graduation. [I wish] to have a nice place to live in. *(Woman, 40)*

After home ownership, a car is the next acquisition desired by the upwardly mobile. A car offers immediate absolution from the considerable indignities of urban public transport. But cars are more than a convenience. They represent conspicuous consumption; a signifier of success. This child saw owning a car as an ambition alongside wealth: 'Being beaten by my parents [changed my life]. [My greatest worry is] getting fat; failing to enter university. [I wish] to have a car and to become rich.' Brands are chosen with care. Bright red hatchbacks make the young feel fashionable. The middle-aged and better off seek to demonstrate sombre good taste and luxury. This seven-year-old girl lived in Hemu Lu, the area where the farmers had been relocated. Owning a car here is rare, but she could proudly say: 'We've got a car.'

The number of cars flooding on to the gridlocked streets led the government to ration new licence plate numbers in 2010, creating long waiting lists and an active grey market in new registrations. Too many cars, such a visible sign of change in Chinese life, are an irritant to some: '[My greatest worry is] public transportation. Some cars just don't follow the rules. [I wish] to have a better transportation order.'

Travel too is a symbol of prosperity, business success or status. Travelling within China, now undertaken freely by everyone except dissidents, has grown enormously. At the Buddhist caves at Da Zu, the World Heritage Site a few hours from Chongqing, or in the beautiful restored gardens of Suzhou, half an hour on the bullet train from Shanghai, or at the lakes of Hangzhou from where the Grand Canal takes water to Beijing, groups of Chinese tourists are led around, chattering happily, by a guide talking incessantly into a mini-megaphone. Girls in denim hot pants and rubber sneakers pose for cellphone photos with a cocked head, a big grin and a 'V' for victory sign, adopting a coquettish air. The reasonably well off can take the train from Shenzhen for a weekend in Hong Kong. The raised walk-ways of Hong Kong's Central or Wan Chai districts are crammed with mainland Chinese people at the weekend. The international-style resorts on Hainan Island attract wealthy Chinese people, along with Russians, to the standardised luxury of Sheratons and Marriotts and the special services of upmarket prostitutes. Only the extremely well off can tour Europe or USA, unless sent on a Party-organised junket. This woman wants to succeed in the new society, but is conscious of the strains placed on family life. She talks of her dreams and wants to travel as well as owning a home:

> [I am] employed. My job [changed my life]. [My greatest worry is] the changes in the family and relatives departing from the family. [I wish] to live happily; to realise my dreams through hard work; to travel and to have my own property. *(Woman, 33)*

One nine-year-old girl's vision of her bright future includes seeing the world: 'I want to travel around the world when I grow up and I want to enter university.'

Travelling is not just a way for the curious to have fun and the high-minded to acquire worldly knowledge. Studying abroad greatly improves employment prospects. Many students who study abroad never come back. Opportunities are greater for the diligent and the talented in the

USA, Europe or Singapore despite the grievous loss of family, food and friends – the great staples of social life in China.

Cafés and restaurants flourish and coffee is now fashionable in a country where the centuries-old traditions of tea drinking seemed to run in the lifeblood. As a counter-current, traditional teahouses for the discerning are also making a small but welcome comeback. In Starbucks and its local imitators I often eavesdropped as young people gossiped with friends, flirted, discussed movies, pop music and up-and-coming fashion brands, planned their weekend, dreamed of foreign travel, criticised their 'stupid', demanding bosses and wondered disbelievingly why some people seem not to relish the new society. Shopping has become a continuous form of leisure and distraction. Buying lots of cheap clothes in ever-changing fashions is particularly popular, though is not without its own capacity to create anxiety: '[I'm] a warehouse keeper. My marriage [changed my life. I'm worried about] getting too fat to fit into beautiful clothes. [My wish] is to have my own house' *(Woman, 40)*.

Another Western obsession is taking hold: dieting, the dangers of getting fat and the never-ending search for self-improvement:

> Through fitness activities I changed my shape and became healthier and more confident. [My greatest worry is] whether I could find a good job from now on. [I wish] to lose weight until I reach the ideal weight. *(Woman, 21)*

These hopes and dreams of middle-class life may have filtered into the minds of the young and well-educated, but few will realistically benefit. The pyramid of social mobility is still wide at the bottom and very narrow at the top. According to the McKinsey Quarterly in 2006 only one per cent of the population earned more than *RMB*100,000 a year.[15] Incomes may rise, but so do demands on those increased incomes. Housing, health and education are significant drains on money. Housing and utilities are estimated to take up 16.6 per cent of household income. Many may aspire to middle-class lifestyles, but in truth only a few will achieve them and lots of strings will be attached.

Considering all this uncertainty the best most can hope for is peace of mind; freedom from worry. This teacher seems to reject vaulting material ambition. The 'true way' of 'ordinary' health and happiness might be lost and forgotten once and for all, she believes:

> I have been engaged in education for decades and this has taught me the sweetness and bitterness of being committed to teaching. I hope everyone can live in happiness and spend every day in health and happiness. This is the true way even though it is ordinary. There is no better life than this.

The wish for security and happiness rather than the wilder shores of ambition was by far the most frequent aspiration mentioned by more than a third of those who expressed ambition. People never had much before and their future expectations are pragmatically limited. This middle-aged man's simple views were the archetypical concerns from the Wish Tree: 'Losing my job [changed my life. My greatest worry is] education of my child; getting ill. [I wish] to live a safe and sound life.' *(Man, 48)*. Many hoped for a life without worry. Even at 21 this young man remained realistic: '[I'm] a driver. My job and family [changed my life. My greatest worry is] not being able to afford my living expenses. [I wish for] a life with no worry and sadness.'

Others made the connection between health and happiness:

> [I'm] a healthy woman with a healthy attitude to life. Good health and a happy family [changed my life. My greatest worry is] the health of my family. [I wish for] peace, healthiness and joy. *(Woman, 32)*

The phrase 'safe and sound' *(ping an)* was used many times, for example:

> I'm a mother of a child. Becoming an urban resident [changed my life. My greatest worries are] health of my parents, my child, my husband and myself. [I wish] the whole family is happy and safe and sound all their lives. *(Woman, 35)*

Older people in particular welcome security: 'The steadiness of life [changed my life]. I'm worrying about suffering from severe illnesses. [I wish] to be safe and sound' *(Woman, 76)*. Many hoped for a moderate, gradual social improvement, though they feared that might be thwarted by political upheaval, as so often in the past:

> Our country is becoming prosperous and our life has been gradually improved. [My greatest worries are] war and social harmony. [I wish] people can live happily and work happily and life can be gradually improved. *(Woman)*

> Development of society [changed my life.] I'm worrying about social order. I feel insecure. I want to be a happy woman. *(Woman, 34)*

Others were more positive and optimistic. This young man thought, like many others, that getting a job would be the route to happiness: 'Losing my job [changed my life. My greatest worry is] health. [I wish for] a good job, good health and a happy life' *(Man, 28)*.

Having a job certainly makes people more optimistic, as these two believed:

> I have a steady job now. [My greatest worry is] education of my child. I wish for a rosier future. *(Woman, 31)*

> Having got this ideal job [changed my life. My greatest worry is] losing my job. [I wish for] a more beautiful life.

After being secure and happy and becoming a middle-class professional, more money was the third most often mentioned ambition. People wanted more money not to achieve wild hopes and dreams but to ward off anxiety about the future. They wanted it for greater security and happiness, the outcome most wished for. Many people were worried about money:

> I have no savings in the bank. [My greatest worry is] not being able to afford my living expenses. [I wish] to change my life. *(Man, 39)*

> There are so many things in life we can't change. I'm worrying about so many things – money, health and lots of things. [I wish] all kind people could have a peaceful life. *(Man, 52)*

Losing my job [changed my life.] I can't live a secure life because I don't have enough money. [I wish] to get a job and have enough money. *(Man, 29)*

Money could change everything. [My greatest worry is] getting ill and going to hospital. *(Woman, 74)*

Especially for those without much money, security and contentment also stem from the spirit of community. The old blocks of flats adjoining factories were cramped, scruffy and uncongenial. Consequently people spent a lot of time in squares, parks, noodle bars, markets, or just on the pavements. They chatted, played cards, chess or mah-jong. They did exercises or joined in *taiji* sessions, sometimes with swords or fans. The adolescents played ping-pong. Old men brought caged birds out for fresh air and to meet and sing with other caged birds. Grandma brought the grandchild out to play, doing her knitting while gossiping with her neighbours. In the evening on the pavements or town squares spontaneous singalongs sprang up or ballroom dancing. Life with all its hardships was still convivial.

In the old estates these public squares are often ugly, treeless and concrete, but they are nevertheless the heart and hub of community life where gossip is exchanged, old arguments are resolved (or rekindled), new friendships nurtured, people fall in love, sadness and losses are disclosed and discussed, advice is sought. The full range of human emotions is expressed in public, not in the living room or by telephone. People still want these spaces – as places for public entertainment as well as private encounters: '[I wish] to build a big entertainment square' *(Woman, 52)*.

In most open spaces in traditional factory neighbourhoods exercise equipment has been installed and is regularly used, particularly by older people. There is no place to exercise in the new neighbourhoods, with high-rise blocks of flats, little public space and a disagreeable lack of warmth and friendliness. A strip of grass in a canyon-like shadow between two high-rise blocks or a car park has to do duty for *taiji* or exercises. Many people commented on the continuing need for somewhere to do their exercises:

Taking exercise [changed my life]. I worry about the condition of my body. [I wish] to build a square to take exercise.

I cannot find any green in my neighbourhood. [My greatest worry is] the city would get over-developed. There would be no places for me to do exercises. I just wish there would be a place where I can do exercises.

[I wish] they would build an activities centre for the elderly in Ciqikou and let elderly people have a place to exercise. *(Man, 72)*

Another respondent is looking for more modern gym facilities, rather than just the old open air exercise equipment:

'I worry about the condition of my body. We hope to get enough gym facilities.' In addition this man wants a theatre: '[I wish] to have more gym facilities and a theatre on the playground' *(41)*.

The Beijing Olympics in 2008 were heavily promoted as an extremely significant national moment. That particularly resonated with children – who noticed that the Olympics sports facilities being built in the capital were rather superior to those they were used to in Chongqing: 'I hope we can have more sports grounds – I want to be a part of a new generation of Olympic athletes' *(Boy, 10)*.

Chairman Mao was a keen swimmer and swam in the River Yangtze with much attendant publicity. Late at night in the dog days of summer, if the schools are on holiday, children dive into a roped-off portion of the river to cool off, but the fast-flowing Yangtze does not freeze in the winter and so ice skating, another great outdoor communal activity, is not possible.

I suffered from severe illness when I was young and my health has been poor since. I wish we could have a pond in our community where we can swim in summer and skate in winter. *(Girl, 11)*

Old people are much more isolated than in the past. Families are smaller and family members are not so close at hand. They spend more time indoors because there are fewer congenial outdoor spaces. Many wanted somewhere to meet. But many newly built community centres were dispiriting places, lifeless and sterile, always with a police officer or two present, with the ineffable atmosphere of bored bureaucrats: they were not places of spontaneous and intimate community life – the best antidote to isolation and depression.

[I'm] a retired worker. Retirement changed my life. Build a community activity centre for entertainment and enrich people's lives. *(Woman, 55)*

I'm very interested in traditional art and this makes my life colourful. I'm worrying the traditional art and culture couldn't be passed down. I think we could make use of the discarded factory storehouses to exhibit traditional arts and crafts. *(Woman, 56)*

[My greatest worry is] getting ill and nobody asks how I am doing. [I wish] to have a cultural public square in Ciqikou and provide the citizen with leisure and to build an activity centre for older people. Let older people have a place to do different activities.

In Chongqing alone 16,000 community workers are supposed to help people cope with the consequences of change and to support the most needy. Their behaviour is sometimes clumsy and ill-judged and they can exacerbate rather than resolve tensions. Nevertheless, judging by these quotes, some at least make a significant contribution in arranging community activities to combat loneliness. This support is especially valued by the elderly, for whom isolation was both unexpected and unwanted.

There are lots of things [that have changed my life]. There's nothing for me to worry about as I am being taken good care of by the social workers in my community. I want to state my appreciation to those who have ever cared about me. *(Woman, 82)*

Good service for the elderly from my community [changed my life. My greatest worry is] whether this kind of service will keep on. I hope I can still enjoy this service in the future. *(Woman, 78)*

In line with traditional attitudes, men were more likely to have big financial ambitions and wish for more money in their responses on the Wish Tree. Women were more likely to want security and happiness. The residents of

Hemu Lu, the newly established community for farmers divested of their agricultural land, gave markedly different responses to the people in the other two communities. They were much more likely to have humble aspirations for security and happiness and much less likely to have big financial or professional ambitions. Farmers have always been denigrated and it seems they still know their place. Those with little don't expect much more.

Ambition is also greatly influenced by age. Children were the most likely to wish for great wealth and extraordinary career success. Young adults and middle-aged people were the most likely to aspire to a middle-class profession and lifestyle. Old people were keen, most of all, to ensure security at the end of turbulent lives in which they may have seen war, revolution, famine and social chaos. These generational patterns were evident in political as well as economic attitudes. Older people were far more likely to explicitly praise the Party, its leaders and the Reform and Opening policy. Young adults and middle-aged people were more likely to be silent on politics, and children were more likely to express general idealistic views about wanting to make the world a better place. Being a Young Pioneer was the extent to which Communist politics intruded on their consciousness. These shifts in social attitudes are intertwined. People of all ages are still less individualistic than their counterparts in Western countries, but through the generations they are becoming less committed to strict Party hierarchies and more concerned with their personal goals and lifestyles. People have become more entrepreneurial and self-reliant in part because government policy has been to end the expectation of jobs for life in state-owned enterprises and to withdraw social safety nets. Their decision to look out more for themselves has been forced upon them by the government.

Ordinary people in poorer neighbourhoods now recognise that a new middle-class way of life has opened up for some. The well-educated and well-connected can start businesses or enter professions, own houses, buy cars, travel and make money. These new values have superseded the old bogus Communist claims of equality, but hundreds of millions of ordinary people do not identify with these positive possibilities. Instead they feel they have been left behind. Responses to the Wish Tree questions showed that they worry about their family's well-being, keeping their job, not getting sick, affording medical treatment, paying for their child's education, having enough to live on in their old age and living in a neigh-bourly, supportive community. These more modest ambitions are the true Chinese dream and they are almost universally felt. Making this dream a reality would bring peace of mind, security and happiness, but being excluded from the benefits of change while feeling the full force of losses brought on by the same changes means that for many that the short-lived dream has died.

CHAPTER 6

Unhappy Families

Two interlinked principles lie at the heart of Confucian thought. First, those with power should be exemplary in their moral character and personal demeanour and protect those over whom they rule. In return those who are ruled over and protected should be obedient. Second, all types of human relationships must be connected for harmony to prevail. To the Confucian mind people are connected to the world through five cardinal human relationships: ruler and subject; father and son; husband and wife; older brother and younger brother; and friends. Rules of proper conduct were prescribed for each type of relationship by Mencius, who interpreted Confucius's sayings: 'love between father and son, duty between ruler and subject, distinction between husband and wife, precedence of the old over the young, and faith between friends'.[1] Concepts of family and society are closely interwoven and can seem almost interchangeable to the traditional Chinese way of thinking. Social harmony is an amplification of the principles and rules for family life. The emperor was deemed the Son of Heaven and his public officials, extensively trained in Confucian thought and rules of behaviour or 'rites', were expected to act as benevolent parents to the masses; they were referred to as *fumuguan*, literally parent-official. Communist propaganda has extended some of this identification between the family and society to include the Party. Children are taught at school, 'Love your country, love the Party, love your mother.'

Since family members, and by extension members of the same society, are permanently bound together for better or worse, conflict must be regarded as temporary, and overcome. A parent must provide for a child whatever their hardships and a child must look after their parents in old age regardless of whether they were kind parents. All these obligations are reciprocal across time and space, drawing in the dead as well as the living. Ancestors must be cared for and served and then they too will protect. Neglected, they become angry and malign, hungry ghosts. Obligations to ancestors are most visibly expressed at the annual *Qingming* grave-sweeping festival. People visit their ancestors' graves, maintain and clean them, feed the ancestors and propitiate them with offerings, including burning fake paper money. Piles of ashes are all over the city streets for the next few days. After the lunar New Year, also a festival that celebrates family life, *Qingming* is the most popular and widely observed Chinese festival. Whatever discord arises either among the living, or between the living and the dead, mutual obligations remain. So from a Confucian point of view, discord, instability and conflict do not have their roots in reality, but instead represent an unnatural imbalance of no lasting significance which should be eradicated. The overall tendency of the universe is towards unity, order and, the most important Confucian concept, harmony.

An updated version of Confucian thought is being reclaimed by ordinary people. In part this is simply the reappearance of a belief system that never really went away but is now no longer proscribed and campaigned against by over-zealous authorities. Confucian values are also seen by many ordinary people as an important antidote to rising materialism and shallowness in rootless contemporary urban life. With monolithic political identities and belief systems retreating in the face of a fast-changing and unpredictable society, the revival of Confucianism is a rediscovery of something more profound and a re-establishment of a proud, traditional, distinctive and universal Chinese identity. Parents commonly arrange extracurricular tuition on Confucianism for their children. A self-help book (a very popular genre in China) first published in 2007, *Confucius from the Heart*, on the relevance of Confucian thought to modern life sold 10 million copies. The author, Yu Dan, was an academic who had presented a popular television series on a similar theme. He took Confucius's teachings and, in a simple way, related them to contemporary Chinese society. Confucius 'can teach us the secret of happiness, which is how to find peace within us'. Because so many people have suddenly become extremely wealthy 'there is always something to make ordinary people feel that their lives contain unfairness'.[2] Even Hu Jintao would return an echo to those sentiments.

But, just as neo-Confucianism has gained some official recognition and popular support, the lifestyles endorsed by Confucius, particularly the importance of family life as the keystone of a harmonious society, are being structurally undermined. The fragmented, insecure labour market undermines feelings of permanence and predictability, scattering people all over the country. But more than that, the traditional Confucian way of thinking is fundamentally undermined by the one-child policy. This has brought about two lasting changes in the structure of society: a disproportionate number of old people, and six boys for every five girls. It has also, as responses to the Wish Tree showed, produced many more subtle damaging psychological and emotional effects. At a time when the state has in many ways pulled back from interfering in people's day-to-day life (so long as they stay away from political criticism of the regime) the government has interfered at the heart of their private and intimate existence through the one-child policy. Embracing Confucian values emotionally may be as much a consolation for the loss of old certainties in family life and employment security as a re-establishment of those values in reality. Values thrive in people's minds, to some extent in the face of the facts, partly and paradoxically because they are hard to sustain on the ground. Traditional values become a refuge even as these traditions disappear from lived experience.

In the 1970s Deng Xiaoping became convinced the rate of population growth needed to be drastically slowed for economic reform to succeed. Under Mao efforts at population control were denigrated as an anti-Chinese Western conspiracy. Malthus, who had warned in 1798 that the earth's resources would not support an infinitely growing human population, was dubbed anti-Communist. But by the 1970s, policy was dramatically reversed. Initially the new policy of encouraging people to have only one child was persuasive rather than coercive. Chinese citizens were used to an endless succession of campaigns and slogans promulgated by the government to influence public attitudes. These familiar techniques were deployed to promulgate the new family policy. From the early 1970s the government promoted the 'longer, later, fewer' policy, stressing the benefits of late marriage, small families and spaced births. This policy 'yielded quick results: the birth rate plummeted'.[3] But not fast enough for the Party leaders. The leadership adopted rapid 'one childization' (*yitaihua*) in 1980 to keep the population below 1.2 billion by the year 2000. The irony of this change to a more coercive policy passed largely without comment. Just when the leaders of the Chinese Communist Party were abandoning the failed planned economy and collectivist economic structures in favour of the free market and greater individual freedom, their enthusiasm for inter-fering in people's private and social lives was stronger than ever. Unlike in the economy, in the realm of family planning, individual choice and decision-making was not thought a useful route towards social progress. This resort to authoritarianism in family planning as early as 1980 was a sign that economic liberalism was not going to be accompanied by social freedom.

From 1983 the approach became more direct. Women were compelled to use contraceptive devices if they already had a child. Sterilisation of one parent was compulsory after the birth of the second child. Provinces and local authorities were assigned targets for sterilisations. In 1983 there were 21 million sterilisations, four times as many women (16.4 million) as men (4 million) and about 14 million abortions. When these numbers are compared to the years on either side it is obvious that the overwhelming majority of the procedures were compulsory.[4] Village walls were painted with lurid slogans such as

Better to let blood flow like a river than to have one more allowed.
    You can beat it out! You can make it fall out! You can abort it! But you cannot give birth.[5]

Harsh incentives were deployed to meet birth control targets. Women in Guangdong province who refused to have abortions risked having their water and electricity cut off, roof tiles removed and houses sealed.[6] Party administrators only agreed to hand over land to peasants if the recipient signed a side contract not to have any more children while working the newly acquired land. Another child meant forfeiture of the land. In these villages people were recorded fleeing sterilisation teams.[7] But not all got away. In 1981 the Wall Street Journal reported that women were 'hand-cuffed, tied with ropes or placed in pig baskets' before being forcibly removed for abortions.[8] Steven Mosher was a PhD student at Stanford who witnessed forced abortions while conducting fieldwork in agricultural communes in Guangdong. He attended a meeting at the commune's headquarters where the Party cadre in charge told 18 women who were between five and eight months pregnant what was to be their fate:

> None of you has any choice in the matter. You must realise that your pregnancy affects everyone in the commune and indeed affects everyone in the country. The two of you who are eight or nine months pregnant will have a caesarean; the rest of you will have a shot which causes you to abort.[9]

Population growth has undoubtedly slowed dramatically since the 1980s. The target of limiting the population to 1.2 billion by 2000 was almost met. The final figure was 1.25 billion. The government estimates, controversially, that the one-child policy has reduced births by about 300 million. But academics still disagree about whether these policies, treating citizens as biological entities and ignoring emotional lives, were necessary to reduce population growth. Official data shows that the greatest reductions in the country's total fertility rate occurred before the sterilisations and forced abortions became widespread. Better-educated people with rising incomes living in urban areas in every society choose to have fewer children because childrearing is becoming relatively more expensive and provides few economic benefits. The experience of other developing countries confirms that coercive policies are not necessary for population reduction. Between 1970 and 1980 the birth rate in China fell from 5.5 to 2.3. During the same period the fertility rate in Thailand dropped from 5.6 to 2.1 and in Brazil from 5.0 to 2.8. In short, the birth rate in China was already falling before the draconian measures were introduced, would have carried on dropping and will continue to decrease even without the one-child policy. Economic development and prosperity are the best contraceptives.

The economic benefits of population control are also neither intrinsic nor inevitable. India, which also had a painful encounter with forced sterilisation policies under Prime Minister Indira Gandhi in the 1980s, has, according to some, enjoyed a demographic dividend from having so many young people. Nandan Nilekani, one of India's leading businessmen, has argued that patterns of rapid growth across states in India reflect demographic transitions. He argues that regions in the transition from relative poverty to relative wealth are marked out by large numbers of young people with the education, skills and flexible cast of mind to exploit new economic opportunities in business process outsourcing or IT.[10] From this perspective, China's overwhelming official ambition to control population may prove a drag on economic growth and, in particular, reduce China's capacity to migrate its industrial base from low-value manufacturing to high-value, high skills, high-tech industry. China has yet to produce world-leading technological innovations in the way that Korea and Japan have done and the skills base of its workforce – linked in part to demography – is one of the reasons for this.

Despite all this the government has no plans to abolish the one-child policy. The National Population and Family Planning Commission announced in 2008 that the policy would continue for at least another 10 years. Having a child still requires permission and having more than one child without permission is punishable by a substantial fine, calculated by a factor of local average disposable income. The amount varies from place to place but it is punitive and a powerful deterrent. People with more than one child may have their work registration documents revoked: they may lose their jobs, never to get another one. Communist Party membership is withdrawn from senior people who do not comply, however exemplary their previous conduct. The professional consequences are devastating. Officials who do not rigorously enforce the policy may be censured and lose their job.

In recent years the rules have been slightly relaxed. People in rural areas and ethnic minority communities can, with permission, have more children. Urban couples who themselves are both single children may be granted permission to have a second child, so long as sufficient time has elapsed since the first child was born. Ways of avoiding or getting round the policy are few and fraught with difficulty, though nevertheless widely practised. Rich people sometimes treat the fine as an expensive tax. If people cannot find a legal exemption from the policy they resort to illegal and emotionally painful subterfuges. During the 1990s, China saw the appearance of tens of thousands of 'extra-birth guerrilla troops': couples whose household registration is in a one-child area moving from place to place to shield their two or three children from the authorities.[11] Second children are kept hidden away, emerging outside only after dark. They are sent away to the countryside to be brought up by relatives. Alternatively, foster parents are paid to bring them up. The child may be given up for adoption or simply abandoned on a rubbish heap or wasteland. Some are found and saved by charities and social workers; others just die.[12]

Mothers forced to abandon their babies take great care about where the baby is left to maximise the chance of her being found. In cities like Beijing and Shanghai, where many foreigners live, the mothers seek out alleys and doorways which foreigners frequent. In 2010 Patti Waldmeir, the *Financial Times* correspondent in Shanghai, found a baby in an alley by Dunkin' Donuts, a few steps from the best hotel in Shanghai. The mother often leaves the baby with the means for her survival (unless the baby is sick or disabled, it's always a girl). The baby is dressed in several layers of baby clothes, or extra clothes are wrapped in the bundle. Tins of infant formula, packs of nappies and clean bottles are also left with the baby. Having abandoned the baby, the anxious mother may also wait and watch out of sight from a nearby darkened corner to see who picks up the baby and to make sure she is safe.[13] This is not heartless indifference to girl babies or unfeeling abandonment, more an act of desperation when all the other options have run out. Once the baby has been abandoned many mothers are consumed by feelings of loss and guilt akin to bereavement. One mother told Xinran about her painful memories several years after giving up her baby girl:

> I'm two different people now. By day, I'm just like any other woman of my age, working away like mad, wanting recognition for everything from the way I look and dress to my intelligence and my work. I long for love and I do love my boyfriend. But by night, I become the lonely woman I have grown into, weighed down with guilt of having abandoned my daughter. The pain of missing her so much tears me apart, until I actually feel it's giving me a real, physical heart attack.[14]

Ultrasound and sex-selective termination is a less horrifying alternative and has meant that abandonment of babies is becoming less common. The Chinese authorities have also become more concerned about abandoned babies. Perhaps mindful of the negative impressions created both at home and abroad by the consequences of the one-child policy, conditions in orphanages have greatly improved and procedures for international adoptions have been tightened and regularised. But these improved arrangements have created a perverse incentive because abandoned and adopted babies may now have better life chances than a poor mother could give them. This applies particularly if the babies are sick or disabled because a poor mother cannot afford the treatment, and abandonment might increase the chance of the baby receiving free medical care.

By the end of 2007, 120,000 Chinese orphans had been adopted by nationals of 27 countries; almost all the orphans were girls. In her book about mothers and girls given away for adoption Xinran notes how some mothers are 'peasant women who have never left the confines of a mountain village'.[15] Others are 'lively but naive young girls who know nothing about life, still less about how men and women create life together'. Or maybe the mother was 'a good traditional woman who put her family first but was caught between the one-child policy and the need to produce a son'. The mother may be tormented by her conscience every day and condemned by her friends and family as cold-hearted. Or perhaps the mother 'paid for giving birth with her life'.[16]

The effect of the one-child policy that most bothered Wish Tree respondents was the rapid acceleration in the ageing of China's society. Estimates of future age distribution vary. No demographer, however, disputes that the proportion of people over 60 will increase from 10 per cent of the population to at least 30 per cent by 2050, perhaps more; from 128 million old people to at least 430 million. In 2015 relatively small numbers of children will reach the age of 15 and large numbers of people will reach retirement age. From then on the working-age population as a proportion of the total will decline rapidly. In 1995 there were more than four times as many children under 14 (327 million) as people over 65 (76 million). By 2050 the number of people over 65 is forecast to quadruple to 300 million, while the number of children under 14 drops by nearly a third to 211 million. From an economic point of view, in 1995 there were ten adults between 15 and 65 (808 million) for every person over 65. In 2050 there will be just over three working adults (962 million) to support each person over 65 (300 million).[17]

Other factors have also contributed to falling birth rates. As they get richer all societies get older. Better nourished, healthier people are less prone to disease.[18] Fertility rates also fall because children cease to be

economic contributors and become 'cost centres'. Women have greater
economic independence and more choose to have fewer children or no
children at all. All these natural effects present complex challenges to rich
societies, but they have been artificially accelerated in China by the one-
child policy, moving demographers to observe that 'China will become old
before it becomes rich'.[19]

The effects of an ageing society on individual elderly citizens are profound.
Because of the one-child policy, elderly people in China increasingly have
the lifestyles of the elderly in developed countries without the incomes to
maintain, much less enjoy, their 'third age' independence. In the developed
world almost all old people receive a state pension and public expenditure
on pensions is between 6 and 18 per cent of GDP. In China nearly 80 per
cent of people over 85 are financially dependent on their children and relatives. Around 70 per cent of people over 60 live with children or relatives
and just 0.8 per cent live in institutions. Public expenditure on pensions
accounts for 2.7 per cent of GDP. In other words, single children are forced
to look after and financially support their elderly relatives because old
people, especially the increasing number over 80, simply have no other
financial choices and nowhere else they can afford to live.[20] Children have
to support their relatives because the state doesn't. At the same time as being
financially dependent they are also more isolated; more reliant on other old
people for companionship and more worried about having to cope on their
own because their child will not be able to support them.

Respondents to the Wish Tree were, of course, concerned about the consequences of the one-child policy for them and their family rather than big
national trends. The emotional territory they charted in their responses
was: fear, foreboding, anxiety, sadness and loss. This woman explicitly
highlighted the one-child policy as a contributor to her feelings of vulner-
ability. It has made her particularly worried about who would look after
her if she became sick:

> I'm worried about the medical problems because we are a one-child
> family. I hope I can be taken care of when in illness and the retirement
> salary will increase at the same rate as food prices rise. (*Woman, 59*)

Some people were more generally worried that having only one child means helplessness in old age: 'I have only one child. I am worried no one will care for me when I'm old' *(Man, 62)*. Because their single child had many problems and preoccupations, many of the elderly just felt worried that there was no one to look after them in their later years:

> The loss of my family and friends [changed my life]. I'm worrying about my life when I'm old. What shall I do if I haven't got anyone to take care of me? [I wish] to love my life and to cherish my time and to stay happy.

> Retirement [changed my life]. I worry about my child's employment. It's hard to see a doctor. I fear nobody will take care of me when I am old. We hope to have a bank branch to get our pension and get medical care distributed more fairly. *(Woman, 57)*

This woman's son died a year before the family lost their land. Her husband was ill and she had no job:

> I lost my only son in 2000. I became an urban resident in 2001. I don't have any job. [My greatest worry is] having nobody [to] take care of me when I get old; my husband suffers from cancer and we can't afford medical expenses. [I wish] 1. my husband recovers from cancer. 2. I could get financial support when I get old. *(Woman, 55)*

This man, like a lot of other older people, would have preferred to live in the traditional extended family way when he retires: 'Being laid off [changed my life. My greatest worry is] that I couldn't afford my medical expenses. [I wish] that I could live with my daughter for my later life' *(Man, 54)*.

People worried about being a burden to the children, because only one child bears the burden:

> I'm afraid of getting old as I don't want to be a burden to my child. [I wish] everything goes well with my child. *(Woman, 70)*

Poverty [changed my life]. I couldn't afford to get ill and I'm worrying about becoming a burden to my child. I can afford the basic living expenses. I just want to live a peaceful life.

In particular some respondents worried about who will look after them if they get sick when they are old:

[My greatest worry is that] no one will take care of me when I'm sick. I'm worried there will be no security when I'm old. Cancel the health access fee. The medical costs are too high. *(Man, 54)*

Some older people had sufficient independent means to look after themselves. That made them feel more secure on their own account, but did not remove their worries about their children's future. Having only one child understandably meant older people were more concerned their child should do well and be happy. A resident of Ciqikou noted that employment security in a humble job has given her a degree of independence. Consequently she did not have to lean on her child. But knowing she could be more independent did not stop her worrying about the future happiness of her child: 'I'm a cleaner of my community. Having this job [changed my life]. At least I can live by myself. [My greatest worry is] whether my child would have a happy family' *(52)*. Such hopes for the well-being of their child were most profoundly undermined by the prospects of their child losing their job. That had consequences for all generations of the family: 'My children do not have jobs. [My greatest worry is] low salary and difficulty seeing a doctor. I wish there was no health access fee.'

The problems associated with the disability of this person's daughter had been made worse by unemployment:

My children have lost their jobs and my daughter is disabled. It's difficult being in hospital because of my age. I hope my country will grow more prosperous and strong and all people will have a better life.

These older people explicitly linked their children's having lost their jobs with being unable to pay their own medical fees, so the obvious port of call for financial help was closed:

I'm becoming older and I do not have enough money to see a doctor when I'm sick because my children have lost their jobs. *(Woman, 76)*

I have several children but they are all unemployed. [My greatest worry is] being ill and having no money to see a doctor.

If their children lost their job and they too have prematurely lost their job, the old person inevitably worried about who would care for them when they are old: '[I am] a worker who has lost his job. [My greatest worry is] no medical insurance. I worry about my children's jobs. [I hope] I am cared for when I am old.'

Another woman was worried about her child losing her job and recognised she needed to be financially independent. A more equitable retirement pension would help: 'Retirement [changed my life. My greatest worry is] my child's job. I hope the retirement pension can reach the same level as other municipalities' *(Woman, 58)*.

This woman had lost her land and livelihood. She feared that her children might lose their job and leave her without access to financial and other support, particularly for medical care: 'I have no income and my child couldn't support me either, plus my land has been expropriated.'

Older people felt they would have to be more self-reliant but the loss of the old social protection made that harder. They may not have a retirement pension and, in particular, without health insurance they cannot afford health care. This person felt the government should do more to support the elderly:

My two children have lost their jobs and this influenced my life. [My greatest worry is] the pension is low and when I am sick I have no money for hospital. I hope the government can care for us and solve the problems of the retired.

A grandmother was worried that her son's having lost his job might make it difficult for her grandson to stay at university, where paying tuition fees is challenging, even for people with jobs: 'My son has lost his job and my grandson went to university. We're worried about my son's employment. [I wish for] medical care reform' *(Woman, 74)*.

With a single child, grandparents also had to worry about the welfare of the single grandchild, because there are no aunts and uncles to step in to look after the grandchild if anything happens to the parents. Employment and family security are seen as prerequisites of happiness down the generations. This retired person was looking out for the welfare both of the child and of the grandson, also grown up. The grandson was facing the added challenge of finding a wife amid a shortage of women:

[I am] a retired worker. [My greatest worry is about] my child's employment and family. [I wish] for good health and [that] my grandson would find a good job and a good wife.

In their old age circumstances and having a single child may conspire to give grandparents childcare responsibilities once again. This grandparent had a disabled grandchild, and that was a source of worry to her: 'Disability of my grandchild [changed my life]. [My greatest worry is] there would be nobody to take care of my grandchild.' Another grandmother had been obliged to look after her grandchild because the child's mother was mentally ill and homeless:

I took care of my granddaughter as her parents are incapable of doing so. My daughter has no home to live in. My daughter is mentally ill. I hope she will be cared for by the community and receive adequate treatment.

The absence of family members nearby and the increasing number of old people meant elderly people were often isolated. Instead of looking to the family for companionship and occupation, they had to find social activities for themselves, relying on the community to organise those activities and spending more time with other older people:

[I'm] a lonely old fellow. [I have had] good service for the elderly from my community. [My greatest worry is] if this kind of service would keep on. I hope I can still enjoy this service in future. *(Man, 78)*

I'm a retired woman. Taking part in the social activities in my community [changed my life. My greatest worries are] social order; health insurance;

too much stealing and robbing; retirement pension gap is too much. [I wish to] get the pension in the local China Construction Bank. Build a big department store. Build a cultural public square and an activity centre for old people.

Isolation and idleness had led some to contemplate the lonely safety of an old people's home, a dispiriting aspect of life in the developed world that is being imported into China. Though this can't have been how they imagined their old age, as circumstances had turned out, without other forms of support and with many anxieties, it had come to seem the least worst option. As this respondent said: 'Retirement [changed my life.] I used to be busy, now I have a lot of free time. I hope the government medical system will be changed. I hope the old people's home can be completed quickly.'

Health insurance, unemployment and the security of his children's employment were all worrying this man. He hoped the lonely prospect of an old people's home might ease his anxieties: '[I am] a worker who has lost his job. [My greatest worry is] no medical care insurance – My greatest worry is my children's jobs. I hope the old people's home can be built quickly' *(Man, 58)*.

Older people with only one child were worried about whether they would have anyone to look after them, particularly if they get sick. They had lost the self-reliance gained through the old social protection system and they worried they would have to turn to their child for help. But they knew that their child might not be able to support them, perhaps, because they had lost their job or had problems of their own, including problems with a grandchild. Detached from the traditional three-generation family, old people were isolated, reliant on community support and hoping in desperation to be able to live in an old people's home. This is all a far cry from traditional family ways of life and Confucian reverence for elders. The old way has collapsed and the growing army of older people in China are listless and lost, pessimistic and frightened.

Things have changed for younger people too. In Mao's day people had to get permission from Party officials in the work unit to get married, to have a child or to move house. These rules have been relaxed and romance is back, with all its joys and apprehensions – or at least it has re-emerged from the secrecy and hiding to which Mao consigned so much of the deeper essence of human experience. The exhilarating and frightening prospects of looking for love are now managed without state interference. A young couple felt they had found true love. The young man had made up his mind about his desired future: 'Falling in love [changed my life.] [My greatest worry is] I couldn't spend my life with her. [I wish] to marry her' (*Man*, 20). His girlfriend shared these feelings:

> Having met my Mr Right [changed my life]. [My greatest worry is] whether I could spend the rest of my life with him; whether my family could have a happy life. [I wish] to live a happy life and to spend the rest of my life with (name). (*Woman*, 18)

Adult single children, having got married and become parents, have simultaneous obligations to their parents and to their child. The long-standing and persistent government campaign, rising prosperity and greater female economic independence have combined to raise the age at which people get married and parents have their child, so the 18-year-old young woman quoted above may have a long wait for her wedding. Delay is a tried and tested means of reducing family size, but it also means that grandparents are older when the grandchild is born. Consequently they can help out less and are more likely themselves to need assistance from the middle generation while the grandchild is still young and in need of maximum parental attention. Confucian tradition, along with human kindness, creates the obligation to care for elderly parents. This woman, in the middle generation, faced the common situation of worrying about two generations: 'I worry about my son growing up. [I wish] the whole family is secure and my mother is healthy' (*Woman, 43*).

This middle-aged man gave one of the longest and most vivid responses to the Wish Tree questions. He had the common combinations of concerns, including health care for old people so they can be independent, and the cost of children's education at the other end of the age spectrum:

> I'm a worker at the tyre factory and I changed from rural to non-rural urban registration and the tyre factory went bankrupt. I'm already in my

fifties and I'm getting old. It's very hard for me to find a job. I don't have enough money for food and my living expenses. I don't see a way to solve my problems and we don't have health insurance. I'm jobless and I don't have health insurance. I can't even afford my living expenses and I also need to support my parents. I don't know what to do. [I wish] to get some compensation and to get health insurance when I retire. *(Man, 52)*

Adult children may also have to move far away in search of work, meaning that they cannot offer day-to-day support to their parents. This soldier did not feel he was fulfilling his filial duty because he was away from home in the army: 'Being a soldier [changed my life. My greatest worry is] my parents are living alone' *(Man, 21).*

In relation to their own child, parents compound and concentrate all their aspirations and expectations on the hoped-for achievements of a single child. Many parents expressed strong hopes for the happiness of their child:

My marriage [changed my life]. My greatest worry would be one of my relatives gets ill. I wish my son would have a productive life and every one of my family would remain happy and healthy.

In particular, in contemporary China, those hopes and expectations relate to educational attainment, an unreliable passport to future success, as these respondents made clear:

Losing my job [changed my life. My greatest worries are] getting ill; job; my child's education. [I wish for] good health; a good job; my child receiving good education.

Being laid off [changed my life. I wish] that my child could receive a good education and grow up healthy. *(Woman, 25)*

Many parents worried about their children's future: 'Everything about my kid's future [worries me]' *(Woman, 30).*

A woman living in Hemu Lu, who became an urban resident after her land had been expropriated, worried about her child's employment and future happiness: '[My greatest worry is] whether my child could get a steady job. I wish my child could live a happy life without too much burden' *(Woman, 51)*.

Unemployment and the collapse of social welfare meant many people worried about themselves as well as their children. They had health concerns alongside worries about their children's future. They knew their own ill health would be a burden to their children, particularly, if they could not afford medical costs themselves: 'My child's future is my biggest concern, as well as my health. [I wish] every one of my family would stay happy and healthy.' This man's worries about health insecurities sprang from having lost his job, but his most important wish was about his children's future: 'Being laid off [changed my life. My greatest worry is] no guarantee against falling ill. I wish for the happiness of my children' *(Man, 54)*.

Many parents worried about their children getting sick, such as this woman with a young son: 'I would be heartbroken if my son got ill. [I wish for] good health and a happy life for my son; a peaceful life for my family' *(Woman, 29)*. The extended family are also included in the circle of anxiety and obligation: 'My marriage [changed my life. My greatest worry is] the health of my brother's son. [I wish] to make sure everyone has health insurance' *(Woman, 53)*.

An adult couple, both of whom are single children, have to be concerned about the welfare of four older people. Those older people may be less able to support themselves because of a lack of social welfare services and poor retirement pensions. The adult couple may also find it difficult to support their parents from a distance if they have moved away. In addition they face the stresses and strains of ensuring their own child's well-being. Their child's educational attainment will be another pressing concern. All these worries about others will have to be borne alone, as there are no other siblings. Employment and financial insecurity in their own life will exacerbate all these anxieties. Adults are beleaguered with cares for themselves and for the generations above and below.

For children the biggest anxiety that stems from being an only child is the ever-present fear of being abandoned, isolated and unloved. These concerns came through repeatedly in children's responses on the Wish Tree. Some children simply feared their parents' love for them would diminish. This child was also worried about friends, 'My greatest worries are my parents wouldn't love me this much in future, my friends would leave me and I couldn't do well in exams.' Other children feared they would have no one to love them more generally, not just their parents:

[My greatest worry is] I wouldn't have anyone to love me.

[My greatest worry] is lack of loving and caring. *(Boy, 11)*

Some children feared losing their parents altogether. This child implied that his greatest fear would be the premature loss of his parents before he could cope without them: '[My greatest worry is] to lose my parents at an early age.'

Less extreme than parents dying is the fear that they might become sick. The divorce of this child's parents would have exacerbated his anxieties about their health: 'My parents' divorce [changed my life. My greatest worry is] my parents suffering from illness' *(Boy, 12)*.

Many other children were concerned about what might happen to their parents: 'I'm worried about my parents' health. I hope to give my parents something in return' *(Girl, 11)*, and another child: [My greatest worry is] my parents suffering from severe illnesses.

Some children were already dealing with parental illness, not just fearing it:

I'm worried about my parents' illness. *(Boy, 12)*

[I wish] to cure my mum's illness and to be a good student. *(Girl, 11)*

The love from my parents [changed my life]. I'm so sad my parents got sick.

My wish is my parents could love me more and my mum would be recovered soon from illness.

This girl extended her anxieties about adult infirmity to the mother of her friend: '[My greatest worry is] the illness of my friend's mum. I wish I could make 10 wishes every day.'

Connected to anxieties about abandonment and isolation, children also wished for the longevity of their parents:

[My greatest worry is] whether my mum could live 100 years. *(Girl, 11)*

Let my parents live 100 years. *(Girl, 10)*

This teenager had already lost one parent and so was concerned that the other should have a long life: 'My father's passing away [changed my life. My greatest worry is] to lose my mum. [I wish for] longevity for my mum' *(Girl, 17)*.

Some children had explicit anxieties simply about being left or abandoned by their parents:

[My greatest worry is] my parents would leave me. *(Girl, 9)*

I hope my parents won't leave me. *(Girl, 11)*

One or both parents leaving home to look for a job, perhaps in another city, is increasingly common. The parent who is away from home may return just once or twice a year for the official holidays at New Year and in the autumn Golden Week. People from the countryside seeking work in the city often have no choice but to leave their children back home with grandparents for months and sometimes years on end. Perhaps this fuelled some of these fears about being left alone, as this child made clear: 'Parents trying to make money [changed my life. My greatest worry is] my parents would leave me' *(9)*.

The converse of being left by parents is that the child will be forced to leave the comfort and security of the family home. Some children were worried about that:

I'm worried I will have to leave my family when I grow up. *(Girl, 10)*

I'm afraid of having to leave this community and this country. *(Girl, 11)*

I'm worried I will have to leave the school and the community. *(Girl, 11)*

Parental separation and divorce is another potential trauma, perhaps the most serious of them all. These children feared that the separation of their parents might be made permanent and irreversible by divorce:

'Arguments and separation of my mum and dad [changed my life. My greatest worry is] my mum and dad would get divorced. [I wish] Mum would come back home and Mum and Dad would get back together.' *(Girl, 11)*

Separation of my parents [changed my life. My greatest worry is] divorce of my parents. [I wish] my parents would get back together and Mummy would come back home. *(Girl, 11)*

For some children, it was too late. Their parents were divorced, though some hoped they would get back together: 'Divorce of my parents [changed my life. My greatest worry is] not having a complete family. [I wish] Mum and Dad would get back together' *(Girl, 11)*.

The prospect of being an only child living with a single parent is obviously even less appealing and more worrying. The lone parent has to face all the pressures. There's no opportunity to choose which parent is more likely to consent before asking permission to do something. One parent cannot be played against the other; nor can a disciplinary decision by one be ameliorated by consolation from the other. This boy was worried that his father, who seems to have left home, would no longer look after him from a distance: 'Divorce of my parents [changed my life]. I'm worried my dad would not care for me. I wish my mum and dad could get married again' *(Boy, 10)*.

Even if parents remain together, marital conflict is also felt especially acutely by only children. This girl feared domestic conflict: '[My greatest worry is] Mum and Dad fighting' *(Girl, 10)*. Another child connected her own poor health with a wish for parental harmony, so she would be looked after in the event of illness recurring: 'I suffered from a severe illness when I was young and my health got poor since. [My greatest worry is] whether my parents would get along' *(Girl, 11)*.

Without siblings to conspire or collaborate with, parental disapproval or control is likely to be felt more strongly. This child was in conflict with her parents: 'I have become mature. My parents don't trust me. I wish to have my own computer. My mum brings me trouble' *(Girl, 10).*

Childhood is normally characterised by the love and care of parents, the companionship of siblings and friends as well as carefree joys and personal pleasures, enjoyed both alone and convivially with others. The positive experiences of childhood are, however, as every child eventually finds out, accompanied by less-discussed, sometimes taboo, dark shadows of fear and anxiety, conflict and possibly violence at the hands of other children or by adults; even parental beatings. Corporal punishment of children is becoming less common in China, but, anecdotally, still seems more frequent than in Western countries. These four children commented about being beaten:

> [My greatest worry is] my dad beats me. *(Girl, 10)*

> [I wish] my mum would beat me no more. *(Boy, 9)*

> Being beaten by my dad [changed my life. My greatest worry is] to get beaten again by my dad.

> Being beaten (by parents) [changed my life]

Even as a teenager, this boy was still being beaten:

> '[I wish] my parents would beat me no more.' *(Boy, 15)*

These multifarious concerns do not weaken people's commitment to family life. On the contrary, the traditional Confucian sense of obligation is still strong and is being made stronger by the withdrawal of other formal and informal forms of social support. The presence of so many simultaneous insecurities puts a premium on family relationships. People have fewer and weaker family relationships just at the time when changes to the economy and labour market mean they need more and stronger family support. Although family relationships are fewer and further between, the need to depend on them has grown.

As well as the rapidly ageing society and the concerns it has brought to all three generations reported on the Wish Tree, the other big social consequence of the one-child policy is a socially destabilising gender imbalance. A preference for boys over girls has an ignoble cultural history in China, long predating the one-child policy. In remote rural areas, the perception is still that a girl child is an unwanted economic burden. In poorer rural areas, where sentimentality can seem like extravagance, girl children were sold for domestic service or marriage, or abandoned, killed or simply ignored, neglected and starved. In 1971 Mao told Edgar Snow, an American journalist highly sympathetic to Mao and the Communists, about the preference for boys among rural Chinese people: 'In the country-side a woman still wants to have boy children. If the first and second were girls, she would have another try. If the third one came and was still a girl, the mother would try again. Pretty soon there would be nine of them.'[21]

This traditional preference has evidently been reinforced by the one-child policy. China has about 120 boys for every 100 girls, compared to roughly parity in the developed world. This phenomenon is not confined to China. The established norm for sex ratios at birth is 105 boys to 100 girls. Boys typically have a higher early mortality rate than girls so the balance between girls and boys reaches parity by the age of five. The Chinese government says the ratio is 119: 100, though demographers estimate 121: 100. In India, with strong patriarchal traditions and a deplorable record on women's equality, the government estimates the ratio is 113 boys to 100 girls.[22] Pakistan, Bangladesh, Bhutan, Taiwan, Afghanistan and South Korea also have above-average ratios, but none as high as China's. The causes, according to Amartya Sen in his groundbreaking *New York Times Review of Books* article, are female infanticide and neglect of girls.[23] Contrary to trends elsewhere, in India and China the early childhood mortality rate for girls is higher than that for boys. To put it more straight-forwardly, boys are cared for when they get sick whereas girls are neglected.

Others such as Mara Huistendahl have argued plausibly that the wide-spread availability of ultrasound techniques to determine the sex of foetuses, followed by relatively cheap abortions to terminate female foetuses, has also played a big part in creating the gender imbalance. Mass-produced ultra-sound equipment became available in 1982, two years after the intensifica-tion of the one-child policy. In 2008 in Jiangsu province a sex determination test report cost RMB1,000 in bribes to ultrasound technicians. The fine for having a child without a birth permit was ten times that.[24] Nor is sex selection confined to the unenlightened rural poor; some of the highest sex imbalances are recorded in prosperous urban districts where ultrasound equipment is widely available and affordable by the middle-class residents.

The absolute imbalance is not the whole problem. Certain types of boys get ahead and others are left behind. The young men with talent, money and opportunities get the girls. The poor and unskilled do not. Those with little enough to hope for, without the prospect of marriage, have even fewer reasons to be optimistic. The Chinese call these young men 'bare branches' (*guang-guan*). In China and India, the 'bare branches' make up 12 to 15 per cent of the young male adult population. The prospective difficulties boys face in finding a wife came out in responses to the Wish Tree, expressed by parents and grandparents as well as boys and men of all three generations. This woman worried about her adult son: 'I wish my son could find a wife' (*Woman, 63*). Another middle-aged woman, on the other hand, expressed relief: 'My son getting married [changed my life]' (*Woman, 57*). Grandmothers also have anxieties about their grandsons' prospects for marriage. '[I wish] when my grandchildren get out of university they get a good job and find a good wife.'

Young men certainly worry about finding a good wife: 'Getting a job after growing up [changed my life. I wish] to marry a good wife and have a good family.'

This young man had been a soldier in the army: 'After that I got a good job. [I wish for] the best job. That my parents have a long life. That I have a harmonious family and a good wife.' A man was approaching middle age and was still looking for a wife: '[My greatest worry is] to make money and to get a wife' (*39*).

Recent events in his personal life had concentrated this respondent's thoughts. He seemed to sum up the thoughts of many boys, men and their families: finding a suitable wife is part and parcel of succeeding in life: 'Breaking up with my girlfriend [changed my life. I wish to have] a good marriage and a successful career' (*Man, 26*).

Even young boys seemed to have internalised anxieties about the shortage of girls as potential marriage partners. An 11-year-old boy whose ambition was to be a flying squad leader said: '[My greatest worry is] I won't find a wife.' Another boy, aged 12, who wanted to be a trillionaire was also worried he 'couldn't get a wife'.

Some women also had marriage on their mind, but their requirements from a husband betray the shifting balance of power in China's marriage market. Boys and men just want a good wife; girls want to marry rich and successful men, not just good husbands:

[I wish to] become rich and to find a good husband (that means he should have his own car and property). (*Woman, 22*)

[I wish to] marry a rich man so that I can depend on him. (*Woman, 23*)

The men have good reason to be worried. By 2013 one in ten Chinese men will lack a female potential marriage partner. By the late 2020s, one in five men will be surplus. According to forecasts women will remain scarce until 2045, so about 15 per cent of men overall will lack potential wives.[25] Professional young women with economic independence, in my experience, are already becoming more critical and fussy about the suitability of young men as partners. Wealthier bachelors without sufficient appeal to city girls seek wives from the countryside or from abroad. About four million girls are estimated to move from the countryside to get married.[26] A dispiriting but profitable trade has been established in marriage broking in Vietnam. Rural women live in cramped conditions in Ho Chi Minh City awaiting selection by a foreign husband. The cultural fit between China and Vietnam is believed to be better than it might be with, say, girls from Cambodia or the Philippines. Chinese men can expect Vietnamese women to share their Confucian values, their commitment to ancestors and a patriarchal family structure. All countries involved can only hope that their 'bare branches' cross borders to make love, not war.[27] Another option for parents concerned about their son's marriage prospects is finding him a child bride; a once common bad habit in China now making a comeback. At the extreme, girl children are simply stolen from their parents. This problem is sufficiently significant for the police to have set up an online registry, Baby Come Home.

Social unrest can also be a consequence of male/female imbalance. Historically, China has plenty of experience of this. The Nian uprising against the Qing in 1850 was born of poverty, charismatic leadership and the rootless gangs of bandits that had roamed the Chinese countryside for centuries. These bandits were *guangguan*, 'bare branches', men detached from family, community and conventional social prospects who had turned into feral robbers, kidnappers and violent criminals. The historian

Jonathan Spence noted that 'a profound imbalance in the region's sex ratios' contributed to the uprising.[28] Government figures from 1874 for the area in Jiangsu province where the uprising began show there were 163 men for every 100 women. Trouble was therefore inevitable. The Taiping Rebellion at about the same time further south also featured a charismatic leader drawing support from the frustrations of young men.

In the past, governments in many countries dealt with 'bare branches' by sending lone young men to war, sponsoring construction of large, dangerous public works, such as building railways, with a high male fatality rate, exporting them to under-populated areas and co-opting them into the military or the police. None of those options are designed to produce social cohesion and calm, nor are they equal to the extent of the problem. A more repressive approach may yet be needed. 'The need to control the rising instability created by the bare branches has led governments to favour more authoritarian approaches to internal governance and less benign international presences.'[29]

In modern times young men are the main causes of crime and social unrest everywhere. Single young men gather together in groups and gangs battle each other for territorial and other forms of dominance, with socially disastrous results. Crime rates rise, particularly violent crime. Drug use and drug dealing become endemic in their neighbourhoods. Weapons smuggling and trading become more common. The trafficking and prostitution of women increases. This man who responded to the Wish Tree had been in prison and was now a lost soul: 'I'm an old fellow. Going to prison [changed my life]. I have no home to go to and no support for life. [I wish for] a place to settle.'

Since Reform China has experienced a crime wave. Between 1992 and 2004 crime in China doubled. Crime and its causes are multifaceted, and isolating the impact of a single cause such as sex imbalance on a wider trend is difficult and unreliable. But regressions done by academic economists at Hong Kong and Columbia Universities have led them to conclude that 'the increasing maleness of the young adult population may account for as much as a third of the overall rise in crime'.[30] In 2007 a statement by the Central Committee recognised that these single men were 'a hidden danger' that will 'affect social stability'.[31] Family life is in trouble in China and its problems have brought trouble to the whole society.

CHAPTER 7

Educational Pressure, Hope and Despair

Established in AD 606 during the Han dynasty, the Imperial examination system in China was the first full system of educational testing in the world, remaining in place until the fall of the Qing dynasty thirteen centuries later. Examination results were the only way of achieving status and wealth, ordaining lifelong position in the social hierarchy. Those with the highest marks could aspire to become a scholar-administrator at the apex of the Confucian social order. The top students were admitted to a government academy from which officials were appointed. During the Imperial heyday in the Ming dynasty between 1368 and 1644, the students with highest scores in civil service exams joined the Grand Secretary of Advisers or worked in one of the ministries south of the Meridian gate in Beijing around a T-shaped courtyard called the Heavenly Streets (*Tianjie*). These ministry buildings survived until the 1950s, when they were demolished to make way for the revolutionary triumphalism of Tiananmen Square. A vast bureaucracy worked under this elevated elite. By the middle of the sixteenth century 200,000 bureaucrats ran a government that ruled 150 million people. Their principal qualification was knowledge of Confucianism. Little emphasis was placed on technical or scientific skills.

Since time immemorial, endless study in preparation for constant tests and super-significant exams has been the bane of Chinese children's lives. They don't just have to pass the exams; they must get the highest mark possible because that too will influence their destiny. The initiator of the Taiping uprising during the Qing dynasty was provoked to rebellion and taking control of large swathes of Imperial territory by a lack of success in exams. Study, revision, testing, scores and results tables are deeply embedded in education, in family life, and in society as a whole.

During the Cultural Revolution Mao attempted to overturn the old order in education and exams. Traditional book learning was labelled reactionary and pointless. Encouraged by Mao, students became Red Guards. They were intent on denouncing the past, shaming and hounding those they saw as being associated with it. Professors were paraded through the streets and downgraded to menial jobs, like cleaning toilets. Libraries were destroyed and books burnt. School students were forcibly removed from their families at a moment's notice and sent to live in the countryside. Many were not allowed to return for many years. Some never came back. One respondent to the Wish Tree had been sent to the countryside during the Cultural Revolution, and used a common euphemistic description of that experience: '[I'm] a retired teacher. Intellectual young people being sent to the rural places [changed my life].'

Educational institutions were in the front line as an air of denunciation, hysteria, intimidation and chaos came to dominate society. Higher education was virtually shut down and a rising generation of students, graduates, teachers, technicians, scientists and professors were lost to the world of the intellect. For many people the deficit was never recovered. After all this Deng Xiaoping noted, 'Everyone here is scared – the youth, even more the elderly. That is precisely why our technology is so far behind.'[1] Putting education back together again after the Cultural Revolution has seen a return to old ways. Learning by rote, copying out characters hundreds of times, disciplinarian teachers, incessant testing and impossible mountains of homework are once more the order of the day for schoolchildren.

In the first phase of Reform after 1978 education was rapidly turned back into a rigid hierarchy. Bringing on the brightest and best with technical skills was urgently needed for modernising the economy. Eighty-eight 'key' universities were designated. Admission was strictly on merit and educational authorities were told to identify gifted children well suited to the fast track. The school system was also rigidly stratified. The best were the officially designated 'key' schools. 'Non-key' schools differ greatly in the equipment, resources, teaching staff and educational quality they can offer, thus increasing the imbalance in access to high-quality compulsory education.'[2] The schools that are not key are further sub-categorised into general and vocational schools. Only the children who attend the 'general' schools can apply for higher education. Students at 'vocational' schools can only apply for technical education, widely perceived by parents as a dead end. Whether children attend general or vocational schools is decided by exam performance at the age of 12 or 13.

The other big change to education in the Reform period is that the cost of tuition fees paid by parents has exploded. After 1978 the commitment to free education both in the countryside and the cities disappeared almost over-night. In the countryside the break-up of the collective farms led swiftly to the collapse of the free public services they provided, including health clinics and schools. The demands on farmers' new-found income, which rose after the break-up of the communes, also quickly increased. People in the coun-tryside are spending up to half their income on educating their children. In 2005 a typical rural primary or middle-school student's family would need to pay between RMB300 and RMB500 a year for textbooks and other additional fees. Their annual per capita cash income was about RMB1000.[3]

After the accession of Jiang Zemin with his allies from Shanghai and Deng Xiaoping's Southern Tour in 1992 the Beijing government's commit-ment to market-based reforms accelerated and intensified. Managers in loss-making state-owned enterprises could determine, and reduce, labour costs. Unsurprisingly they reduced the head count and employee benefits. But cost reductions were not enough to turn around many loss-making enterprises. They had to close or be sold off. Tens of millions of people were rendered unemployed without welfare benefits, health insurance, pensions or any way of subsidising education costs. Such was the fate of the people working in the chinaware industry in Ciqikou and in the tyre factory in Banshanercun. The funding and delivery of education and other public services became the responsibility of local government. In the rural areas these responsibilities were delegated to the lowest and least well-funded levels of local government. No mechanism was established for equitable redistribution of funds from richer provinces, mostly those containing the successful cities of the eastern seaboard, to the less wealthy provinces. Funds for education are so limited that many townships can barely afford staff costs, and can afford little else in the way of buildings or equipment. This lack of funds has led to 'the widespread policy of making public service providers, such as schools and clinics, responsible for their own financing through the collection of fees.[4] Consequently, 'the financial burden of compulsory education fell on local people, who were now subject to paying tuition and miscellaneous fees.'[5] Education can absorb one third of family income. The average is about 20 per cent, and as much as half in the countryside. As children go up the school system the costs rise and therefore the proportion of household expenditure absorbed. Xu Anqi of the Shanghai Academy of Social Sciences found that if, as in most cases in Chinese cities, there is one child in a family, his or her education demands 46 per cent of the family's total expenses for secondary school, 51 per cent for high school, and 52 per cent for university. Sending a child to study abroad costs much more.[6]

The charging of fees by local officials has also created plenty of opportunities for graft and illicit gouging of money from parents.[7] Schools have invented myriad ways of charging unauthorised fees. No satisfactory method of controlling illegal and corrupt practices has yet been found. In 2004 the *China Daily* noted, 'extra fees are chargeable for everything from the very start of a child's learning to a university student's graduation.'[8] These extra charges include additional stipends for teachers in public schools, contribution to school building repairs (the state of school buildings in China is variable and often disgraceful), 'office expenses', purchase of books, newspapers, sports and other equipment.[9] A report by the National Development and Reform Commission found the unauthorised charging of fees for education was the leading cause of complaint about the price of goods and services in 2006.[10]

The government prides itself on having increased the proportion of children receiving the statutory minimum nine years' education, as well as improvements in literacy, and a big increase in the number of graduate and postgraduate students. These achievements, however, were brought about by transferring a substantial proportion of the cost to citizens, not by raising public investment in education to international standards. The proportion of educational expenditure borne by the government has been declining, down to 62 per cent of the total by 2003. In 2004 public expenditure on education in China was 2.8 per cent of GDP compared with the average for middle-income countries of 4 per cent. By 2010 that figure was scheduled to reach 4 per cent of GDP and by 2020 it will be between 4.4 and 4.5 per cent, still below the international average of more than 5 per cent.[11]

The two groups of citizens worst affected by education charges are rural dwellers and migrants to the city. In the urban areas the children of migrants are either not admitted to school or have to pay even higher fees than the children registered in the city. As with rural dwellers, school fees for children of migrants to the city can be 50 per cent of the household income. Consequently these children frequently drop out from school because their parents cannot afford the fees.[12] According to a paper produced for the Ministry of Agriculture, 'naturally education expenses have produced heavy financial and psychological pressures on poverty-stricken families and when illnesses or disasters happen students from such families usually drop out because of debts'.[13]

Although the one-child policy was vigorously enforced everywhere for many years, people in rural areas are now permitted to have more than one child. However, many parents can only afford to educate one of their children beyond the basic level. Available family funds are invested in the child with the best scores in the dreaded exams. The other children have to be removed from school for lack of funds. Higher education is simply out of the question for rural families. The tuition fees, according to the *China Daily* in 2006, would exceed their entire annual household income.[14] Rural people make enormous sacrifices for their children's education. One farmer told Hong Zhang, a researcher, what Chinese farmers have thought for centuries: anything is better than being a farmer.

> I hope they [a son and a daughter] will not end up a farmer like me. That is my biggest hope. I will do all I can to get them out of the countryside. To be a farmer is utterly meaningless.[15]

The government introduced 'two frees and one subsidy' in 2005. The 'two frees' are that children in rural areas are exempt from tuition fees and receive free textbooks. Many pupils have to board because schools are few and far between in remote parts of the countryside and parents can receive help with boarding fees, which is the 'one subsidy'. However these subsidies are cash limited and do not cover extraneous charges, so virtually everyone is still paying something towards their children's education and most people are paying a lot. China is still a long way from free, universal school education.

Many of today's parents and grandparents would have been school-children and students (and indeed Red Guards), during the Cultural Revolution. They are members of the lost generation. Although not forgotten, these experiences are rarely discussed with children. Parental optimism is a duty and rehearsing the traumas of the past sullies that. Losing out themselves has, however, redoubled their commitment to their child's education. In addition, having only one child stacks expectations on both parent and child. Educational attainment is a building block in career success and prosperity. Parents understand the importance of getting a good job with a decent income for the child. For boys educational failure and the consequent lack of professional success may prove substantial handicaps in the highly competitive marriage market. Also, their child's prosperity is important for them in their old age when filial duty, another strong Confucian tradition, may be called upon – but with only one child to fulfil the obligations. They will make as many sacrifices as they can for their child's education. New opportunities in a restructured labour market also mean increasing social stigma for failing to educate your child properly, whatever the anxieties and sacrifices.[16] Children are constantly reminded that success in exams is their most significant contribution to making their parents and grandparents happy. Education is even thought to bring honour to your ancestors (*guang zong yao zu*).

As a result of all this, the extreme pressures of education, revision and examinations are felt continuously by children. These children who participated in the Wish Tree all desperately wanted to do well at school:

Study [changed my life. My greatest worry is] I couldn't do well in my studies and my dreams won't come true. [I wish] for a productive life. (*Girl, 12*)

I'm thinking of my study every day. I'm worrying whether I could do well enough at school. [I wish] to be a good student and to become an artist.

[I'm] a student. Dance changed my life. I worry I will not be good enough in my studies. [I wish for] good health and the opportunity to help the country be prosperous. (*Girl, 11*)

Since the 1950s excellence in schoolchildren has been recognised by teachers selecting a small proportion of school students as *san hao xuesheng*, a 'three good' student: good morals, hard study and physical prowess. The system has been criticised for being too selective, too opaque and not validating practical qualities or achievements. Education researchers have pointed out that applying such rigid categories to young children creates few incentives to improve educational performance across the board and de-motivates the majority.[17] Chasing this recognition, children are on a roller-coaster ride between hope and despair. Since 2005 reforms have been proposed and piloted, but judging by children's responses to the Wish Tree, striving for this badge of merit still had an undiminished appeal. Being a 'three good' student was a commonly held ambition. This and being a Young Pioneer, were both valued badges of adult approval:

Being a Young Pioneer [changed my life] I'm worried about failing to be a 'three good' student in the future. [I wish] to be able to make a great contribution to my society and my country when I grow up. *(Boy, 10)*

[I'm] a student. Becoming a Young Pioneer [changed my life. My greatest worry is] whether I could be a 'three good' student next term. I wish for a better environment in my community.

Being a Young Pioneer [changed my life]. I'm worrying if I could be a 'three good' student at school. My wish is to enter a good university. *(Girl, 11)*

Being a Young Pioneer [changed my life]. I'm afraid I will not be graded as a 'three good' student. I hope to be teacher when I grow up – and my parents will be healthy and their jobs go well. *(Boy, 10)*

Admission to the best middle schools is strictly by exam marks. Examinations are not just pass or fail. The exact score makes the difference for entry into a good middle or high school and then university.[18] Because of this highly sensitised stratification children are desperately worried about doing badly in exams, as illustrated by these comments:

Studying in school [changed my life. My greatest worry is] my school results are not satisfactory. *(Girl, 11)*

Study [changed my life]. I'm worrying I couldn't do well in exams. [I wish] I could do better in exams.

Burn on my hands [changed my life. My greatest worry is] bad results at school. [I wish] to get high marks in each exam.

Some pupils feared low marks across the board: '[I'm] a student. Reading and writing [changed my life. My greatest worry] is to get 0 [zero] in my exam. [I wish] to have my own computer' *(Girl, 11)*. Or they were concerned about low marks in a particular subject, especially an important subject like mathematics: 'I'm a girl. Reading and writing [changed my life. My greatest worry is] I may get 0 [zero] in maths exam. I want a Barbie doll' *Girl, 11*.

Many simply wanted full marks in exams, such as this boy and girl:

[My greatest worry is] I couldn't get a 100 in my exam. [I wish] to get 100 in exams. *(Boy, 10)*

My classmates changed my life. [My greatest worries are] books. [I wish] I could pass the entrance exam and enter a university; to get 100. *(Girl)*

This child had other ambitions but knew getting full marks must come first: 'Study [changed my life. My greatest worry is] to fail to enter a university. [My wish is] to get 100 in every exam and to become a singer and painter when I grow up.' Another child's ambitions were only marginally more modest: '[My greatest worry is] poor results in exams. [I wish to] get 90 or above in every exam in every subject.'

Chinese and mathematics make up more than half of the curriculum in primary school, so doing well enough in the exams to go to a good middle school depends upon a high score in these two subjects, as this child knew: '[I wish] to get 95 for Chinese (exam); to get 98 for maths (exam); to enter a good university; Mum and Dad could earn big money.' This ambitious young teenager wanted to be the best: 'I want to work hard and be the top student in my class *(Girl, 13)*.

Exam results are a passport to a good school. Children are in no doubt about the importance of getting into the right school, as this child said: 'I'm worried about being sick and not going to a good school and not serving my home town.'

Another child's first love was clearly dancing, rather than study, but she was still worried about getting into a good school: 'Dancing changed my life. I'm worried I will not be able to go to a good school. I hope I can give a performance abroad' *(Girl, 11)*. One girl also had recent artistic interests and, in her own opinion considerable achievements, but nevertheless saw the importance of getting into the right school.

> [I'm] a student. I started to learn violin when I was 10 and I play it well now. [My greatest worry is] failing to enter a good school and couldn't make a contribution to my country. *(Girl, 11)*

One of the youngest respondents at 9 years old, this girl nonetheless knew the importance of a good school. She also knew what she wanted to do when she grew up: '[I'm] a local resident. [My greatest worry is] to fail to enter a good school. [I wish] to be a stewardess.' *(Girl, 9)*

Children enter middle school at 12 or 13 and high school at 15 or 16. Many children were concerned about entering good middle schools: 'Being a Young Pioneer [changed my life. My greatest worry is] continuing to be rated a "three good" student. [I wish] to enter an excellent middle school' *(Boy, 12)*.

Although going to high school is some years away for many of these children, high school entry is even more competitive than entry into middle school. Getting into a good high school is already causing anxiety for these two children:

> The progress I made in my study [changed my life]. My greatest worry is whether I could enter a good high school. [I wish] to study hard and to enter a good high school.

> [My greatest worry is] to fail to enter a good high school. [I wish] to get into a good high school. *(Boy, 12)*

More than a third of the children who mentioned education talked about wanting to go to university. This was the topic most commonly mentioned by children even though most of them were not yet 12. Even at a young age they knew that higher education was their best hope for a prosperous and successful future – and failing to get into university their worst fear: '[I'm] a pupil. Going to school [changed my life.] I'm worried about my parents' illness. I hope to go to a good university and to serve the country and its people' *(Boy, 12)*

Another patriotic child whose loyalty and leadership qualities had led to her being made a Young Pioneer also echoed a popular Communist political slogan, 'Serve the People': 'Being a Young Pioneer [changed my life]. My greatest worry is I couldn't enter a famous university. My wish is to become a teacher and to serve the people' *(Girl, 11)*.

The history curriculum in schools teaches a partisan version of the war with the Japanese and, in particular, paints a rosy portrait of Chinese heroism in resisting the oppressive invaders. Children are taught that the Communist 'liberation' in 1949 ended a bitter century of national disaster and depression which started with the 'unequal' Treaty of Nanjing. This girl seems to have absorbed this description of events:

> The heroes in our victory over the Japanese [changed my life. My greatest worry is] other countries get involved with China. I hope to go to university and have good friendships with other countries. *(Girl, 11)*

This child was concerned about going to university, but also, more immediately, about the generosity of relatives at the traditional gift-giving time of the lunar New Year, when adults give children money in red envelopes: '[My greatest worry is] to fail to enter university. [I wish] to have lots of red pocket money.' Another girl had other pleasures in life, but university was still the biggest anxiety: 'Dancing and singing [changed my life]. My greatest worry is if I could enter a good university.'

This boy also had artistic interests and wanted to go to university: 'Learning the violin changed my life. I hope I will be graded a "three good" student in the future. I hope I can go to a famous university and serve my country' *(11)*. Despite having suffered an accident, another boy was still ambitious about going to university, even though he does not seem to come from a wealthy background: 'Burn on my face [changed my life. My greatest worry is] to fail to enter a good university. [I wish] to get a scholarship' *(Boy, 9)*. Many others also wished to go to university but also had other ambitions: 'When doing exams sometimes good, sometimes bad. [My greatest worry is] to fail to enter a famous university. When I grow up [I wish] to be a scientist.'

Judging by what was wished for, this child was a long way from entering university, but it was already a concern: 'Study [changed my life. My greatest worry is] to fail to enter university. My wish is to have a history book and to understand the origins of the human being.' Another child expressed a rather less serious-minded wish. Presumably he had a toy in mind: 'Study not good. [My greatest worry is] to fail to enter a famous university. [I want] to have an automatic machine gun.' *(Boy)*

Enormous amounts of homework and high expectations mean conscientious children need to spend a lot of time in libraries, like these two:

[My greatest worry is] I won't get into university. I wish libraries could be built near our school so we could enrich our knowledge.

I learned a lot from reading. [My greatest worry is] the library is small but many wish to read. I wish we could have a bigger library and more books. *(Girl, 12)*

One boy had high academic ambitions, but was concerned about his handwriting. Calligraphy is still a valued skill: 'My poor handwriting [changed my life]. [My worry is] I fail to enter university. I want to pursue a doctor's degree' *(Boy, 10)*. On the other hand, this child's handwriting had been an asset but he is still worried about getting into university: 'Having good writing [changed my life. My greatest worry is] I may not get into university. [I hope] I can serve my country when I grow up' *(Boy, 11)*.

Some children, even before they go to middle school, aspire to university abroad: 'I have passed the Cambridge English exam. I hope I will continue to be rated as a "three good" student. I hope to go to Cambridge University' *(Girl, 10)*. But in the main, young adults are the ones interested in postgraduate study:

Graduation in 2005 meant I could become a teacher. I don't want to be deterred by anything. I hope my family will be safe and sound, work goes well and I am able to get a doctorate degree. *(Woman, 24)*

Studying abroad is the highest ambition: 'I wish I could study abroad and get a good job' *(Woman, 24)*.

Going to university, though so dearly wished for, is by no means a guarantee of security or success. Since the massive expansion in higher education that began in 1999, between a quarter and a third of graduates, about two million young people each year cannot find a job. They move to the outskirts of big cities looking for work and live in minuscule rooms in vast makeshift buildings with many other young, hungry graduates. Seventy to 80 people share a toilet. These packed student enclaves are the 'ants' tribes'. [19] The salaries of graduates, even when they do find a job, are on a par with the wages paid to migrant workers. Many graduates from rural families lost their jobs in the downturn of the 1990s. Out of shame, they did not return home or tell their proud parents that they had no job. They stuck it out in the 'ants' tribes'. This recent graduate was feeling nervous and dissatisfied and looking for peace of mind using a typical Chinese description:

> Graduating from university [changed my life. My greatest worry is I] can't find a job to look after my parents. [I wish] to get a good job and for good health of my parents. All my family [to be] safe and sound and everything is plain sailing ('single sail, gentle wind'). *(Man, 22)*

Parents' criticism of their children, including invidious and demoralising comparisons between different children, seems to many Western observers harsh and sometimes even humiliating. [20] Parents' disappointment, disapproval and anger in the event of poor results is a common fear for children. This girl was all too conscious of her parents' views of her ability and the requirement to fulfil her educational potential: 'Going to school changed my life. I am afraid my school grade will not reflect my ability – my parents are concerned.' *(Girl, 11)*.

These two boys were worried about acquitting obligations to parents by going to university:

I'm worried I will not be able to go to a good university and give my parents something in return. [I wish] to be successful and serve my country. *(Boy, 12)*

I'm worried in the future I will not be a good student and I will disappoint my parents. I hope I can go to university and make a positive contribution to my homeland. *(Boy, 11)*

As well as her parents' expectations, this girl was also concerned about what her teacher wanted: '[My greatest worry is] poor results at school, I can't live up to parents' and teachers' expectations. [I wish] to make contributions to the world in future' *(Girl, 11)*.

Teachers are quick to blame children's indolence and fecklessness. Punishment is swift, public and humiliating – and sometimes violent:

Getting told off by my teacher [changed my life. My greatest worry is] how to do well in study. [I wish] to enter a university. *(Girl, 11)*

Study [changed my life. My greatest worry is] my school results are not good and I get told off by my teacher.

Parents almost always endorse punishment by teachers, never challenging mistreatment or complaining to schools. Instead they reinforce the teacher's message: do as you are told and work harder. That message can be made more memorable by the accompanying beating. The need to do well in exams translates inevitably into pressure to do unlimited homework. Tiny, thin shoulders carry home a plastic rucksack full of heavy textbooks. Children routinely study for hours and hours late into the night, sometimes long after their parents have gone to sleep. This child put it straightforwardly:

I have too much homework to do. [My greatest worry is] being poor. I wish our community would be better.

Many children are constantly exhausted, perhaps like this little girl:

I am a lovely girl called (name). I have little time to get rest because I need to study very hard every day and to learn singing. [My greatest worry is my] study is not good and not being able to sing well. [I wish] to be a very good student and to become an artist when I grow up.

Parents also pressurise children to do more and more homework. This boy preferred playing computer games, incurring parental wrath: 'My parents forced me into doing homework. [My greatest worry is] poor results at school so I'm not allowed to play computer games' *(Boy, 10).*

This parent was a lone voice concerned about the amount of homework children have to do: '[My greatest worry is] my child has got so much homework she doesn't have any spare time. [I wish] to release the students' workload so they could have a happier childhood' *(Woman, 36).*

From a child's point of view, validation matters. Being rated an excellent or a 'three good' student is a high priority. They focus on good exam results as a way to please their parents and teachers and to achieve their own ambitions. The pressure of homework and preparing for tests and exams is extreme. Getting good enough results in exams to get into good schools and universities is an all-consuming obsession for young minds who long to be more carefree. Education is deeply traditional, expensive and highly competitive; it is stratified to produce 'winner takes all' benefits for a few, disappointment for most and has an infinite capacity to make almost all children and their parents unhappy. Extreme educational pressure becomes intolerable for some children, making them anxious and depressed. This is often ignored, so great is the need for relentless study. But, at the extreme, such stress leads to suicide, which cannot be ignored. Exam stress, career worries and relationship problems are the leading reasons why suicide has become the main killer of people aged between 20 and 35 according to a Ministry of Health survey. Newspapers regularly feature articles about student suicides and official reports now confirm a common problem. A two-year survey by Beijing University found that over 20 per cent of 140,000 high-school students had considered killing themselves.[21] Accurate figures are hard to come by but the *China Daily* reported that 2009 was the worst year on record for student suicides.[22]

It's not only children who feel the pressure of the education system. Parental and grandparental concern about education came top of the list of education topics mentioned in responses to the Wish Tree, closely followed by the ambition to get into university on the part of both children and parents. Parents also frequently mentioned worries about the cost of education. This community worker was a secure state employee, hence her contentment with her job. She was nonetheless concerned about her child's education: '[I'm] a community worker. Getting a satisfactory job [changed my life. [My greatest worry is] my child's education' *(Woman, 43)*. Others had similar hopes: 'My daughter [changed my life. My greatest worry is] education of my daughter. [I wish] my daughter will grow up independent and intelligent' *(Woman, 31)*. This woman was a widow, so her hopes for her son's education were understandably intense: 'My husband's passing away [changed my life. My greatest worry is] my son. [I wish] my son could be more educated' *(Woman, 46)*.

More children go to school than ever before, but, as noted, many children, particularly in rural areas and among urban migrants, drop out because their parents cannot afford the fees. Knowing this, some were still worried about access to education: '[I am] a teacher. [My greatest worry is] education and health of my child. Let no child be deprived of education' *(40)*.

This respondent felt that guaranteed universal education was needed, prioritising more than just grades and test results: '[My greatest worry is] education of young people. [I wish] every child could get well-educated. Emphasis shouldn't just be put on their grades.' The outcome of a decent education should be moral strength as well as narrow educational attainment, for this woman: '[My greatest worry is] education of the new generation. [I wish] everyone will be morally well-educated' *(Woman, 53)*. Wider education reform with practical benefits was needed, according to this respondent: '[My greatest worry is] the education of my child. I wish the reform of the education system would be practical and bring us people real benefit.'

The purpose of education for this respondent and no doubt many others was, of course, employment and the likelihood that a good job would help their child to support their elderly parents: '[I wish] my child could have a good education so he can get a good job' *(Woman, 38)*.

Parents, like children, worry enormously about exam results: '[My greatest worry is] whether my child could do well at school' *(Man, 34)*.

Parents' highest ambitions were for their children to go to university, even if they did not have the opportunity themselves:

I'm a social worker. I have a good son and a sweet husband. I was once laid off but I got re-employed [because of] the good policies of the government. I'm living a happy life. My son is going to attend the college entrance examination this year. I'm worrying about his health. I wish my child could pass the exams and enter a good university.

According to a survey by the China Youth Research Institute (Zhongguo Qingshaonian Yanjiu Zhongxin) 91.4 per cent of parents expect their children to study past undergraduate level and 54.9 per cent hope they will get a PhD. In 2005 gross enrolment in all forms of tertiary education was, however, only 20 per cent, signalling disappointment for most parents.[23] These three parents wished their children's exam results would be good enough for them to be accepted by a good university:

[My greatest worry is] poor results of my son at school. I wish every one of my family live a happy life and my son could enter university.

I'm worrying my son couldn't pass the exams to enter university. *(Man, 42)*

[My greatest worries are] medical care and social welfare for the elderly. I hope my daughter will be selected by the university after her examinations. I hope my family will be secure and happy. *(Man, 43)*

Grandparents had similar hopes: '[I wish] my son would become wealthy and my grandson could enter university' *(Woman, 55)*.

This woman with an adult child was concerned that her child's university education should help in getting a well-paid job: 'My child's going to university [changed my life]. [My greatest worry is] whether my child would have a good job which ensures a steady income' *(Woman, 53)*.

This man's child had also gone to university but now his concerns were with his own old age:

My daughter going to university [changed my life. My greatest worry is] there would be no retirement pension when I get old. [I wish] to have a retirement pension and to live a better life. *(Man, 55)*

Some respondents feared they would simply not be able to afford tuition fees:

> My kid's going to school. [My greatest worry] is I couldn't afford the increasing education fee. [I wish] my child gets a good education. *(Woman, 35)*

> [My greatest worry is] failing to afford educational costs. [I wish] my son could enter university and every one of my family be secure and healthy. *(Woman, 47)*

University fees, which are much higher than school fees, are a particular anxiety. For many people they are unaffordable. The child's effort in study and exams might mean they achieve the required results, but the cost may prove too much, for example:

> [My greatest worry is] the tuition fee for my son to go to university will be too expensive. *(Woman, 36)*

> [My greatest worry is] I couldn't support my child to go to university. [I wish for] a very good education for my child. *(Man, 43)*

Even secure government employees were worried about paying university tuition fees:

> [I'm a] community worker. The varieties of cultural life [changed my life. My greatest worry is] my daughter's tuition fee to go to university. [I wish] city people's lives will improve. Life is rich and colourful. *(Woman, 50)*

Unemployment, of course, greatly exacerbated worries about paying tuition fees and educational charges for these two respondents:

> Losing my job and my child going to university [changed my life]. I can't afford to pay my child's education fee and I can't afford my medical expenses either because I don't have health insurance. I wish my child

could find an ideal job after graduation and I wish for good health for every one of my family.

Losing my job and living a hard life afterwards [changed my life]. [My greatest worry is] no money to afford my children's education. I am afraid of being sick. [I wish] to improve the poor's living standard.

Rising prices were an added dimension to the concerns about tuition fees for people on low incomes. Inflation in the price of other goods may leave less funds available to pay tuition fees: '[I wish] the tuition fee would decrease. I hope we will have stability in the commodity prices' *(Woman, 32)*. Inflation may increase the tuition fees as well as other prices: 'I hope the price of commodities does not rise too high – nor the tuition fees' *(Woman, 28)*. This man had fallen on hard times and he too was worried:

[I am] living in a bachelor dormitory in Banshanercun district. Bankruptcy of state-owned enterprise [changed my life. My greatest worries are] prices of commodities are increasing and the tuition fee is too high. I wish to have a good job. *(Man, 40)*

Anxiety about the cost of education sat alongside equally, if not more, frightening worries about their own health and old age. These relatively young men were already concerned about old age as well as about education costs and medical expenses:

Losing my job [changed my life. My greatest worries are] medical care, insurance for the elderly and children's education fee. I can't find a job. *(Man, 43)*

Losing my job [changed my life. My greatest worry is] I couldn't afford educational expenses for my child and medical costs. [I wish to] get a job, to afford my child's education and medical costs. *(Man, 35)*

This person was worried about education fees because of their own poor health and unemployment.

I've got poor health. I'm worrying about my child's education fee because I can't afford that. [I wish for] good health and a good job. I wish I could support my child's education.

These two people felt the obligation was on them to find another job so they could afford the educational fees:

[My greatest worry is] I couldn't find a job and couldn't afford to go to hospital and I'm also worrying about my child's education fee. [I wish] to find a job to support my child's education and to have health insurance. *(Man, 42)*

[My greatest worry] is I couldn't find a good job and therefore couldn't afford my child's education fee. I wish I could find a good job and my child could receive good education.

Others felt the fees should be reduced. Some felt they fees should be reduced specifically for children of unemployed parents:

Both me and my husband are lay-offs. We have no income, no health insurance or endowment insurance. I wish my daughter could be exempted from educational charge. *(Woman, 46)*

Losing my job changed my life. [My greatest worry is] no security in life after I lost my job. [I wish] to cut down the tuition fee for the kids of the lay-offs. *(Woman, 50)*

Losing my job [changed my life. [I wish] to get my child's education fee paid and to have health insurance and retirement insurance. *(Man, 51)*

As well as all this, mismanagement of the education system has thrown up other dramatic problems. The May 2008 Sichuan earthquake drew attention to another even more terrible set of failings in the education system: the shoddy and dangerous construction of many school buildings. A Ministry of Education official, Han Jin, told the media a few days after the quake that across Sichuan 6,898 classrooms collapsed. According to media reports 4,737 students had been killed and more than 16,000 injured.[24] The tragedy of the parents' loss was greatly exacerbated by the discovery that many other build-ings around the area had not collapsed and those in them had survived.

The Fuxing school was completely shattered by the earthquake but many buildings surrounding the school remained intact, towering over the debris. According to an eyewitness, 'the whole building crumbled to ashes in about 10 seconds'. More than half the students were killed in hallways while trying to escape. About 100 metres from the Fuxing school is a shop opened in 1982 and recently classified as a dangerous building because of its age and poor construction. Despite its condition it survived the earth-quake with just a few cracks while the school, built in 1988, collapsed. Builders had added the third floor at the request of school officials, even though the original plan was for only two storeys. Similar things happened in other cities affected by the earthquake, including Mianyang, Mianzhu and Shifang. Two buildings at the Juyuan Middle School were the only structures totally destroyed in the city of Dujiangyan, killing 240 students. As the schools collapsed, many of the buildings that survived largely unscathed were government and Party buildings.

Premier Wen Jiabao rushed to the scene of the earthquake and helped to dig out survivors. Parents held vigils for their lost children, but soon these came to the notice of foreign reporters and the parents were told to stop their memorials and protests and not to speak to reporters. Those that resisted were dragged away by police. One man did speak on the telephone to a reporter from the *Guardian* newspaper:

> Now they do not even allow us to gather together. The officials asked us to be patient. They told us we need to support the Olympics, and after the Olympics they will sort this out. But we have been waiting for such a long time . . . I guess they hope that if the time is long enough we will just forget this.[25]

Of course the parents did not forget – and neither did the authorities. Activists who had been investigating the earthquake, Tan Zuoren and Huang Qi were imprisoned. Tan received the maximum sentence for subverting state power, allegedly because of online comments about the Tiananmen suppression in 1989, but no one doubted that his involvement with earthquake survivors was the real provocation.[26]

As part of the central government's massive, five-year investment in rural schools, Sichuan received *RMB*700 million in 2007 to improve dangerous school buildings, a year before the earthquake. According to official records in Sichuan and elsewhere, however, few improvements were apparently made. In 2000, for example, just 13 million square metres of the nation's 9.6 trillion square metres of classroom space were reported to the central government as dangerous. But some 2 million square metres were shattered by the earthquake in Sichuan alone, affecting many schools that were not on any list of dangerous buildings.[27]

Like the rest of the education system school buildings are totally controlled by a local educational hierarchy. Local officials are responsible for fund-raising, lining up design and construction bids, and quality appraisals. No third party supervises the process. *Caijing*, a finance and business maga-zine, investigated five schools that collapsed. None had undergone a geolog-ical survey prior to construction. 'From day one, a combination of problematic design and poor construction, coupled with geological peril, meant these schools were time bombs waiting to be triggered by a natural disaster.' A few weeks after the earthquake, *Caijing* obtained a review conducted by the Sichuan Construction Bureau. It showed that the wide-spread destruction at the schools was linked to failure to meet earthquake prevention standards, and to poor structural design and substandard construction. A government investigation was promised into the possible corruption involved in the tragedy; however, no results have been published.[28] The central government's education and construction minis-tries are still divided over whether to blame the size of the earthquake or poor-quality construction.[29]

Official dishonesty and concealment, bureaucratic wrangling, scape-goating and the vain search to find where public money went are, as in so many other situations in contemporary China, the depressing aftermath of the tragic earthquake. Chinese leaders, however senior and scientific, are not oblivious to the widespread and ancient superstition pervading Chinese culture that natural disasters presage the collapse of dynasties. Before the Sichuan earthquake the last great seismic event had been the Tangshan earthquake in 1976, the year that Mao and Zhou Enlai died – confirming in some more mystical minds the predictive power of the old superstition. The year 2008 was planned as Beijing's year of triumph culminating in the

Olympics. But in April 2008 the government had to suppress uprisings in Tibet and in the Tibetan areas of Gansu, Qinghai and Sichuan. The Sichuan earthquake struck a few weeks later in May. In unguarded and less rational moments Party leaders heavily protected in their compound in Zhongnanhai in Beijing may have momentarily wondered what fate had in store for the Communist dynasty.

CHAPTER 8

Failing Health

A letter sent to *Time* magazine on 8 April 2003 shook the Chinese leadership to the core. Written by Jiang Yanyong, a 72-year-old retired doctor, Communist Party member and People's Liberation Army veteran, the letter claimed that health workers in military hospitals in Beijing were, on their superiors' orders, concealing cases of SARS (a potentially fatal virus with pneumonia-like symptoms). Contrary to the government's public assurances, the disease was spreading quickly across the capital. More than 100 cases had already been identified.[1] 'I felt I had to reveal what was happening,' he said afterwards, 'not just to save China, but to save the world.'[2]

First identified in Guangzhou, where millions of migrant workers live in intense proximity, the virus spread to Beijiing and Shanghai. As migrant workers fled Guangzhou and returned home to escape the virus, the epidemic threatened to spread across the country. Hu Jintao, who in 2003 had been leader for only a year, had yet to consolidate his grip on power. His predecessor Jiang Zemin was still powerful and the old guard insisted on covering up the SARS outbreak. The leadership was once more divided and paralysed. Inaction is the perfect breeding ground for an epidemic. Once Dr Jiang's letter was published international pressure grew and eventually Hu Jintao prevailed over the warring factions, publicly demanding the release of accurate figures. Senior officials, including the Health Minister and the Mayor of Beijing, were sacked. The authorities were forced to admit that the figures were much higher than previously stated – more than 2,000 cases in Beijing alone. To make matters worse, during the 1980s and 1990s public health services had collapsed after market reforms. Many clinics and hospitals closed and those that remained were drastically short of equipment, including simple things like face masks. In the countryside the situation became desperate. Public health had been starved of funds by cash-strapped local authorities. Healthcare services almost entirely disappeared. Even where limited treatment and facilities were available, most people did not have the insurance to cover the cost. Only 10 per cent of rural dwellers and just over 60 per cent of urban dwellers had any health coverage.[3]

Jiang Yanyong had forced the government into introducing stringent quarantine measures, setting up infection control checkpoints, following up people who had been in contact with affected individuals, opening fever wards and even temporary hospitals and, as surprised foreign visitors were to discover, universal airport surveillance. Treatment for SARS was made available free of charge. Eight hundred people died of SARS in China before the epidemic was contained.

While the world's gaze was still on China, Jiang Yanyong was shown respect for his courage, but things were soon to turn sour for him. Having embarrassed the leaders in 2003 for lying about the extent of the SARS outbreak, in 2004 he broke the biggest political taboo in Chinese politics: he criticised the Communist Party for dishonesty about the Tiananmen uprising. In 1989 he had been a surgeon at a Beijing military hospital treating some of the protesters. He could see from the injuries that the protest had been peaceful and, notwithstanding all the official denials, the People's Liberation Army were the unprovoked aggressors. Echoing the views of the banished leader Zhao Ziyang, who had been deposed from power in 1989 for his tolerant views of the student protesters, he said, 'My proposal is that the 4 June student movement of 1989 should be reappraised as a patriotic movement.' Dr Jiang had written this in a letter dated 24 February 2004. He later added: 'Errors committed by our Party should be resolved by the Party. The sooner this is done, the better.'[4] An emboldened Dr Jiang reminded people of the moment when the Chinese leadership had been simultaneously at its weakest and most brutal. He was arrested and subjected to political re-education for 45 days, but his hero status in China and internationally meant he was released without charge. He was denied the right to travel to the USA to receive an award in 2007.[5] He told an American journalist, Philip Pan, that he knew he was under constant surveillance and he was trying not to antagonise the authorities because he wanted to visit his daughter and grandson in California.[6]

A health scandal even bigger than SARS was to come in 2008, however: contamination of formula baby milk powder. It stemmed from the great expansion in the production and consumption of dairy products in China, and the shift in the habits of mothers towards feeding their babies formula milk rather than breastfeeding. Hundreds of thousands of babies were to be made seriously ill by contaminated milk. The market for milk had grown on average 23 per cent every year since 2000. Premier Wen Jiabao, echoing a more famous dream, said 'I have a dream to provide every Chinese, especially children, sufficient milk each day.'[7] He wanted everyone to have one *jin*, or half a kilogram. According to the UN Food and Agriculture Organization, China's consumption of milk rose from 26 kilocalories per person per day in 2002 to 43 in 2005. This shift to dairy is particularly perplexing in the light of a traditional Chinese lactose intolerance. The majority of Chinese adults suffer a deficiency of lactase, the enzyme needed to break down the lactose in milk and the common trigger for lactose intolerance.[8] The Chinese government has nevertheless made every effort to increase milk production. China is now the third-biggest producer in the world behind the US and India. Businesses, including foreign-owned agribusiness, are creating massive industrial-style dairy farms with imported Friesian cows.

I visited one of these mega-dairy-farms an hour or two outside Chongqing. The municipal authorities were keen to show me what they saw as a showpiece of rural development. Having displaced a substantial group of farmers, the owners of Cow Dream Works, as it was called, had imported 2,800 black and white Friesian cows from the Netherlands to the relatively temperate and green hills of rural Sichuan. The cows had been installed in long metal sheds with bright blue roofs. Most of them wisely stayed inside, away from the sticky summer heat. Outside there was a square mud compound for any cows in search of fresh air and open skies, but never again for any of these cows the long, green grass of the cool, flat, wet fields of Friesland. Nuffield farm scholar Emma Hockridge, visiting Chinese dairy facilities like this on a research trip, noted:

There does seem to be a really strong government push to eat more cheese and dairy. There is very much an aspirational Western diet. It is quite a new industry for China, but they are trying to be very technical about it. I saw 3,000 cows kept in pretty bad conditions. It did seem that they were trying to mimic the Western-style dairy unit. The whole climate isn't really suited to dairy farming – there's very high humidity.[9]

Efforts like this to intensify dairy production and consumption turned dramatically sour at the time of the Olympics. On 1 August 2008 the Olympic torch was carried through Shijiazhuang, the capital of Hebei province, on its way to the opening ceremony in Beijing a week later. The lucky employees of the dairy farm company that sponsored this part of the torch's journey were the proud bearers. But the senior management of the company were to meet the next day to discuss a crisis that could have national repercussions and cause deep embarrassment and loss of face to the Chinese government across the world during the Olympics.

The company was Sanlu, a dairy products firm which had been built up from a single farm using intensive farming methods like those at Cow Dream Works. The company had been receiving reports of melamine contamination in their milk for months. Babies fed the company's milk formula were coming down with serious kidney complaints. The evidence of melamine poisoning was irrefutable. The crisis meeting was chaired by the founder of the company, Tian Wenhua. Inevitably for such a senior executive she was also a senior Party member locally. She would have known that the Propaganda Department in Beijing had announced, among other directives in advance of the Olympics, that 'all food safety issues . . . are off limits'. The meeting lasted ten hours and ended at 4 a.m. Eventually they decided to cover up the evidence of the contaminated milk, not to withdraw the tainted products that had already been distributed. What remained on the shelves of their warehouses would be quietly disposed of and replaced. The board met by phone the next day, including its international members; the company is partly owned by a New Zealand dairy producer. Under pressure from international members, the board reversed its decision to cover up the scandal and decided that the contaminated milk must be publicly recalled, only to be overruled by local Party officials. The ensuing cover-up was comprehensive, including internet search engines shutting out any reference to the contaminated milk and sick babies.[10]

The authorities in Beijing were kept out of the picture until the Olympics were over several weeks later. Once informed, they knew that the situation was too serious to continue with secrecy and denial. On 17 September 2008

Health Minister Chen Zhu announced that tainted milk formula had made 6,200 babies sick. One thousand three hundred were in hospital and 158 were suffering from acute kidney failure. Four children had already died. Within a week a further 10,000 cases had been identified. By the beginning of October the government had decided to stop issuing embarrassing and alarming official figures, but Reuters calculated that the numbers of children affected had risen to 94,000.[11] In an official survey of just over 300,000 babies in Beijing, nearly a quarter had been fed tainted milk formula.[12] By December 2008 the official news agency Xinhua was reporting 290,000 cases and 51,900 children, mostly babies, in hospital. Only children who had fallen ill after the scandal was officially acknowledged on 12 September were entitled to free medical care. The treatment of those that were sick before had to be paid for by their families or they received no treatment at all. Wen Jiabao apologised for all this in characteristically circumspect terms:

> This incident makes me feel sad, though many Chinese have been understanding . . . The government will put more efforts into food security . . . What we are trying to do is to ensure no such event happens in future by punishing those leaders as well as enterprises responsible. None of those companies without professional ethics or social morals will be let off.[13]

Once the scandal was out the news got worse every day. Exemplary retribution for a few of those involved was not far behind. Mrs Tian was stripped of her Party membership and a number of local officials were dismissed. The Mayor and the Party Secretary resigned soon afterwards. By the end of the year more serious punishments had to be contemplated and people were being arrested, including Mrs Tian. She pleaded guilty, telling the court she had known of the problems from May 2008 onwards but had not told officials until 2 August: she was sentenced to life imprisonment. Other executives also received long sentences. Two people who had produced the contaminated milk, Zhang Yujun and Geng Jinping, were executed. The company was besieged. Hackers attacked its websites. Long queues formed at its offices demanding refunds. Internet bulletin boards seethed with anger. Sanlu soon went bankrupt. Many parents of children made sick by contaminated milk sought compensation with the help of lawyers working for free. However, as in the aftermath of the Sichuan earthquake, the authorities instructed lawyers to drop these cases in the interests of 'stability'. All civil lawsuits have been extensively delayed and remain unresolved. Further tests have shown that other Chinese companies are also producing contaminated milk formula and there are many more concerns about food safety; in relation to chicken and eggs, for example. Many better-off parents have shifted to feeding their babies imported formula, but it is much more expensive and many people cannot afford it. So they and their babies continue, apprehensively, to consume locally produced food. In the Sanlu scandal as in others, the familiar sequence of events unfolded: official denials and dishonesty, cover-up, public panic and anger, grudging acceptance by the authorities, scape-goating of a few and finally interminable, inconclusive official inquiries.

In addition to these concerns about deadly infections and official cover-ups the permanent anxiety for many people remains simply what to do if they get sick. Will they have access to medical care and treatment and, crucially, will they be able to afford it when they need it? Hundreds of millions of ordinary Chinese people now live with these anxieties, but it was not always like this. In many ways things were better for many people in the past. While China has become so much better off in so many ways, how has basic healthcare gone from being free to being prohibitively expensive?

The massive, inefficient, depressing farms in the countryside were decollec-tivised and broken up following Reform in 1978. Farms that could produc-tively be worked by a family became once more the norm. They could produce enough for themselves as well as a surplus to fulfil government quotas and to sell in local markets at competitive prices for profit. This increased productivity eased shortages of essential foodstuffs and raised rural incomes. But the welcome closing of the collective farms had an unwelcome consequence: shared public services also disappeared. The village co-operative medical insurance systems that had provided rudi-mentary healthcare at no cost to rural citizens collapsed instantly although that system had achieved higher standards of health care in China than in many comparable countries. After this collapse, funding health care provi-sion became a local government responsibility at roughly the same time as changes to the tax system decreased local government revenues. No redistributive or equitable subsidies came from Beijing; all revenues had to be locally generated. Public health and medical agencies had to collect fees to keep their services going. The managers, as elsewhere in the public sector, were encouraged by market reforms to incentivise their staff by paying them according to the revenue they collected. So healthcare staff over-prescribed medical treatment even if patients could not afford the costs. In the case of mental health, hospitalisation and incarceration rapidly increased while treatment rates for anxiety and depression declined.

By 1997 the World Bank reported, 'only about 10 per cent of the rural population is now covered by some form of community-financed health care, down from a peak of 85 per cent in 1975. As a result some 700 million rural Chinese must pay out of pocket for virtually all health services.'[14] Sixty per cent of the population of China are rural residents but only 25 per cent of health expenditure is made in rural areas, conforming to an ancient and ignominious Chinese tradition of extorting the maximum taxation from the peasants, even during famines, and spending as little as possible on their welfare when they need it most, such as after natural disasters.[15] In 2003 the SARS crisis drew attention to this collapse of public health services. The clinics were overwhelmed. They simply could not administer treatments fast enough for people to recover or to contain the epidemic. Ironically, the situation was made worse because some rural people, whose income had risen after agricultural reform, could afford to pay for treatment – but there were no clinics to provide it. Many rural people cannot afford healthcare, however, and are left to fend for themselves. So, many millions of people simply do not seek advice or treatment if they are sick. In 2003, 48.9 per cent of those who had been sick for more than two weeks had not sought medical care, up from 36.4 per cent in 1993.[16]

In urban areas, as with education, free healthcare vanished with the closure and reorganisation of many state-owned enterprises. The old health facilities in the factory units were either closed or privatised. The new modern facilities were reserved for that small minority who could afford to pay or were adequately insured. In the new factories the new private sector employers showed no appetite for such generous employee benefits. The government, in part having learnt from the experience of the rural health-care collapse, set up an employment-based medical insurance system during the 1990s, funded by mandatory contributions from the employer and the employee, not by the government. But by then many people had already been laid off with no health insurance. Because free healthcare has disappeared and few have insurance cover, the amount people spend on healthcare from their own limited savings has risen more than a hundred-fold from a total of *RMB*3 billion in 1980 to *RMB*485.4 billion in 2006. As a proportion, personal expenditure on health has risen from 21.2 per cent of the total in 1980 to just under half, 49.8 per cent in 2006, having risen as high as 60 per cent in 2000.[17] Chinese people bear a far higher proportion of health costs themselves than the population of most other countries. China was rated 188 out of 191 countries listed for equitability by the WHO in 2000.[18] In 1995 each member of an urban family spent 3.1 per cent of their income on health and medical care. By 2005 this proportion had more than doubled, to 7.6 per cent. Per capita medical expenditure in rural households grew from 4.9 per cent in 1995 to 6.5 per cent in 2005.[19] In the same period incomes rose dramatically, meaning people were spending a much larger proportion of a larger income – a massive increase in actual money spent on healthcare by citizens themselves.

Against the background of this recent history of health panics and collapsed health services, anxieties about health were unsurprisingly the largest group of concerns mentioned on the Wish Tree. The most frequently mentioned was getting sick in the future. Nearly one in five people were concerned they did not have medical insurance. Almost as many people expressed a more general worry about affordability. Having no healthcare, simply stated, was a concern for more than one in ten people. The health access fee of *RMB*800 for an initial medical consultation, exclusive to the Banshanercun neighbourhood, was mentioned by 72 people, nearly one in five in that neighbourhood. The health access fee was a concern for 40 out of 42 elderly respondents from Banshanercun.

In Banshanercun the local clinic and small hospital connected to the tyre factory were privatised when the factory closed. I visited the hospital on the day the Wish Tree was erected. It is a square building with a dozen or so rooms each with eight or ten beds. The patients were sprawled on their beds, half asleep and bored. They were almost all on intravenous drips, the preferred way of administering drugs in China. Patients shuffled slowly along the corridors in their pyjamas pushing a tall thin silver frame with a the plastic bag of fluid hanging off it connected to a vein in the back of their hand. The small hospital was the only place for medical treatment and had been free, but since privatisation the charges were prohibitively expensive. Seeing a doctor meant paying a health access fee, as this woman notes: 'My greatest worry is we need to pay *RMB*800 health access fee every time we go to the hospital.' *(Woman, 65)*. Many of the respondents in Banshanercun wanted the fee lowered or, better still, abolished. This single issue caused enormous concern to the people who lived there. This person expressed a simple anxiety: '[I am] retired. I'm worried about getting ill because the health access fee is too high' *(63)*. Many relied on minimum living payments (about *RMB*210 a month), making *RMB*800 for a single consultation simply unaffordable, as this man pointed out: 'I don't know what to do if I get ill because I've only got *RMB*210 a month' *(63)*.

Because of the lack of affordable medical care many people simply worry about the general costs of medicine and healthcare, convinced the health access fee should be cancelled. These were responses from retired people for whom the fee was just unaffordable:

[I am] a retired worker. The medical fee is too high and I can't afford it. I hope they increase the retirement pension and cancel the health access fee. *(Woman, 53)*

I'm afraid to get ill and not be able to afford hospital. [I wish] the retirement pension will be increased – and the health access fee will be cancelled.

The health insurance system that has emerged since the disappearance of free public health services is built on contributions by employer and employee. In return, a cash payment (limited by the level of previous contributions) is paid towards healthcare costs. This system is still relatively new. Many people do not have a health insurance policy and even those who do know it will not cover the full costs of a serious illness. They would then have to pay from their income, savings, or borrow from family and friends. For many, particularly the retired living on pensions, that would be an impossible situation. Even for residents who had it, health insurance scarcely paid out enough to cover even initial consultation costs:

Because of the concerns of the party we got the Minimum Living Standard. When I am sick I can't afford to go to hospital. My children are getting older and don't have a job and haven't settled down. They are living with me and I also need to pay their expenses. The pension is very low and our medical insurance is only *RMB*23 a month. [I wish] to raise pension and cancel the health access fee. *(Woman, 67)*

One in six Wish Tree respondents specifically mentioned Deng Xiaoping's Reform and Opening from the late 1970s onwards. All supported Reform, but many were nevertheless critical of the government's policies:

The Reform and Opening [changed my life]. Medical expenses and health access fee are too high [so] we can't afford to go to hospital. [I wish] to live a better-off life.

For some people anxieties had become real; the worst had already happened. They were ill and were struggling with the costs of medicines and healthcare. This man was worrying about not being able to pay for the treatment he needed: 'The pension is low, the medicine fee is high and I have got a serious illness. The fee for getting a physical check-up is high.' *(Man, 75)*.

Such concerns were not confined to older people. Everyone who gets sick is worried about medical costs even when young, like this woman in her twenties: '[My greatest worry is] I couldn't find a job and couldn't pay my medical expenses. [I wish] to get a job and be able to pay the medical cost.' *(Woman, 22)*. 'A traffic accident made me disabled. I am sick so I worry about illness. I don't have a job and live on low income insurance.'

Winning the lottery was seen by this woman as a way of escaping the anxieties of health costs when she was ill: 'Being laid off and being ill [changed my life. My greatest worry is] getting ill and not managing to pay the medical cost. [I wish] to win the lottery and get my disease cured' *(Woman, 45)*. Another woman who had been ill could not pay her medical costs. The strain on her finances was also making her worried about the costs of her child's education:

'Not being able to pay my medical expenses [changed my life. My greatest worry is] the high medical cost and my child's education fee. [I wish] to be able to pay my medical expenses and to have good health.' (*Woman, 39*)

One man's illness convinced him of the need for more comprehensive social welfare. He also wanted somewhere decent to live: 'Illness [changed my life. I wish] to have health insurance and retirement insurance and to have my own house.' (*Man, 56*).

Illness in the family casts a pall of anxiety and depression over everyone, not just the person who is sick. This man was trying to cope with his wife's illness: 'My wife suffering from illness [changed my life. My greatest worries are] high medical costs and the health of my wife. [I wish for] the good health of my wife' (*62*).

This woman's husband was seriously ill but social security payments were not yet guaranteed:

My husband has got high blood pressure and there was bleeding in the brain. We are worried about our living security. I hope my husband gets well and passes the physical check – and gets the retirement payment from social security.

A sick mother was a cause of worry for this young woman: 'I'm worried about my mother's illness – and my father. [I wish] for the whole family to be safe and this country to be prosperous.' (*Woman, 21*).

Even if people were not sick they were nevertheless worried about the lack of medical care. Retirement left these two men worrying about their old age and the lack of medical facilities:

Retirement [changed my life]. I'm worrying about getting ill. [I wish] to reform the health insurance system and to ensure the retired can get adequate medical care. (*Man, 60*)

[I am] a retired worker. [My greatest worry is] medical care and my children's life in the future. [I wish for] a perfect medical centre. (*Man, 60*)

Low incomes and pensions are a problem in themselves, but paying for medical care turns a low income into a wellspring of fear. This person was concerned about calls on their expenditure, including potential medical fees:

'State-owned enterprise bankruptcy [changed my life]. I'm afraid I can't go to hospital. I wish the retirement pension was improved. I hope I have enough money to pay the cell phone fee, electricity bill and medicine fees.' *(68)*

Another person was specifically worried about the costs of medical care for children under six: 'Being laid off [changed my life. My greatest worry is] medical treatment problems. I wish all children under six be exempted from medical charges.'

Nearly two-fifths of the people who mentioned health were concerned about getting sick in the future. Many people just said they were worried about 'getting ill'. Even people who felt reasonably good about their lives were nevertheless worried about illness and its consequences. This woman, unusually among respondents, was not worried about her income, but she was concerned about getting ill: 'I have enough money – this changed my life. I'm worried about going to hospital when I'm ill.' *(Woman, 60)*. Similarly this man seemed content with life, relishing the sanguine attitudes of benign old age, except for worries about getting sick: 'The steadiness of life [changed my life]. I'm worried about suffering from a severe illness. [I wish for] a peaceful life.' *(Man, 76)*. Another retired man felt everything was fine except the possibility of getting sick: 'The steady life after retirement [changed my life. My greatest worry is] suffering from severe illnesses. [I wish for] a harmonious society and good health.' *(Man, 58)*.

An older woman liked the social life in her neighbourhood, but she had similar worries about getting sick. Like the man quoted above, she wishes for continuing peace of mind: 'The social environment and atmosphere changed my life. My greatest worry is getting a serious illness. [I wish] to be secure all my life.' *(Woman, 72)*. While content with her lot, this older person worried about getting sick and saw doing something about it as the government's job:

[I've had] a harmonious and long life. I'm worrying about being sick as I can't afford the medical expenses. I wish for the efficiency of the government, they could serve our people with all their heart and soul.

Despite feeling that people in the neighbourhood had been treated well, this older woman was still worrying about pensions and medical costs:

The right leadership gave us a salary so this changed my life. [My greatest worry is] a low income. We are all retired workers and hope to increase the retirement workers' pension and we hope the country can make it easier to see a doctor and cheaper to see a doctor. *(Woman, 68)*

Although these women had jobs, not having health insurance was still an anxiety:

I was laid off but I'm re-employed and I'm living a happy life now. And I even feel I'm getting younger. The factory I used to work [in] is broken down and I've lost my health insurance. I'm worrying about getting ill. [I wish] to find a good husband.

The Party and the country have taken care of me. I have a job and life has some sort of guarantee. At present the society is ageing and I'm afraid of getting ill. The health access fee is too high. Salary is too low and school fees are too high. *(Woman, 66)*

Even with the good fortune of housing, this woman was still worrying about the costs of ill health:

Because of the good work of the community I've got a place to live in now. Although I've got some basic guarantee for life I'm still worrying about falling ill as I couldn't afford all those medical costs. [I wish for] better medical care and insurance. *(Woman, 38)*

Stoically, this man felt he simply could not afford to get ill but was nevertheless seeking to be optimistic: 'Losing my job changed my life. There is no security for life. I cannot afford to get ill at all. [I wish for] a good attitude towards life' *(Man, 30)*.

But many more people did not express optimism, content or sanguine feelings. They had a range of anxieties about their and their families' health, the availability of health insurance, healthcare and the cost of it. Many were simply worried about medical costs. One woman said simply: 'No money stops me seeing doctors' *(Woman, 66)*. This woman felt that unless medical fees were decreased, going into hospital was out of the question: 'Losing my job has changed my life. Life is a little tight. I'm worried I cannot afford to be in hospital when I am sick. [I wish for] the medical fee to be decreased' *(Woman, 54)*. One man felt he could not afford to see a doctor, having been laid off, let alone go into hospital: 'I couldn't afford to see a doctor. [I wish for] a happy life' *(Man, 50)*. Another man also felt he couldn't afford the medical fee and wanted the pension raised, though that would hardly be enough to pay any medical bills: '[My greatest worry is] being sick when I'm old. [I wish] to afford the medical fee. I hope the pensions will increase for those over 60 and their life improves' *(Man, 70)*.

The following two respondents fought for the Communists in the 'liberation' of China in 1949. A hint of bitterness, or perhaps just wistful regret about unmet expectations, comes through in their responses. As patriots they might have hoped for something better in their old age; at least covering their health needs:

> I took part as a soldier in 1949. I'm worried I haven't got enough money to cope with illness. We hope the treatment of ex-servicemen will improve.
>
> I am a retired soldier of the year 1949 with a very low income. I ask for better medical care/insurance.

Even a retired health worker was worried about care costs: [My greatest worry is] I couldn't afford the heavy medical expenses. [I wish] general prices were stable; to raise the retirement pension; to have a better environment' *(64)*.

Reform and Opening led to the removal of price controls in the countryside and consequently inflation in the price of food and day-to-day necessities. Rising prices also undermine people's sense of well-being, particularly the unemployed or those on low incomes. Concerns about the cost of living generally were connected to medical fees, as for example by this older person: 'My wish is to lower the cost of living. The medical fee is too expensive. [I wish] to increase the [welfare] payment for medical care and for the elderly' *(69)*. These worries about inflation were only made worse by the cost of seeking medical advice and the absence of health insurance: '[I am] retired. Health insurance is too low. [I wish] to raise retirement pension and to have steady general prices' *(Man, 71)*.

Those without jobs obviously had more reasons to be concerned about health and the costs of healthcare. Losing their jobs meant losing free health services and health insurance. This middle-aged man felt the only possibility of being able to afford medical expenses was by getting a job:

> Losing my job [changed my life. My greatest worry is] falling ill and not being capable of paying the medical fee. [I wish] to be able to pay the medical expenses, to get a good job. *(Man, 48)*

One's twenties should be an aspirational time of life but without a job even the young share these worries. This woman had many of the same anxieties as much older people: 'I am out of employment. If there is a job then there is change. I'm worrying I have no income because I have no job. And my greatest worry is getting ill' *(Woman, 26)*.

Two new healthcare systems have been belatedly put in place to replace the pre-Reform arrangements. In the countryside a 'rural co-operative medical system' was established. In urban areas a 'basic medical insurance' scheme was introduced. The government's target was that the latter should cover 200 million unemployed people by 2010, leaving those with jobs covered by contributory workplace insurance schemes.[20] In 2005 medical insurance coverage for employed people was just over 60 per cent, but under 50 per cent in some western areas of China. Even assuming the government's target to cover 200 million unemployed people is met, there will still be hundreds of millions without health insurance. The insurance payments are also limited, on average *RMB*782.7 annually for urban residents and less than *RMB*500 in the rural provinces.[21] So even those who are covered face strict cash limits on the amounts of healthcare expenditure insurance will pay for. These people saw the lack of health insurance and the associated worries as linked to their unemployment:

> I've been looking for a job and cannot find one . . . [I wish for] a job, health insurance and retirement insurance. *(Man, 27)*

> I'm out of employment from a state-owned enterprise. Enterprise bankruptcy changed my life. I have no income now. I wish I could get health insurance when I retire. *(Man, 53)*

Like others, this person connected unemployment and lack of health insurance to more general concerns about social welfare. A steady job if possible, and social welfare if not, seemed to be the limits of most people's ambitions: 'I'm out of employment. I have no job and no income. [I wish] to have a steady job, retirement insurance and health insurance.'

Concerned about unemployment, which left her without health provision or insurance, this woman saw it as the government's job to rectify the situation: 'I'm out of employment. Enterprise bankruptcy and illness [changed my life. My greatest worry is] having no income and no health insurance. [I wish] the government could provide a better health insurance' *(Woman, 52)*.

One resident in Banshanercun was also worrying that the absence of health insurance and a pension would mean they could not support themselves during their old age:

> Becoming an urban resident [changed my life]. I don't have health insurance and national insurance. I'm worrying I couldn't support myself when I retire. I wish I could have income and financial support and I wish the government could do something about it.

Similarly, another man was also worried about the prospects for his old age:

> '[I am] a retired worker. Retirement [changed my life] I'm worried about getting ill. [I wish] to reform the health insurance system and to ensure the retired can get adequate medical care.' *(Man, 60)*

Even this woman in her forties was worrying about the prospects for her old age without health insurance: '[My greatest worry is] getting ill when I am old because there is insufficient health insurance. I wish to have retirement insurance' *(Woman, 43).*

Alongside worries about unemployment, old age and the costs of healthcare, people connected the stress of these financial and health problems with difficulties in paying school fees. These respondents, having lost their jobs, were worried both about educational expenses and medical costs. Getting a job was, to them, the best way of solving both problems, as these two women confirm:

> Losing my job – I have no money to see the doctor. My greatest worry is medical care, the education fee for my children's education. There is no money for getting cured when I fall ill. [I wish] to find a good job. Medical service to be provided for us. To have enough money for my children's education. *(Woman, 39)*

> Being laid off [changed my life]. [I wish] to get a good job, to be able to afford seeing a doctor, to get my child's education fee paid and to have good health. *(Woman, 40)*

Desperate to find a new job to meet his potential financial obligations this man also hoped health insurance would bring security: 'Losing my job [changed my life. I worry] I cannot get a job and won't be able to afford to go to hospital. And I'm also worrying about my child's education fee. [I wish] to find a job to support my child's education fee and to have health insurance' *(Man, 42).*

Since the healthcare crises the government has sought to rebuild the supply chain for healthcare provision. More hospitals, clinics, childcare centres and disease control centres (after the SARS panic) have been built. The numbers of doctors, nurses, pharmacists and health inspectors has doubled. The government has also sought, since 1997, to establish a network of community health clinics. One such is the community health centre in Nan Hu, a neighbourhood in the south of Chongqing which has not yet undergone comprehensive redevelopment. I was shown round the new clinic, not far from the university, with a group of graduate students. It was painted in a bright combination of stark white and sky blue. The colours and the unforgiving fluorescent lighting gave the place an icy feel, signifying hygiene rather than hospitable warmth. However, the pharmacists and nurses in uniforms were friendly enough. They smiled and looked efficient. Curiously, above the glass doors of the clinic was a sign in both English and Chinese: 'Nan Hu Community Healthcare Station in Hua Yuan Road'. Outside the clinic a big sign listed many different types of drugs, comparing prices charged at the clinic with higher prices charged elsewhere. According to this chart prices at the clinic seem to be between 10 and 20 per cent lower. The social workers said this was a new government scheme to address the healthcare crisis. No doubt discounted prices for drugs were welcome to local people on moderate incomes but the bigger problem remained that the vast majority of those who need medical treatment have to pay for it themselves at the point of delivery, even if they do get a small discount. The cost may still turn out to be exorbitant and, over time, simply unaffordable. Small discounts on commercial drug prices are a benefit but not an adequate or permanent solution to the costs of healthcare. Like the community schemes I had ben told about in the Wish Tree neighbourhoods, this scheme was well intentioned and worthwhile, but woefully inadequate.

Even including the various government plans and schemes, public expenditure on health remains low. Many less wealthy countries spend a far higher proportion of their GDP on healthcare. China is ranked 156 out of 196 countries for the ratio of government health spending to GDP. Even where public money is being spent on health provisions it is not being spent efficiently and there is much waste. At county level, in the middle of the local government hierarchy, the utilisation rate of hospital beds is 78.3 per cent and at town and township level the rate is 48.3 per cent.[22] There are overlaps in supply and endemic problems in accessing healthcare. The World Health Organization has noted that confusion in the Chinese healthcare system could mean that more and more money is spent on healthcare provision by the government at the same time as the cost to the citizen, and the proportion of healthcare costs paid by the citizen, also continue to rise. The Chinese government is no longer the producer and provider of healthcare. It has become partly a funder, partly a licence giver and partly a regulator. It plays none of those roles efficiently.

The deepest wounds and scars wrought by economic transformation have been felt in healthcare. Because people cannot afford the services that do exist and are poorly served by health insurance, as well as being concerned about unemployment, education costs, low incomes in retirement and inflation, they have no alternative but to save money as a meagre and inadequate insurance against their future expenditure on ill health. People in China save on average about half of their income, one of the highest savings rates in the world. This is the continuance of a long-standing savings tradition in China but also suggests that people retain an understandable scepticism about government guarantees of future prosperity and stability. Savings rates in rural areas are proportionately even higher, suggesting even greater uncertainty among rural dwellers.

Family members of friends of mine have been diagnosed with chronic conditions like cancer. The treatments are frequent and expensive. People sell their houses to pay. Once the proceeds are spent they once more contemplate ending the treatment. Their only child may then have to sell their recently acquired home. Since many of these homes are weighed down with enormous mortgages the proceeds from the sale are small. Once these resources are exhausted nothing more can be done other than to abandon the treatment and die. Serious illness is in the first instance the death of ambition, then the death of security and then perhaps premature death itself. They just turn away from the world, give up the ghost and die

CHAPTER 9

Lifelong Financial Insecurity

Like the other laboratory of Marxist economics, the Soviet Union, Mao's regime comprehensively failed in economics and industry – though it was not evident even to Western critics that failure was inevitable until the late 1970s and early 1980s.[1] Contrary to the propaganda, efforts to build urban industry did not produce anything like the intended economic outcomes, but nevertheless they did cause profound social changes in cities. The organisation of urban society into factory units, though designed for (never achieved) efficiency and productivity, had the semi-intended effects of building social solidarity among the workers and inculcating and embedding expectations of social protection. These feelings grew in part from Communist rhetoric and propaganda about equality, 'serving the people' and building a utopian industrial future, but also drew inspiration from an older Confucian world-view. Dynastic rulers are patriarchs, who must protect as well as rule. Their power came from ruling, but their legitimacy came from personal moral integrity and protecting the social order. People must know their place in family and society and keep to it, even beyond death. Society is an extended family; temporary disorder must be quelled and harmony must prevail.

Mao was no economist; nor was he an anthropologist and, despite a penchant for philosophical rumination himself (noted, for example by Henry Kissinger in their famous encounters in the 1970s),[2] he abhorred Confucius. He believed that societies should turn a blank page and start anew, but despite his vigorous and destructive efforts Chinese society, though obviously not immune to change and even transformation, is an inventory of historical, traditional and cultural traces which have proved hearteningly ineradicable. Ironically, the industrial effort, designed to destroy traditional ways of thinking, reinforced the old belief among the workers that the powerful had obligations to protect those beneath them. From the 1950s until the 1980s the state guaranteed full and lifelong employment to all able workers in the cities, a promise made possible by public ownership of firms and a centrally planned economy. Each worker belonged to a work unit (*danwei*) through which employees of state-owned enterprises and their families received not just work but also a multitude of benefits. Labour welfare was seen as a way of promoting economic growth and restoring the worker's faith in collective production methods discredited during the ill-fated attempt to accelerate industrial modernisation between 1958 and 1962, the so-called Great Leap Forward.

Because enterprises did not keep their profits or bear responsibility for their losses, generosity had no price. Though services and benefits were much exaggerated for propaganda purposes, many provided insurance (covering retirement, sickness, injury, healthcare, funeral expenses and maternity expenses), subsidies and allowances (to help purchase food, housing, bathing, haircuts and transport), collective welfare (such as clinics, nurseries, kindergartens, schools, canteens, clubhouses, libraries and sports facilities) and services for individual staff who found themselves in difficulties (through job placement, family mediation and assistance with care of the poor and elderly). Wages were low but life for the vast majority of workers revolved around their *danwei*, which functioned like extended families or 'small societies' (*xiao shehui*). This was the 'iron rice bowl' (*tie fanwan*): it never broke regardless of how often it was dropped. But it is broken now.

Provisions for people in the city not employed by the state were less generous. The minority of urban residents who were not members of a *danwei* could apply either for regular social welfare (*shehui fuli*) or temporary relief (*shehui jiuji*), if they met eligibility criteria. People were classed as having 'three-Noes' (*san wu*): no ability to support themselves, no employers with a duty to assist them and no relatives with responsibility for them. After a rigorous process of testing an applicant's means, capability and kinship, benefits were available, in theory up to the average living standards of the region. The central government gave no subsidies to poorer local authorities to spend on welfare so they could afford little. The poorer the area, the less the local authority could afford. This system, now known as the Minimum Living Standard, is still more or less in place and poor people still describe themselves as a '*san wu*'.

Until Reform in the 1980s welfare – distributed through work units and communes – was intertwined with employment from cradle to grave. Unable to use wages to attract people to work, welfare became the incentive. Those outside this system were marginalised and could not fully participate in society. The state insisted local areas were responsible for funding and administering their own welfare regimes. But Party leaders ensured cities were more generous than rural areas, since the best opportunities for economic growth were in the cities and the peasantry had anyway long grown bitterly accustomed to being disproportionately taxed, exploited and conscripted in the service of their leaders' plans. Similarly, those working in industry or for the Party were systematically favoured, as were army veterans and their families. Social welfare sat at the heart of Chinese socialism; it was seen as the most promising route to the nation's developmental goals.

In Mao's day most people in the cities worked in factories. Only the lucky and the well-connected got jobs in government or, best of all, in the Party. The factories were self-contained communities, like the tyre factory at Banshanercun. The scene was usually drab and uniform. The work was repetitive, joyless and unrewarding. The conditions were smoky and dirty.[3] The work wasn't always arduous, however and many opportunities for malingering cropped up. Hours could be spent keeping warm around the brazier. Time off was taken to join long queues for goods which appeared only fleetingly in markets. There were no incentives to work hard, you didn't get paid more and promotion was dependent on Party status rather than performance. Few left their home neighbourhood for work or study elsewhere. Jobs for life created stable communities. Living cheek by jowl with the same people for decades meant everyone knew one another. Over time, as people married partners in their own communities, neighbours became kin – bound together by family obligations, particularly influential to a Confucian way of thinking. New relatives were at hand to help, and could also call for help. Reciprocal obligations created shared benefits. Life was routine but stable; predictable but secure; repetitive but convivial.

During the period of Reform and Opening the social welfare system was completely overhauled. Systematically, the state retreated from provision and regulation of social welfare, and left funding to local authorities. The principal financial burden now falls on individuals and their families. Officially this is known as 'socialisation' (*shehui huan*), basically a euphemism for privatisation. Starting with pension reform in the mid-1980s, responsibility for covering insurance and benefits has been shifted from enterprises to 'society'. Contributions to insurance and pension funds are made by both employers and employees and paid into pooled and individual accounts. These are collected and managed at local government level.

The new social welfare system claimed to hold 'three lines of defence against urban poverty'. The first was a transitional arrangement for urban workers made redundant (*xiagang*) as a result of economic reforms. Wang Wei was one of these. He worked in the Boshan porcelain factory in Shandong province that closed in 2002:

> When the factory hit real difficulties, the higher authorities came to us and organised the workers to sing the Internationale, tell us we must help ourselves. It was pointless. At first workers were sent home and told they were merely 'off duty'. Salaries were cut again and again. Production fell lower and lower until one day it stopped completely. No one bothered to tell the workers the plant was closing. It was like a car without a brake: the crash came quickly.[4]

The majority, not protected by unemployment insurance, risked poverty. In cities like Chongqing, where many state-owned enterprises suspended production or were near to suspension, the retraining and redeployment effort struggled to cope. There were simply not enough jobs. Failing that, unemployed workers received a basic living allowance, but the scheme was grossly under-funded in some areas. Many laid-off workers received no allowance at all. Draconian criteria and exclusions had to be applied to keep expenditure within limited budgets. Many people ended up out of work in short order with poor re-employment prospects and no financial safety net worthy of the name.

The second line of defence, unemployment insurance, was made compulsory in 1993 for all workers in state-owned enterprises and by 1999 covered all work units. Contributions are made by both the employer (usually 2 per cent of the total salary bill) and employee (usually 1 per cent of the individual's salary). Although the fund is mainly managed at municipal government level, including decisions about levels of contribution and benefit, an adjustment fund operates at provincial level. Central government occasionally steps in to support struggling provinces but in essence this is a self-help system for each municipal area and province. Authorities in poor areas have a minimal tax base and so have little to distribute. This has given rise to a massive defect in unemployment provisions: huge variations between provinces.

The level of unemployment insurance benefit is decided by local government and is normally slightly lower than local minimum wages. Participants receive their monthly allowance for a fixed period depending on the length of time they have contributed to the fund. So people who have been with the scheme for more than 10 years receive it for 24 months, those who contributed for between five and 10 years receive it for 18 months, between one and five years entitles one to 12 months' support and those who have been with the scheme for less than a year receive nothing. Over 100 million employees were covered by the scheme and 4.4 million were claiming benefits in June 2003. Tens of millions of laid-off workers fell outside the scheme because they had not contributed while in work or only for a short, insufficient period. Many people in Banshanercun found themselves in this situation.

For those not protected by these contributory schemes the government established a minimal safety net the Minimum Living Standard (MLS), the third line of defence, mentioned by several Wish Tree respondents who gratefully received it's inadequate benefits. The MLS provides a means-tested non-contributory allowance to 'non-agricultural urban residents' whose per capita household income falls below a locally determined Minimum Living Standard (*zuidi shenghuo baozhang xian*), which is defined as 'necessary costs of food, clothes and housing, giving reasonable consideration to water and power and fuel bills',[5] although there is no standard way of calculating it. In Chongqing in 2005 this equated to *RMB*210 per person per month – roughly the same as the internationally recognised poverty line of 'a dollar a day'. This is the amount received by impoverished residents of Hemu Lu and Banshanercun. The level of payments varies widely, but on average the MLS is between 20 and 30 per cent of urban incomes. The *san wu* (those with no family, no income and no ability to work) receive the full amount. Other low-income households and individuals receive a top-up to their actual income. Funding comes from local budgets, although some help is given by central government to hard-up areas. By 2002, RMB10.5 billion had been spent on the MLS to assist almost 20 million urban residents and by November 2003 the government asserted that all poor families received this minimal protection.[6] Judging by responses to the Wish Tree this claim seems implausible, because meeting the eligibility criteria is far from straightforward.

In most areas the local authority uses a public notice to determine whether a candidate is genuine in their application. The person's name, age, number of family members and address is published or put on a notice-board, along with the amount requested. Local residents then comment on – or denounce – the application and reveal any source of income not disclosed in the application. Any disagreement and the investigation is restarted. Often the notice has to be made public three times before any entitlement is approved. People who own pets, cell phones, cars, motorcycles or have a child in fee-paying education are refused. Those in poverty because of illegal activities like gambling or drug use are also turned away. Working-age adults receiving income support must actively seek work or participate in local voluntary work. These arrangements are designed to exclude false claims from the undeserving, but they have perverse consequences. A local official has to certify that no objections have been raised to an individual's claim or that any objections are unfounded. He or she can therefore be bribed into keeping 'one eye open, one eye closed' to objections. That, I was told, is routine. So much so, allegedly, that in some places the only way to get the benefit is to bribe the local officials. In 2000 just four million people in urban areas received the MLS but by 2007 this had risen to 22.7 million.[7] On average, eligible recipients received RMB182 per month. The vagaries of local interpretations of eligibility lead to inconsistencies, disparities and to many people being excluded. The even bigger problem is that spending on the MLS is equivalent to just 0.57 per cent of total government expenditure. The level and coverage of the scheme depends crucially on public expenditure. Meeting growth targets always takes priority over social safety nets in public spending allocation. Even though the benefits are limited and inadequate, the funds are being overspent, unable to afford even the patchy and minimal benefits on offer.

China's inadequate welfare system, such as it is, is grossly under-funded and excludes millions of people who face destitution.

This respondent to the Wish Tree felt particularly aggrieved about what had happened to him when the tyre factory closed. Not only had he lost his job, but he was just short of the required length of service to get a higher pension as well as having suffered an industrial injury in the factory. He responded at length:

> I'm out of employment from a state-owned enterprise. I am a laid-off worker from the tyre factory. When the factory went bankrupt my length of service was one year short and my age was one year short of retirement. I worked for 29 years. I got an industrial injury at work and until now I haven't gone back to work even for a day. Please may I ask what I can do with my life when they closed the factory and my daughter is studying in university? Now the thing that worries me the most is what can I do with my life? I worked so many years on a job which is poisonous and damaging. Now I don't even have health insurance. My wish is to go to the leaders and get some living allowances and in the future when I'm retired to have health insurance. *(Man, 53)*

Being laid off left people with obvious worries about income, security and finding another job:

> Being laid off [changed my life] I have no income and I don't feel secure. [I wish] to raise my income. *(Woman, 38)*

> Losing my job [changed my life]. I can't live a secure life because I don't have enough money. [I wish] to get a job and have enough money. *(Woman, 28)*

This person felt unemployment was a waste of people's talents:

> Being laid off [changed my life. My greatest worry is] whether I can get any support for life (financially). I wish there would be more opportunities and everyone could realise their value. *(Woman, 41)*

Another woman was concerned that her husband's unemployment was making him unhappy: 'My husband's being laid off [changed my life. My greatest worry is] my husband is getting unhappy because he is out of employment. [I wish] my husband could get a job.'

Even those with jobs were worried about losing them. This person, only 35 years old, was already worried about unemployment leading to an impoverished old age: 'I work in a factory. Becoming an urban resident [changed my life]. If I lose my job, how can I live by myself when I get old? [I wish] my child could enter a good university' *(35)*. And although this person had a job they were worried about those who did not: 'Having found a good job [changed my life]. I'm worrying about those who are still looking for jobs. I hope the employment problems could be solved soon.'

Another person thought the response to the growth of unemployment should not just be more job opportunities, but also more support for unemployed people:

> Being laid off [changed my life. My greatest worry is] being out of employment; not being able to afford my living expenses. I wish the government could give more support to the lay-offs and I wish to get re-hired.

Even young adults who should be full of hope are affected by these fears. This young man has graduated but still cannot find a good job: '[I am] a man who is not happy with his life. Graduating from college [changed my life. My greatest worry is] failing to find a good job' *(Man, 22)*.

Despite all the high hopes for education recorded on the Wish Tree not everyone can do well at school and go to university. The situation is much worse for people without a good education, such as these two respondents:

> I didn't go to a good school. I don't have a satisfactory job. [My greatest worry is] no insurance for the elderly – and no fix when things go wrong. [I wish for] stable income, insurance for the elderly and a job. *(Woman, 30)*

> [I'm] a student. Failing the university entrance exams [changed my life.
> My greatest worry is] I won't find an ideal job. [I wish] everyone of my
> family will be healthy and happy and I will find a satisfying job. (*Girl*)

One young man had a job but lost it and he's worried about getting sick,
even though he is only 30: 'Losing my job [changed my life] There is no
security for life. I cannot afford to get ill at all. [I wish] to have a good job.'
This young woman has also lost her job: 'Losing my job [changed my life.
My greatest worry is] the policies for the unemployed. [I wish] to get an
ideal job and my child to get a good education (*Woman, 27*).

Another young woman can't find a job and hopes to get married to alle-
viate her fears for the future: perhaps she knew that young women were at
a considerable statistical advantage in the search for spouses so she could
pick and choose: 'Lack of money [changed my life]. I can't find a job.
There's no security for life. [I wish] to marry a good man to secure my life
and also to have good health' (*Woman, 25*).

By contrast this man is married with a child, but cannot find a job:
'My marriage and my child [changed my life]. I have been looking for a job
for a long time. [I wish] to have a good job and have plenty of money'
(*Man, 34*).

Even young soldiers are worried about what will happen to them when
they re-enter civilian life:

> Being a soldier [changed my life]. I'm very worried I will not be able to find
> a job after leaving the army. [I wish] to be successful in my career. (*Man, 20*)

> Being a soldier [changed my life. My greatest worry is] finding work in
> the future. I hope I will find a good job and let my parents live a good life.
> (*Man, 25*)

> Being a soldier [changed my life]. After retirement from the army it is
> difficult to find work. I hope our country is prosperous, there is peace in
> the world and we have a green earth.

Having a job is no guarantee of security. As well as the risk of losing the job
incomes are low and competition is ferocious. Many people, such as this
man, felt their income was insufficient: '[I'm] a worker. It's too hard to

make a living. [My greatest worry is] no security for the future. I wish I could earn more money' *(Man, 40)*.

One respondent wanted those on low incomes to be able to access some limited social security benefits:

> I am a resident of the Banshanercun community. Our community policy is very good, we have built this community and we have a chance to take part in a lot of activities. We hope we can have more services for low-income people so when people are working they can still enjoy the low-income security services. I am worried about my life – for example, food, clothing and seeing doctors.

Job losses, insecure employment and low incomes taken together make a compelling case for social welfare. This social worker gives a dispassionate view, even though she is employed by the government and therefore professionally discouraged from being critical:

> [I'm] a social worker. My job [changed my life. My greatest worry is] war. [I wish] to have a well-established social welfare system, there would no longer be any problems in medical, employment and retirement issues. *(Woman, 30)*

The familiar interdependency of losing your job and not being able to afford the costs of getting sick without medical insurance are pointed out by these three men:

> [I'm] a worker who is out of employment. Losing my job changed my life. I can't find a job. I worry there is no security for illness. I hope I can get a higher salary and improve my standard of living. *(Man, 55)*

> [I am] unemployed. Losing my job [changed my life. My greatest worry is] health insurance. I hope I can get re-employed and I hope the government could do something to solve employment problems. *(Man, 50)*

> I am out of employment. Being laid off [changed my life. My greatest worry is] getting ill. [I wish] we could have our insurance paid by the state-owned enterprises we are working for. *(Man, 50)*

For the unemployed, concerns about paying education costs come hard on the heels of worries about healthcare and the cost of it:

Losing my job [changed my life]. I have no money to see the doctor. [My greatest worry is] medical care, the education fee for my children's education. There is no money for getting cured when I fall ill. [I wish] to find a good job. The medical care service will be provided for us. To have enough money for my children's education. (Woman, 39)

Losing my job [changed my life. My greatest worry is] I couldn't find a job and couldn't afford to go to hospital. And I'm also worrying about my child's education fee. (Man, 42)

One elderly woman was not receiving social welfare and therefore does not get subsidies with her health costs. '[I'm worried about] not enough money to live. I want the free healthcare card' (Woman, 70).

Although the following three people received social welfare payments, they thought the payments were too low. As they amount to a little more than a dollar a day, they have a point:

[I am] a local resident with no land. A low income [changed my life]. Life is difficult. I couldn't afford the living expenses with my income. [I wish] my financial situation could be improved. Income can be increased a bit more from 200 to 300 or 400 renminbi [RMB].

The Reform and Opening and receiving a monthly allowance of RMB210 [changed my life. My greatest worry is] getting ill. [I wish] to get more allowance from the government. (Man, 72)

[I'm a] common resident. Getting the Minimum Living Standard [changed my life. My greatest worry is] insurance for the old, medical care. There is not enough money for medicine. [I wish] the Minimum Living Standard would increase, as well as medical care.

This woman, who had been a farmer and moved to Hemu Lu, was evidently living a hand-to-mouth existence, picking up rubbish and selling it for recycling. She was encountering administrative difficulties receiving her minimal payments: '[I'm a] rubbish picker. Growing crops [changed my life. My greatest worry is] I haven't yet received my allowance for January' *(Woman, 56).*

Even if people are in work themselves they wanted relatives to be secure with social welfare, either parents or children:

> My job [changed my life]. I wish for a better job. I hope my parents are healthy and receive social welfare.

> The birth of my children [changed my life. My greatest worry is] my kids and their families. [I wish] social welfare for those on low income will increase, as well as medical care.

The hardships brought about by unemployment, difficulties finding a job and no, or low, social welfare payments are all compounded by rising prices. Urban development has continued apace; city boundaries have pushed ever outward, encompassing more and more farmland. The successful middle classes have begun to consume more food, in partic-ular pork and other meats the rearing of which is more land-intensive than crop production. Food prices have rocketed: food price inflation in 2008 stood at 18.2 per cent. Since the proportion of income that households spent on food in 2009 was 36.5 per cent for people in the city and 41 per cent for those in the countryside, this has obviously become a serious concern.[8]

The Chinese economy since reform in 1978 has fought a continuous battle with price volatility. In July 2011 the inflation rate was 6.5 per cent and rising despite several increases in official interest rates.[9] In 1994 infla-tion reached 27.7 per cent and in the aftermath of the Asian financial crisis dropped to −2.2 per cent in 1999.[10] This elderly woman worried about the price of things and felt her retirement pension was too low:

> [I'm] a mother with six children. Getting retired from the factory [changed my life]. I'm worrying about cost of living in the future; my health and the pensions not matching the price of goods.

Others also worried about inflation, for example:

I hope prices are stable and living standards improve continuously. *(Woman, 70)*

Prices are increasing quickly but incomes are only increasing slowly. *(Man, 41)*

Widespread access to the internet [changed my life]. Commodities are more expensive than ever – the price increases are quickening. *(Woman, 36)*

One woman ascribed the increasing cost of living to spreading urbanisation: 'Cost of living's increased because of the local development. I'm worrying I won't be able to afford my living expenses' *(Woman, 52)*.

Concerns about inflation were connected in some people's minds with medical costs. They knew they had little enough money to live on. That could be eroded by inflation, and paying more for medical care, education fees or looking after old people would place an enormous strain on them. For example:

[My greatest worry is] security for the old and medical care. I hope the price of commodities does not grow too high – nor the tuition fees. *(Woman, 28)*

I'm afraid of falling seriously ill and not being able to afford the hospital. [I wish for] improved retirement pension and more stable food prices.

The arrangements for old-age pensions are highly unequal. Former government employees receive pensions of up to 88 per cent of their former salaries, but workers in state enterprises have to build up personal pension pots through employer and individual contributions.[11] Similar arrangements are in place in rural areas and for self-employed people. Citizens must build up individual pension pots from their own contributions, enhanced by state subsidies, calculated as a proportion of their income and on condition the individual maintains his or her contributions. On retirement the pension reflects the amount contributed. The effect is that some people already either have pensions or can look forward to claiming them, like these two people:

[I'm] a retired worker. Having a retirement pension secured my life. *(Woman, 63)*

[I wish] to get retired so I can receive a retirement pension. *(Woman, 49)*

Others didn't have a pension: '[My greatest worry is] there would be no retirement pension for me when I get old. [I wish] to have a retirement pension and to live a better life' *(Man, 55)*.

And many others had a small and inadequate pension:

[I'm] a retired worker. [My greatest worry is] no money. [I wish] to raise my retirement pension.

[I'm a] retired old man. Retirement [changed my life. My greatest worry is] health. There is no money in case I am ill. I hope older people will be taken care of – and that the retirement pension will increase.

Having built up people's expectations between the 1950s and 1970s, a previously overweening state that controlled all aspects of the economy has pulled back dramatically from social obligation. To cope with a rapidly ageing population, massive movements of people across the country looking for work, huge gaps in income between the top and the bottom and an increasingly diversified and unstable labour market, an integrated welfare system is essential with an element of redistribution between richer and poorer areas and people. The sudden withdrawal of the safety net and an inadequate, inequitable replacement with millions of casualties abandoned in the transition means people are left to fend for themselves as best they can if things go wrong, and because so much has changed so quickly, things are more likely than not to go wrong. The administration of these inadequate arrangements is hopelessly fragmented between different government departments: 'departmental interests and policies, more often than not, are mutually conflicting'.[12] Overall, 'associated risks are rather large'[13] says the United Nations' *Human Development Report*. That's putting it mildly.

CHAPTER 10

Exodus from the Suffering Land

To the Confucian mind the world is governed by a triad of heaven and earth with mankind in the middle. Heaven's force and creativity is the will that drives the earth and the emperor has the mandate of heaven to guide and rule over mankind. Earth's role is to bring forth the produce of heaven's will to support mankind. The emperor's most important ceremonial function was to perform the yearly harvest rites at the marvellous Temple of Heaven in Beijing. He ploughed a ritual furrow, interceded with heaven for good harvests and made amends for human frailty. The job of humans as instructed by their social and intellectual superiors is to invest their energy and ingenuity in realising the potential of the earth and, by so doing, create a moral and harmonious human civilisation with correct observance of propriety. In practice that meant taming rather than protecting nature and Chinese folk tales are full of stories of the human struggle to conquer nature and bring it under human as well as divine will. Mao often invoked the folk tale of the old man Yu (*Yu gong yi shan*) in which a stubborn, persistent old man believes that he can move mountains with the help of many generations of his family. In the face of his persistence the emperor of heaven decides to grant his wish and move the mountains out of the way.

This philosophical outlook has mutated through the dynasties into a pattern of successive generations of leaders up to and including the current leadership who see it as their duty to put forward schemes to conquer nature. Sun Yatsen proposed many projects including a Three Gorges Dam in 1919. Mao actively supported the project, which was finally completed in 2009 having received the determined sponsorship of former Premier Li Peng, who made sure all objections were overridden. Notions of environmental balance or the earth being a sustainable living system in which humans play a minor role has not been part of the Confucian tradition. So, unlike the situation with family life and social harmony, Confucian tradition has not offered an intellectual and emotional refuge against the radically accelerated pace of economic transformation and the negative consequences of environmental degradation.[1] Some have argued that Confucian thinking gives an intellectual justification for putting economic growth before environmental sustainability.

In most developed countries debate about environmental collapse is theoretical and futuristic; linked to concerns about climate change and global warming. In China the degradation of air and water quality is now a reality, the consequence of accelerated economic transformation, rapid urbanisation, loss of agricultural land and increased demand for food and water. Global warming will only add to environmental problems that have already become intractable. Much of China's terrain is desert and mountains. For such a large population, there is relatively little land suitable for agricultural production. The too rapid exploitation of the available agricultural land reduces the fertile ground even further. People in the countryside live with the despoliation and loss of land through over-cultivation, desertification, pollution, drought and climate change.

The expansion of the cities turns country dwellers into involuntary city dwellers, as in Hemu Lu. Nearly 350 million Chinese people are expected to migrate to the cities before 2030.[2] Urbanisation has already triggered large-scale construction of infrastructure and residential development, generating huge demand for cement and steel. Once the people are living in cities demand for transport, medical care, drainage and landscaping will rapidly grow. All this activity, both construction and maintenance, obviously creates more intensive energy use than rural lifestyles. To cope with urbanisation China may need to build more than 50,000 new high-rise buildings and 170 cities may need new mass transit systems, more than twice the number that currently exist in Europe.[3] Highways, railways and ports will all be needed and the road network will have to expand 60 per cent by 2030.[4] Car ownership has been rising by 30 per cent a year. Nonetheless, by 2010 it had only reached 6.2 per cent of the population; it is expected to continue to rise rapidly.[5] The population of the metropolitan areas of Chongqing is set to double from 10 million to 20 million by 2020.

Half a million people become city dwellers in Chongqing every year.[6] One boy who participated in the Wish Tree expressed his worries about the impact of the city's growth: 'The construction of my home town [changed my life]. My home town is getting over-metropolitanised, and this results in heavy pollution' *(Boy, 12)*

Adults, having lived through the city's transformation, knew that widespread environmental harm and particularly pollution was the result of rapid urban economic development, as these people observed:

> The development of the world economy, industrial development and the air pollution around the globe changed my life. I'm worried about people living in a bad environment due to air pollution. Protect the environment and keep the ecological balance. *(Man, 32)*

> The changing of society brings changes to life. [My greatest worry is] environmental pollution following the advance of society. *(Woman, 71)*

> The development of the society and the prosperity of my country have changed my life. I'm worrying about environmental pollution. *(Man, 72)*

The lived experience of environmental damage caused by urbanisation is serious air and water pollution. These were both big concerns for respondents on the Wish Tree. Taking the condition of the air first, China has 16 of the 20 most polluted cities in the world and in 2004 the World Bank rated Chongqing the fifth most polluted city in the world.[7] The following children were concerned about air quality in the city's polluted, humid and fog-bound microclimate:

> [My greatest worry is] pollution in the environment. Air quality is becoming serious. I hope for a safer community and fresh air.

> [My greatest worry is] environment pollution. [I wish] we could have fresh air and clean water. *(Boy, 11)*

Hundreds of thousands of people are thought to die every year in China as a result of respiratory conditions exacerbated by air pollution. More mature people than these children knew that air pollution was a health hazard as well as a discomfort, as this older man points out.

> Environmental pollution; water pollution [changed my life. My greatest worry is] my health will be affected by the environmental pollution. I wish the government could work on improving the environment. *(Man, 60)*

Air pollution, and the consequent ill-health, stem in large measure from the emissions of coal-fired power stations. China has vast coal reserves (as much as 12 per cent of the world's total). With relatively low domestic demand until the early 1990s China was one of the world's biggest coal exporters. Two-thirds of the country's electricity comes from dirty coal compared to 29.4 per cent globally, with a new coal-fired plant built on average every week.[8] China has become the world's largest coal consumer and, despite its vast reserves, is now a net importer. Drive out of Chongqing along the Yangtze for less than an hour and the chimney stacks of coal-fired power stations start to appear along the riverbank. But China's coal mines will not produce enough electricity and increasing imports of fuel for energy will undoubtedly be necessary. Extracting coal is a merciless and dangerous business, causing hundreds of fatalities every year. Chongqing is not the worst affected city by a long way. On still days huge clouds of coal dust hang over cities like Lanzhou in Gansu province and Xian, the home of the terracotta warriors, in Shaanxi province.[9] Linfen in Shanghai province, according to the World Bank, has the worst air quality on earth.

Water has never been plentiful across China, and the north of the country has just 10 per cent of the global average per capita water resources. Polluted rivers, the melting of the Himalayan ice caps and a declining water table in north China are all exacerbating shortages that can only get worse.[10] The northern '3-H' river basins, the Hai, Huai and Huang (Yellow) rivers are already suffering water shortages because of the pressure of the demand from industry, urbanisation and agriculture.[11] Thirty-five per cent of China's freshwater resources come from the Yangtze and the river supplies water to 200 cities in central China and beyond. Human settlement on the Yangtze has increased enormously as farmers have been urbanised and cities have expanded. Around 10 per cent of the river, more than 600 kilometres, is in a critical condition and a third of the tributaries are seriously polluted.[12] The principal source of contamination is the disposal of waste: around 14 billion tons is dumped into the Yangtze every year and the damage is now thought to be irreversible. Pollution by waste in the Yangtze outstrips the speed with which the authorities can build waste-water plants.

When the Yangtze dolphin, a freshwater dolphin found only in China, was feared extinct in 2006 an extensive search by volunteers and scientists yielded no results and the dolphin's permanent disappearance was confirmed. The Yangtze River is the heart of Chongqing, as it always has been, so residents of the city are highly conscious of its decline and present state of decay. This boy was worried about pollution of the river: 'My wish is the River Yangtze would be polluted no more' (11). Seventy per cent of the water in five of the seven biggest river systems in China was 'not suitable for human contact'. The water in most of the big lakes is even worse quality, only fit for irrigation.[13]

Shortage of water and water pollution are one set of problems. At the other extreme flooding will bring another set of dramatic challenges. In 2008 the total rainfall in parts of Guangdong and Guangxi provinces was the highest for a century. Severe floods occurred in the Pearl River Basin and upstream in the Xiangjiang River, causing serious economic losses and human casualties. The sea level is also rising. By 2050 high tides which used to occur every 100 years on the Bohai sea may occur once every 20 years and once every five years on the Pearl River Delta. The high tide at the Yangtze delta will occur once every ten years instead of every 100 years, as in the past.[14] About a tenth of China's territory, containing nearly two-thirds of the population and producing almost three-quarters of the country's output, is below the flood level of major rivers. Global warming heightens the risks of epic floods.[15]

Factories dump destructive chemicals and toxic waste into the atmosphere, rivers and lakes. Mountains of urban waste are rising and added to by waste exported from other countries, some of it toxic.[16] Industrial waste is dumped casually and randomly in the underdeveloped western backlands. Chongqing's biggest landfill dump is at Changshengqiao. It is 350,000 square metres wide and 30 metres deep.[17] Three years after the site opened it contained a million tons of rubbish. None of it was recycled; some was burnt, adding to the air pollution.

Young and old people were aware of the wider ramifications of environmental degradation, not just the immediate effects on them and their neighbourhoods. This schoolgirl seemed to have a good grip on less local environmental effects, information she may have found on the internet: 'The internet [changed my life. My greatest worry is] natural resources around the globe will be exhausted and the hole in the ozone layer will get bigger' *(Girl 11)*.

Natural disasters like earthquakes are regarded superstitiously as premonitions of social cataclysm, such as the demise of dynasties, by many people. Some mentioned their fear of natural disasters, not just for the damage they do, but for the alarming possibilities they postulate. This man seems to link potential natural disasters with worries about social stability, for example:

> The development of Socialist Spiritual Civilization; the economic development; the prosperity of my country [changed my life. My greatest worry is] the environmental problems and natural disasters. We wish for the stability of society, the prosperity and democracy of my country and a stable social order. *(Man, 67)*

Another person links the development of the city with the possibility of natural disasters and health problems: 'The Great Western Development [changed my life. My greatest worry is] natural disasters and severe diseases.' This child also seems to feel the same way: 'I hope we can have a community full of harmony, laughter, happiness and where technology is very advanced and the mountains are green and the rivers are beautiful.'

The superstition about the link between natural disasters and social chaos may not just be an old-fashioned fallacy. It may prove to be a premonition of remarkable accuracy, because China's shortage of energy and water has deep and troubling political and social dimensions. Compared to many other parts of the world, China does not have large reserves of oil; definitely not large enough to meet the country's growing energy needs. Even more problematic, however, oil reserves are confined to politically sensitive places like Xinjiang in the far north-west, the homeland of the unhappy and discriminated-against Muslim Uighurs, or around islands whose ownership China contests with Japan. That has already led to tense relations with Japan and internal demonstrations against the Japanese. Water also poses many political problems because damming projects cause the mandatory eviction of millions of farmers and that can give rise to protests, demands for compensation, and to corruption on the part of administering officials, not to mention the loss and misery of the displaced. The waters of the Himalayas also come through Tibet, which is, pragmatically, another reason for China not to countenance any secessionist tendencies among Tibetans.[18]

Global warming will exacerbate the difficulties with water. Inland lakes, which may initially expand from excessive glacial melting, will shrink over time depriving many communities of water for irrigation and drinking. Irregular weather conditions impact most on the poor, who are more susceptible to natural disasters, such as forest fires, flooding and landslides, and less able to depend on a secure food supply. Yields of the three major grains, wheat, rice and corn, are projected to decline because of rising temperatures and changing rainfall patterns. Food prices are bound to rise and the poor who already spend a large proportion of their income on food will have to spend more. There are also particular concerns about the large numbers of migrant poor living in flood-prone districts of coastal megacities, such as Shanghai.

By 2020 average temperatures in China are projected to rise between 1.1 degrees Celsius and 2 degrees Celsius.[19] Extreme weather events are already becoming more common. China's National Assessment Report notes droughts in the dry north-east, flooding in the middle and lower reaches of the Yangtze River and coastal flooding in major urban centres like Shanghai.[20] In the summer of 2006, while I was travelling in the Three Gorges area, Chongqing suffered a severe drought, the worst in half a century. Several meteorological records were broken. Temperatures soared above 40°C for days on end and rainfall fell by a quarter. The Jialing River recorded its lowest water level since the monitoring station was set up in 1939. As a result about 1.5 million people were left with drinking-water shortages and the government was forced to reduce the hours of public employees working outdoors and in heavy industry. Tens of thousands of peasants were transported to other parts of the country to work in places where the harvest had not failed. Without this drastic means of temporarily propping up their income, famine would almost certainly have been the tragic consequence. Since the drought, there has been an impassioned debate over the extent to which climate change or even the building of the Three Gorges dam could have contributed to the heat wave.

The third aspect of environmental collapse after air quality and water (both too little and too much) is the suffering of the land itself. Acid rain falls on 30 per cent of the country. Farmers use fertilisers banned in other parts of the world. Desertification means that 25 per cent of China's territory is now desert, creating much more frequent sandstorms in Beijing and other cities.[21] Since the 1960s about a third of China's crop land has been lost to soil erosion, desertification, energy projects (hydro stations, coal mining) and to industrial and housing construction. Arable land is in ever shorter supply, because of contamination, over-cultivation or encroachment by urban and other development.[22] Ten per cent of fields are estimated to be polluted. The ancient grasslands of Inner Mongolia from where Genghis Khan's horsemen overran China are rapidly turning to desert as a result of over-cultivation. Grasslands in Tibet, Xinjiang and Qinghai as well as in Inner Mongolia have reduced by up to half since the 1950s.[23] The cities swallow up half a million hectares a year from agricultural production.

The cutting down of forests is also reducing the quality of the land, as well as affecting the biosphere. Forests in Sichuan, the home of the Giant Panda, have been decimated; only 10 per cent remain.[24] Demand for furniture, chopsticks and paper have fuelled a vibrant illegal logging trade. When I visited Wanzhou in the Three Gorges Area I was told that the locals had been forbidden from chopping firewood and had to buy bottled gas for cooking now. I asked if commercial logging had also been banned and the officials confirmed that it had. This order had been passed in the name of saving the much-depleted trees on the steep riverbank. Once it was denuded, soil erosion would undermine the livelihoods of the farmers working fields on the steeper sections. Soon after the officials told me this, two large lorries stacked high with logs drove out of the valley as we drove in. The locals can't cut wood, but illegal loggers can.

Following the end of the communes, and after only a few years of working, small but efficient family farms near the city were engulfed by development. The farmers received compensation, but only the value of farmland, not the development value for a potential luxury hotel, office block, expensive flats or shopping mall.

Hemu Lu, one of the locations of the Wish Tree in Chongqing, was one such neighbourhood, an estate for '*nong zhuan fei*', those whose household registration status has changed from rural to non-rural. Of the 88 respondents to the Wish Tree who mentioned moving to the city, 75 said they were '*nong zhuan fei*'. The transition in 2001 was the defining moment of the lives of the people of Hemu Lu, who received RMB21,000 as one-off compensation, for example: 'Development [changed my life. My greatest worry is] no money to use. RMB21,000 – if I use it up early, what can be done?'

If their land is not swallowed by the greedy cities, most farmers want to hold on to it however hard their circumstances. Many originally rural people who have been living and working in the city for years leave their land fallow in the countryside without selling it. Farmers know land is the best security against misfortune – or another sudden, officially sponsored upheaval, hence their reluctance to accept Bo Xilai's offer of urban *hukou* even though without it they are consigned to inferiority and exclusion in the city or their child is denied education and opportunities. Those who have lost their land once and for all feel keenly the loss of their lifestyle as well as their land:

Cadres requesting my land [changed my life. My greatest worry is] having no land to grow crops. [I wish] to have land to grow crops.

My land being expropriated [changed my life. My greatest worry is] having no land to work on. [I wish] to have my own land and to live my life as a peasant farmer.

In Hemu Lu the administration of these land compensation transactions is bedevilled by incompetence and corruption. This man was angry about his experiences, which had left him feeling alienated: 'I'm a citizen at the bottom of society. My life can only be changed by work. We worry that the central government policy will not be executed well. We would like to punish those who have taken away our land' *(Man, 62)*. Losing land means homes are lost too. Getting a new home involves a tangle of bureaucracy and depends on sufficient housing being available. Sometimes it takes months. For example:

> I haven't got my house in the housing allocation. [I wish] to have an ideal house. *(Woman, 38)*

> I haven't got my property ownership certificate yet after purchasing this house. [I want] to get my property ownership certificate soon.

> Turning into a worker from a peasant farmer [changed my life. My greatest worry is] having no place to live in. [I wish] to have more living places built for the peasant workers. *(Man, 27)*

Their land and housing has gone, and so too has their livelihood. People have to rely on family, but relatives may not be able to support them: 'Local development [changed my life]. I have no income and my child can't support me either, plus my land has been taken away. [I wish] to get more income' *(Woman, 57)*.

People without land or livelihood were obviously beset by worries not just for themselves, but also for their children. First and foremost, as mentioned so often on the Wish Tree, they wanted their child to get a good education so they can get a decent job: '[I'm] a mother of a child. Becoming an urban resident [changed my life. My greatest worry is] no security for the future when I retire. [I wish] my child could have good education so he can get a good job' *(Woman, 38)*.

Grandparents who were once farmers were not immune from anxiety either. Their main concern was that their child could make a success of the new urban lifestyle. There's no going back to being a farmer, and that means needing a job:

> [I'm] a grandfather of a child. Becoming an urban resident [changed my life. My greatest worry is] the future of my grandchild. [I wish] the urban residents who have just changed from rural residents could all get employed. *(Man, 70)*

Concerns about healthcare and costs are a permanent feature of most people's lives: '[My greatest worry is] no security for life; no medical care.

I wish all the living problems of the migrants were solved' *(Woman, 50)*. Social welfare is minimal, so most people feel it is insufficient to live on, particularly older people: 'There is no security for life; no medical care. [I wish] to solve the problems of those who have moved from rural to urban areas.'

According to official estimates, by 2005 40 to 50 million farmers had lost their farmland. Three out of five plunge into poverty.[25] The theory is that compensation should be spent on retirement, medical and unemployment insurance, but the compensation is rarely enough. 'To extend the urban social security system to cover landless farmers is one of the biggest challenges in equalising basic services in China.'[26] Cultural factors are also at work. Traditional country folk feel their children should look after them so why do they need insurance? However, the children cannot work on the land and they must find a job where they can, maybe far from home, in which case they definitely won't be available to look after older relatives.

The requirements even to mitigate the environmental effects of China's current growth model are daunting to the extent of seeming insuperable. Energy efficiency would have to be greatly enhanced to slow the growth of carbon emissions; reducing carbon emissions while maintaining the move to the cities and economic growth is almost impossible to imagine. Dependency on imported oil would have to be reduced. Whole new sectors of green economic development would need to be entrenched, including renewable energy which will require technology transfer from Europe and the USA, which might prove unenthusiastic about co-operating rather than competing.

The environment represents China's most impossible dilemma. In other areas of economic and social policy the government has choices which are not necessarily mutually exclusive. They could for example increase spending on social welfare, build more schools in rural areas, reduce tuition fees, increase subsidies for healthcare and so on. But the leadership faces a straightforward choice between economic growth and job creation on the one hand and less energy consumption and environmental degradation on the other. They believe that the Party's credibility and future legitimacy now depends on job creation, so there is little doubt

that economic priorities will prevail regardless of environmental consequences. The government is making substantial investments in clean
extraction technologies and renewable energy sources, not just for domestic
consumption but also as high added-value exports, but it will not be
enough for 1.3 billion people to live the Western middle-class lifestyle
they aspire to, not to mention the enormous damage that will be done in
the meantime. The needs and wants of Chinese humanity simply cannot
combine prosperity with environmental sustainability.

CHAPTER 11

Losers and their Losses

The agreement I made with the Civil Affairs Bureau when they consented to the undertaking of the Wish Tree was that I would help to train officials in participatory ways of working and methods of community consultation. I returned to Chongqing in October 2007 with two other British experts in community development. The training was arranged at the university, all controversy from earlier in the year had apparently blown over. The idea was that a group of 'street level' officials would participate on a pilot basis in a training course the three of us would run. The university could then continue to run something similar, based on our model, for the vast army of other officials in the city.

A group of about 30 officials turned up for the training. To get things going a training programme based on a case study had been devised. The participants were shown a photograph of a large, empty, derelict factory building in Ciqikou. Assuming funds were available for its rehabilitation they had to devise ways of consulting the community and deciding on its future use. So when I had explained the scenario, the participants were split into groups and asked to decide who they would consult about the future use of the building. All three groups came up with a roughly similar list of local municipal bodies, institutes and departments whose views would need to be taken into account before any decision was made. That was fine, we said, but did they think they should also ask the local people what they thought? And so the training continued. How would you go about seeking their views? What contribution might local people make to the redevelopment of the building? Perhaps they might have some ideas of skills to offer. Maybe they could be givers as well as receivers. Having found out about the community, how would they present their views back to the authorities? And so on.

At the end of the day, the groups were asked to present their conclusions about the future use of the notional building as if they were presenting them to senior officials who could say yes or no. One group suggested it should be a training centre for IT skills where people would also be helped with finding a job. A second group said it should be an activities centre for old people and people with mental health problems. A third group said it should be a place where migrant workers to the city could come to receive advice and assistance. A feeling of astonishment grew in the room, with many gasps of surprise and exclamations of delight at the originality and diversity of the suggestions. I was rather baffled by this since these all seemed entirely practical and rather low-key suggestions to me. So I asked why people were so surprised. The participants explained that it wasn't the suggestions that were surprising to them, but they were amazed that the groups could undertake more or less the same consultation activities on the same project and reach such different conclusions – and furthermore all those different suggestions made perfect sense; one suggestion was not inherently better than any other. One participant, who had been relatively quiet during what had been a lively, sometimes raucous day, observed pointedly that this did not seem 'scientific' to them, but they could see such an approach might go some way towards creating a 'harmonious community'. Through this tiny example, a sharp shaft of light was cast on one of the most profound problems with Chinese public policy. Harmony resides in living with differences; science, on the other hand, depends on the pursuit of a universal, incontrovertible truth. The two are irreconcilable, at least in social policy.

As well as the training, the municipality had nominated a larger group of street-level and junior officials from across the city to attend a seminar to hear about the findings from the Wish Tree. My contact at the Chongqing Civil Affairs Bureau had been as good as his word and successfully persuaded the Ministry of Civil Affairs in Beijing to send a senior official to Chongqing to speak at the seminar; an important endorsement for us and for him. Despite the difficulties while conducting the Wish Tree, relationships with the municipal authorities seemed to have survived in pretty good condition. The seminar was held at the brand new (and therefore empty and very cheap) Intercontinental Hotel in Chongqing. As if to evoke the spirit of the Wish Tree, when we arrived a quiet, orderly group of elderly people were protesting outside the hotel with banners complaining that they had not been properly compensated when their property was confiscated to build the hotel.

More than a hundred officials attended the seminar. At the seminar I presented the findings from the Wish Tree, including quotes and more detailed analysis of the responses. I said that people welcomed the opportunities that reform had brought and they had a dream of prosperity, security and social stability. But reform had also brought anxieties and insecurities. Often Wish Tree respondents saw that they could do little about many of these problems and only the government could solve them; a view I tended to share. I told the audience how worried people were about getting ill and whether they would be able to afford healthcare. I noted that this was the most frequently mentioned concern. Anxious feelings ran especially high in ex-factory work units that previously had free clinics and hospitals, which local residents now had to pay for. For any serious illnesses, which required treatment over a long period, they were just too expensive. Many people didn't have health insurance, or their insurance cover was inadequate.

Education was almost as big a concern. People were worried about tuition fees and other costs of education, which was universally regarded as more important than ever if children were to have half a chance in China's ferociously competitive labour market. Parents and children could see new opportunities but feared they would be passed over. Going to university improved the odds of future success, but provided no guarantee. I also told them grandparents, parents and children were worried about not being able to meet their traditional family obligations and old people were particularly concerned about having no one to look after them. I was less explicit about the one-child policy and the pressures and anxieties it had brought, deeming that too controversial, I talked more generally about pressures on the family. I mentioned concerns about the environment. Finally, I stressed that many people, including young people and graduates, now felt excluded from employment and were not confident that they would ever get another job.

The displaced farmers especially felt they had little chance of raising their incomes and would have to rely on their children – though they were not at all confident that their children would be in a position to support them. People knew that the reformed arrangements for contributory unemployment and health insurance as well as pensions meant that if they were not contributing through employment now, they would not get the benefits in the event of illness or being laid off in the future.

I made no reference to the controversy surrounding the Wish Tree cards. From the floor people asked polite questions about how we had gone about the Wish Tree or for more detail on some of the findings. A few commented in a surprised tone on how much we had managed to find out in a short time. Some said similar concerns often surfaced in their own communities. As local officials they didn't feel there was much they could do about these big problems, but they did what they could to promote a harmonious community.

The speaker after me was the senior official from the Ministry in Beijing; he was in his late thirties, young for his status, with an unusually concise, direct way of speaking. His smiling countenance and easy manner suggested confidence rather than a willingness to be emollient, as the audience were about to find out. Obviously well-educated, he had been abroad on study trips. He spoke in Mandarin but his powerpoint presentation had been translated into English and it set out the Ministry's views about the role of 'communities', meaning the lower levels of local government (rather than the English definition of a neighbourhood where people lived). Beijing's expectation was that the responsibilities of these lower-level municipal authorities would continue to grow. Because cities were getting bigger and more densely populated, 'more and more farmers are to become urban residents. In China more than 500 million people are living in cities and each year sees a migrant population of 147 million. China's urbanisation rate has reached 43 per cent.' He went on to note the 'transformation of government functions ... with lots of social issues and conflicts to be addressed, urban communities need to do more in social administration and service delivery. In sum, communities can not only serve as usual to stabilise the society, but also function to enhance social administration, boost publicity and education, deliver services to resident and advance democratic development at the grassroots level.' That was the official line, but he didn't stop there. He went on to describe 'various conflicts affecting social harmony [that] exist in communities':

China's reform and development has entered a crucial period that is likely to see many conflicts, many of which may occur at the community level. A great many people come to cities for jobs, including laid-off workers due to state-owned enterprise reform, college graduates, demobilised soldiers and surplus rural labour. Issues concerning land acquisition, resettlement and compensation, and migration arise out of urbanisation. There are issues of income disparity, as well as public security issues, for example illegal behaviours, moral disruption, family disputes, misconduct, neighbourhood disputes and so on.

His analysis was straightforward and direct, but senior officials also have to wrap their observations in ringing enunciations of Party slogans, stressing everyone's obligation to obey as well as responsibility to act. Such a top-down enjoinder certainly sounded strange to Western ears.

It is the community that is ultimately responsible for implementing the guidelines, policies and initiatives made by the Party and state government for urban places. It is the community that can understand the residents' desires, wants and needs and then report these to upper-level government. It is the community that is responsible for organising the residents to drive civilizations with respect to production, politics and spirits and advance the drive to build a harmonious society.

He then went into a more detailed critique of the shortcomings of the 'communities' across the country as seen from Beijing. Across China nearly a fifth of 'community' staff have no offices or are using rented offices. Many are 'subject to insufficient finance'. Many have no public buildings for community activities and the staff are badly paid. Community workers have a 'relatively low education level and working competence and lack systematic skills training'. Communities deliver a 'low variety of services and delivery quality has not been substantially improved. Community administration is fragmented. The legal and regulatory framework is weak and incomplete.'

Departing briefly from his script, he began to express some personal opinions. In his view most of the well-publicised problems with land compensation and the administration of social welfare benefits occurred because staff were incompetent in informing people about the rationale for change. Their handling of any disputes that might follow was, if anything, even worse. Too many local officials were simply not the right kind of people. The recruitment methods did not test their ability. They had no training or qualifications. They were either recycled factory workers with good contacts or local worthies, by which I think he meant Party hacks. Put simply, his view was that they were often just incompetent. But his critique didn't stop at the front-line staff. It extended to their bosses who managed them poorly. Decisions were taken far too slowly. Managers obsessed about secrecy and self-preservation, which was generally a recipe for doing nothing. When they finally reached decisions, they took too long to communicate them and rarely thought about how the decision would be received, much less acted upon.

We were listening to a smooth, professional and dispassionate performance by a senior bureaucrat, measured and matter-of-fact. However his analysis, including his criticisms, did not address the bigger structural questions about government policy. Were the policies wrong or ill-thought-out in the first place? Policies and diktats from one part of the system often contradicted those emanating from another department. Ministries, including his own, are long on intentions and short on methods. Resources for implementation were rarely adequate and never distributed equitably.

The officials in the audience looked slightly shocked by his directness, which they clearly hadn't expected, but when the time came for asking questions, one participant was bold and unfazed. A middle-aged woman put her hand up and said in a confident voice that she thought the problems came about because municipal staff were badly paid. In her view the gap between municipal salaries in Chongqing and Beijing was too big and unacceptable. Could anything be done about that? The man from the Ministry paused before replying, looking straight at the questioner, and then said in an even tone that he accepted that pay was too low, but 'if people are not competent, they should be removed and replaced, not paid more.' There were no further questions from the floor.

The Wish Tree and the surrounding controversy about the fate of cards illustrated beyond doubt that the concern of the authorities was to conceal public dissatisfaction and political criticism from foreigners as well as their own citizens. In Wanzhou near the Three Gorges the displaced farmers had clearly not been well treated and the officials did not want me to know that, though their methods of concealment were unsubtle and revealing in themselves. Similarly in Banshanercun the privatisation of the hospital and the introduction of the health access fee were evidently causing considerable hardship. Officialdom did not want that to get out. But most of the resistance I had encountered had been in the junior and middle ranks. They had much to lose from problems coming to light. Senior bureaucrats, especially those in Beijing, were different. They had nothing to gain from concealment and more to lose from either not knowing about problems or leaving them unaddressed.

After the presentations I and the man from the Ministry had a relaxed, cheerful lunch together with a handful of other officials. We chatted openly. He was a good listener and evidently interested in my impressions. Knowing that they are often fed half-truths, senior officials are always keen to gather diverse and independent assessments of the situation on the ground. Contrary to their image as doctrinaire and close-minded many senior or high-flying officials, particularly the ambitious and upwardly mobile, are extremely skilled questioners and listeners in my experience. For my part, I was keen to hear how senior people in Beijing thought things were going, particularly on social policy and especially in Chongqing. He said in Beijing they still had concerns about what was going on in Chongqing. As well as the problem of incompetent officials which he had talked about, concerns about corruption and accountability were just as significant. He smiled and wouldn't be drawn further. He probably wasn't senior enough to know that Bo Xilai would become Party Secretary in Chongqing a few months later, though he may have heard rumours. However, he would have known about some of the problems of corruption that Bo Xilai went on to attack with such vigour. This possibly contributed to the bluntness of his comments during the seminar: he knew his seniors shared his views.

In private I didn't fight shy of difficult subjects like the consequences of the one-child policy, though he said there was nothing he could do about that. He was particularly interested in neighbourhoods with several generations of unemployed residents. I explained that instead they developed an alternative way of life on the social margins, often involving drugs and crime. Family breakdown added to the lack of resilience, application and aspiration. The community leaders and potential leaders had left so there was no safety valve to release tensions within the community, so they easily boiled over. He listened attentively, nodded, and said he had suspected that. He feared something similar would happen in the old factory communities in big Chinese cities unless action was taken. It wouldn't be as bad as in Western countries because the government had more control through state-owned enterprises and policies like household registration, which prevented people from just moving where they liked, but nevertheless he feared there would be problems. He then suggested I go to Beijing and run the Wish Tree in a couple of much-changed neighbourhoods to see if the results were different from those in Chongqing. I said I'd be delighted. We shook hands warmly and parted with promises to keep in touch.

I followed up his suggestion in March 2008. Two neighbourhoods were nominated by the Ministry of Civil Affairs, both near the centre of Beijing. The first was a factory work unit in Dashanzi. The other neighbourhood was Donghuashi near the Ming walls and the Second Ring Road. I was told firmly in advance that this time removing the cards was out of the question; although the difficulties in Banshanercun had blown over, they had evidently not been entirely forgotten. The cards would have to be taken away and analysed by a Chinese university. That was to be undertaken by Tsinghua University, academically probably the best university in China.

Dashanzi was a special place during the Communist era and it's a special place now. In the Mao years it was one of the most famous industrial districts in Beijing. Unusually high-tech for Mao's China, it was still sheltered from the more rapid and dramatic technological innovation in the West, Japan and South Korea. Electronic goods for use by the PLA were manufactured in a collection of factories, built by Russian and East German construction engineers and laid out on a grid of wide streets. The workers in these factories were often visited by senior leaders and much praised in the press. Photos are still on display of large regimented groups of workers, both men and women, all in Mao suits and caps, singing revolutionary songs and performing synchronised exercises to get them in the right frame of mind for another day building China's glorious future. These workers were well looked after by the standards of the times with the best workers' housing in Beijing and good community facilities in the surrounding neighbourhood. In the big concrete community square there were lots of ping-pong tables fixed to the ground and plenty of exercise equipment. On the day I visited one old man spent an extended period hanging (fully clothed) upside down by his feet.

Dashanzi is now home to the 798 art district. Many of the old factories, however modern they were by Maoist standards, were unprofitable and closed. Some, however, are still functioning, including the one where the Wish Tree was erected, but many others have been turned into art galleries and studios. Those huge empty spaces, with high ceilings and natural light from above, are the perfect place to exhibit art. Since the 1990s the contemporary Chinese visual art scene has been hot and notorious, cutting edge by international standards, with artworks commanding high prices in the art markets of Hong Kong, London and New York. Chinese conceptual artists are up with the best in the world in their capacity to shock and sell. Zhang Huan, one of the most internationally famous, covered his body in honey and sat motionless in a public toilet as flies gathered, landed and stuck all over him. Once covered he waded into a filthy storm water drain to shake them off. Photographs of this performance taken by Rong Rong have become icons of an era during the 1990s when artists found symbolic ways to make highly subversive political statements.[1]

In the old communities of factory workers too some more traditional artistic skills remain. In the new community building in the middle of Dashanzi's old housing estate the best paper cutter in China, Jiao Wenjun, taught the locals his extremely refined skills. He made complicated Chinese characters out of red paper by folding and tearing. Using scissors he cut filigree pictures of princesses in palaces as well as dramatically contrasting scenes of stark socialist realism. In the spring of 2008, he, with his team of local volunteer helpers, made paper cuts of virtually all the Olympic sports as played by one of the *fuwa*, the cartoon panda-like characters that the Chinese authorities adopted as part of their branding for the Olympics. All these paper *fuwa* had been pasted on to an enormously long frieze which took about 30 people to unfurl. It stretched a round the four walls of the room. His paper-cutting skills have made him an officially recognised celebrity: when British Prime Minister Gordon Brown came to China, Jiao Wenjun was one of the people invited to meet him.

The other neighbourhood, Donghuashi, had strong historical resonances going much further back than Mao's showpiece factories. The city of Beijing took on its current square layout in the Ming dynasty. Taking the Forbidden City as the centre, a street grid was laid out stretching out to a high grey wall which encompassed the city in a square. Sections of this wall remain, roughly where the second of six contemporary ring roads now runs. Begun in 1419, these walls were built by some 200,000 artisans, engineers and labourers, many of whom were convicts, permanently wearing a *cangue*, a wooden collar, around their neck. It took them three years to build a wall 11 metres high, 17 metres wide and nearly 24 kilometres in circumference. Twelve horses could gallop abreast on the top of the wall without impeding each other. In his history of Beijing, Jasper Becker conjures up 'the sight of Yong Le's troops parading at dawn, the officers' armour flashing beneath their white sable furs and silk embroidered gowns'.[2] Multi-storeyed gate-houses, the largest nine storeys high, were erected for guards at each of the nine gates. From behind these windows archers would keep watch for the marauding armies of the ever disloyal warlords. In front of each was a semicircular space surrounded by a high wall for military drill. According to a Persian diplomat, inside the walls were 'paved courtyards, latticed arcades, magnificent columns and floors of fine cut stone'. Beyond the walls the moats surrounding the city were lined with stone and spanned by wooden bridges.[3]

About two kilometres from Tiananmen to the east at what would have been the south-eastern corner of the Ming city is a watchtower, Dongbian Men, near to where the Grand Canal bringing water from verdant Hangzhou arrives at the dry northern capital. Just outside this stretch of wall, during the Qing dynasty, a flower market spontaneously flourished. Donghuashi stands on the site of this flower market – as its name, East Flower Market, suggests. Aristocrats, senior mandarins and the Imperial household would come here to buy fresh flowers brought up the canals from the countryside. They would also buy handmade silk flowers. According to legend these were the most beautiful and well-crafted silk flowers in the whole of China. Small workshops run by master teachers grew up around the flower market's main street and for decades it was a hive of industry, employment and community. Those that worked in these workshops and the flower market lived hearby in the streets and *hutongs*, the narrow lanes of court-yard houses facing away from the street. All of this was brought to a sudden and abrupt end by the Cultural Revolution; the market was closed, along with all Beijing's markets; the furniture market, the market for horses and donkeys. These were examples of capitalism and rightism and had to go.

Without the market the Donghuashi neighbourhood fell into poverty and in 2003 it was rebuilt. The old 1950s and 1960s brick flats were demolished and much of the land was sold off to private developers. Attracting their interest was not difficult. The neighbourhood, by the expansive standards of modern Beijing is very central, a few minutes from Beijing East station from where the new white bullet trains with noses like dolphins rush to the other big cities. The new homes for sale have been built in high blocks with their south sides glassed over to attract light and heat during the many cold, grey months of the Beijing winter. In the middle of the blocks is a gated courtyard with a strange sculpture of a giant flowering cabbage. The luxury blocks are surrounded by paving and locked gates to keep out marauders. The old flower market has become an upscale security-conscious neighbourhood for busy professionals. On the Saturday morning when the Wish Tree was put up there were not many young adults around; they are too busy shopping. The children are being tended by indulgent grandparents who are mostly unknown to each other. Many of these little emperors, born of newly prosperous parents, have the latest in expensive childhood accessories, including motorised jeeps and scooters that whirr around the square guided by a three-year-old. They are kitted out in designer baby wear, complete with baseball cap at a crazy tilted angle.

Some of the older flower-makers are still around too. They don't live in the expensive gated community. They now live in tiny high-rise blocks of flats nearby, the smallness being the source of much complaint. The developer had to provide cheap replacement housing following their eviction. Much has been lost with the demolition of the old, run-down, ramshackle tenement blocks. Many older people in China still feel superstitious about living above the ground, so that is a source of discomfort. Along with the old living arrangements the sense of community has gone. Amid these high blocks of cramped flats there is nowhere for those communal activities that are the mainstay of Chinese community life, *taiji* and mah-jong. In the older communities based around the *danwei*, like Dashanzi, there is still a place to gather, gossip, gamble; a place for communal singing, ping-pong, exercising, *taiji*, mah-jong and taking the caged birds out for a breath of fresh air and a change of scene. Now the residents of Donghuashi have to cross under the eight-lane Second Ring Road and go to a small patch of grass under the city walls, which is a 20-minute walk. A few people exercise there. Grandmas watch toddlers. Two old women do *taiji*. But the grass patch is not big enough to be a park and it is an island between the walls and the traffic. It is not the same as stepping out of your home and straight into a community. Since the new flats are so small and the interiors often poky and unappealing many old people are forced to spend hours and hours out and about alone or with friends and neighbours. Not so much with families: many of their children have moved away to find work. In the new flats of the old flower market too much time is spent cooped up at home alone or with only your spouse and the Pekinese dog for company. Tracking share prices and watching game shows are the only diversions.

For sentimental reasons many of the elderly residents still make silk flowers as a leisure pastime. They also continued to make fruit out of glass under the tutelage of the acknowledged expert whom they call Master Grape, because his glass grapes were utterly lifelike. There was one other echo of their flower-making past. Along the pavement a flower bed had been laid. Plastic grass had been put down and the real stumps of small trees had been stuck into the ground. To these living branches the local people had attached the silk roses and cherry blossom they had made. These artificial flowers will bloom all year round for ever – never withering; never dying.

The contrasting atmosphere between the two Beijing neighbourhoods, one old and the other new, was stark. Dashanzi showed off the best of the community spirit, shorn of Mao's excesses, that the old factory units had inculcated. People's situations were secure and they were surrounded by familiar people and habits. Living in such close proximity had its downside, but it meant everyone, including the old and disabled, could join in the paper cutting and the spontaneous communal singing. While people were filling in their Wish Tree cards there was a spontaneous, lusty crowd rendition of *Dongfang hong* – 'The East is Red', the most popular of the Maoist songs, practically a second national anthem. Old people always had friends to talk to and enemies to talk about. *Taiji* sessions went on for hours, participants coming and going as they pleased. The children had other children to play highly animated and rapid games of ping-pong with. For the smaller children there was always an adult around to keep an eye out. The contrast in the East Flower Market could not have been more drastic. Children played alone in confined spaces, constantly supervised by a single grandparent. Many old and disabled people just sat around on their own looking bored. There was nothing going on, no activities, no community square. The Wish Tree had to be erected on a pavement. The people gathered around it spilt on to the street, only to be scattered by a stretch limo making its way slowly along and stopping by the locked gates in front of the expensive blocks of flats. Unsurprisingly, although it was a densely concentrated neighbourhood, far fewer wish cards were filled in. Wish cards were completed by 1,159 people in total, 886 in the tightly knit community of Dashanzi, but 273 in the more anonymous Donghuashi.

The analysis of the responses by Tsinghua University, though presented in a dry, factual tone – without the all-important quotes from the people who had written the cards – undoubtedly confirmed that the concerns of Beijing people were similar to those in Chongqing. The analysts noted 'an obvious difference among questions that various age groups concentrate on . . . what has changed the life of youth is study, what has changed the lives of young adults is work and what has changed the life of middle-aged people and old adults is the macro-environment of China'. This seemingly uncontroversial exposition nevertheless describes the shift from a place where lives were entirely controlled to one where citizens are on their own. They also record that 'youth [were] mainly concerned about study, young adults mainly concerned about work and family; and the main concerns of old adults is personal health and disease'. In response to the question: 'What event changed your life?' the keywords noted by Tsinghua were 'nation, Reform and Opening up, family and life, work, education, Olympics, sports, ageing, mental attitude, community, housing, culture, migration to Beijing, disease, love, health, environment and friendship'. And in response to the last question: 'What are your greatest worries?' the keywords started with the Olympics – not surprising since this was in Beijing a few weeks before the start of the Olympics. After that, came health. As in Chongqing, health worries topped the list. After that many similar themes emerged to those that came out in Chongqing: 'family life, work, education, housing and car, community environment, staying young, social security, prices and love'. The Tsinghua analysts noted 'the huge impact of the country's developments on the life of residents. Residents generally expect further development of their nation and a better life that will bring.' Or, to put the same conclusions another way, people had been through enormous upheavals and expected more change to come, from which they hoped they would benefit. Judging by their concerns, however, they were far from sure.

The artist Ai Weiwei (breaking an official ban) wrote an article for *Newsweek* in August 2011 setting out his withering views on the degraded state of contemporary life in Beijing:

> Beijing is two cities. One is of power and of money. People don't care who their neighbours are; they don't trust you. The other city is one of desperation.
>
> Every year millions come to Beijing to build its bridges, roads, and houses. Each year they build a Beijing equal to the size of the city in 1949. They are Beijing's slaves. They squat in illegal structures, which Beijing destroys as it keeps expanding. Who owns houses? Those who belong to the government, the coal bosses, the heads of big enterprises. They come to Beijing to give gifts – and the restaurants and karaoke parlours and saunas are very rich as a result.
>
> You will see migrants' schools closed. You will see hospitals where they give patients stitches – and when they find the patients don't have any money, they pull the stitches out. It's a city of violence.[4]

Beijing is obviously different to Chongqing. Chongqing is a gigantic industrial metropolis with few old buildings or grandiose traditions. It has an important history, but there's precious little of that to see, not least because of the Japanese bombing of the city when it was the Nationalist capital during the Second World War. Beijing, on the other hand, exudes its Imperial history in its buildings and its layout. Its contemporary incarnation as a capital city where power, money and big decisions come together still conveys that sense of grandeur and distance: the feeling that the rulers live here and the rulers are above you. Obviously nowhere conveys the feeling of being in the presence of omniscient power nowadays more than Tiananmen Square and the Great Hall of the People. But beneath the grandeur, the sense of superiority and the rush of power and money, responses to the Wish Tree showed communities with the same underlying relationships, dynamics and concerns as in all cities in China. Mao's work units may have created stultifying and dehumanising uniformity, but they also bound people together in long-term relationships. Mutual obligations and attachments were created over generations and had a strong cohesive power. The wildly overheated property market in Beijing, where prices have almost reached Western levels, and the massive movements of people to the city mean that these communities are now being scattered even faster than in Chongqing. Anonymous modernity is replacing the old communities in Beijing, Chongqing and every other large Chinese city.

Both in Chongqing and Beijing, the Wish Tree experience showed me that ordinary people had strong opinions and were keen to share them. They were neither frightened of speaking their mind nor mistrustful of foreigners. Simple, relevant participation techniques with familiar home-spun resonances, like the Wish Tree, elicited their views easily enough. Although officials, and even the police, were present while people were filling in cards they had simply said what they thought. Although local issues were certainly commented on these concerns did not vary much from place to place. The Communist Party is determined to control from the centre. Ironically they have unified the *laobaixing* – the ordinary people with the old hundred names – in standard discontents. Many had written their names on the cards, including people who were critical of the authorities. The authorities' lack of knowledge of ways to involve local people in decision-making, and the absence of a tradition of doing so, was only part of the problem. The more fundamental difficulty was that the official reason for seeking people's views was not that officials wanted to address or solve the problems. Instead, they wanted to be forewarned of discontent and anger which might escalate out of control. From the official viewpoint, the rationale for consultation was not to improve things but in order to suppress criticism. A depressing conclusion. In addition, addressing many of the problems being raised required changes and decisions about national policy, which were taken unaccountably, without consultation, behind closed doors and mostly in Beijing. Even quite senior officials did not feel they had any say in those, or even much idea of how the decisions were taken. Experts might be involved in taking them on a 'scientific' basis, though Communist Party doctrine was always likely to override 'science'. But in any case that isn't how social policy works. Trial and error, rectifying unintended consequences and balancing competing interests and priorities is a much more common pattern for getting things done, however limited and compromised.

Before embarking on the Wish Tree, I did not know what responses to anticipate. I was sure that people would not mention human rights and democracy, partly because that would obviously be courting disaster with the authorities, but much more importantly, because I knew that sort of politics was not necessarily uppermost in most people's minds, or indeed their biggest concern. Authoritarianism and resistance was made manifest in the lives of the *laobaixing* in more pragmatic, prosaic ways than political discourse and dissident struggle. My strongest impression, once I saw the responses to the Wish Tree, was that in the process of economic and social change, people had been left with many unwanted consequences; many anxieties. The experience of change and their fears for the future had left them shocked and anxious. Not for the first time in many of their lives they had been traumatised by massive upheavals.

Chinese cities are now devoid of the old Communist propaganda and the grey-clad workers on their bicycles. The all too superficial picture of urban, cosmopolitan modernity disguises the loss of protection, security, affiliation, belonging and social stability. Economic growth since the 1980s has been achieved at the expense of another set of traumas to add to those of the 1950s, 1960s and 1970s. The social safety net has been whisked away from more than 50 million people working in state-owned factories in cities.[5] Forty to 50 million farmers have lost their land and many are poverty-stricken and devoid of hope.[6] Hardship is unabated for several hundred million people in the countryside. Up to 200 million migrants float on the peripheries of the cities detached from the past and with no certainty for the future.[7] Communities have been demolished and dispersed by wholesale urban redevelopment sweeping aside families and ways of life with deep local roots. Healthcare, family life, the costs and pressures of education, financial insecurity and environmental collapse are the losses. Despite something of a rehabilitation of Confucius the old social order has gone for ever, along with the old Mandarin script and thousands of different ways to cook *doufu* or practice *taiji*. The family structures that are at the heart of Confucian thinking are unrecognisably altered. Western materialism and fashion are pervasive. The old order cannot be recreated.

The deskilled, the unskilled, the migrants, the unemployed, the still-poor peasants and the old are the losers. The new economy has little to offer them and economic growth, however startling, won't bring these groups many new opportunities. They are the least able to benefit from the hypothetical added-value created by a global economy. As well as their economic losses, they have lost the work-related forms of institutional affiliation, social support, occupational solidarity and locational roots, which once characterised the industrial proletariat. As the historian Tony Judt noted, 'capital can be separated from its owner and move around the world at the speed of sound and light. But labour cannot be separated from its owner, and its owner is not just a worker but also a member of one or more communities – a resident, a citizen, a national.'[8]

Chinese leaders and policy-makers could address all four big challenges – family life, healthcare, financial insecurity and the environment – directly through social policy. A popular change would be to relax or even abolish the one-child policy. The consequences for population growth would not be disastrous. The balance between generations and genders would begin to be restored, though the damage will take decades to correct. State subsidies for education and healthcare could be increased. Larger state contributions could be made to build up health insurance funds, including entitlement to insurance for laid-off workers and rural unemployed people.

Pedagogy and teacher training could be reviewed to introduce a more inclusive approach with more varied levels and types of achievement for children of different abilities, rather than so strongly favouring narrow attainment in exams. The *hukou* system could be liberalised to allow people to move more freely from the countryside to the city without penalising the rural dwellers by the loss of their land. Better access to health and education services could be provided for migrants to the city. Compensation for people who lose their land could bear a closer resemblance to the development value of the land. Compensation could be honestly, fairly and efficiently administered, and paid on time. Financial insecurity could be reduced by increasing the coverage of and the amount paid by the

Minimum Living Standard and retirement pensions to bring them closer to the average wage. All this is achievable.

The environment represents the most intractable policy challenge. China's growth rate is simply not compatible with reducing deforestation, desertification, carbon emissions and air pollution from coal. Nevertheless there are steps that the government could take. It could increase the investment in renewable fuels. Waste management could be drastically improved. A national programme of cleaning up the rivers and the water supply could be initiated. Much more rigorous environmental standards could be applied to infrastructure development, particularly the building of dams.

Courts and judges could be made independent, even drawing on traditional Chinese jurisprudence. This would ensure that people with complaints would have somewhere to seek redress and corrupt officials would be held to account and punished. The Party could build on its tentative experiments in public consultation. At the moment these are confined to trivia like the price of bus tickets in Chongqing. It could extend the experiments in village-level democracy in which Communist Party membership was not a requirement to stand for election. Elections could be held further up the local government hierarchy, as in Wukan in Guangdong following protests in 2012. It could stop discouraging other candidates from standing. The media and the internet could be released from ubiquitous censorship and political criticism could be permitted in public. The privileges given to the children of Party leaders could be exposed, hopefully allowing the oxygen of public disapproval to rekindle the ashes of their consciences.

More than 70 per cent of the economy remains in state hands.[9] Many of the benefits of economic growth fill the state's coffers, though it is far from clear what belongs to the government and what is now the property of the Party. Government budget deficits are not the obstacle. An authoritarian, top-down system run by a factionalised leadership finds it difficult to change systems and policies in an orderly and empirical fashion. They fear a change in economic and social policy risks backfiring into demands for a change in political structures, even though none of the changes suggested here would fundamentally reduce Communist Party control. Much could be achieved without recourse to Western-style democratic governance.

Democracy and human rights are not the answer to everything. For many people, they wouldn't really be the answer to anything. A shift to democracy, which some call for, would not produce a more equitable society at peace with itself without a similarly big change in social policies too. The consequences of a failure to implement more balanced, equitable and humane economic and social policies are to be seen everywhere in China.

Every increase in the amount spent on social welfare has come following a crisis such as SARS, or urban unrest, which has forced open the government's wallet. There has been no systematic attempt to create a national safety net. This would require a set of interconnected reform processes, all of them enormous and complex. Radical developments in policy and the practice of public administration and the financing of public services are required. Above all, a drastic upgrading of public expectations is needed. First and foremost no universal right to basic standards of public services has been established, let alone equitable or redistributive public services. Public administration needs considerable reform with an emphasis on capacity-building, skills development and public accountability. The rooting out of corruption is needed far beyond anything seen in the decades since Reform and Opening. Far greater clarity and accountability are needed about the expectations on central, provincial and local government. An effective fiscal redistribution mechanism is urgently needed to transfer cash from rich local authorities to poorer areas. Otherwise the inequality gap will continue to widen.

If China wants universal access even to basic public services some redress for victims of maladministration derived from the rule of law is essential. Without that, social tensions can boil over at a moment's notice like an untended pressure cooker. Government spending on public services should increase significantly. The government could afford the levels of spending needed as government revenues have risen even faster than GDP. A public finance system that spent sufficient to achieve basic universal coverage and allocated resources equitably across China is also needed. One of the most urgent priorities is to establish a system of access to universal public services that does not continue the long-standing and substantial discrimination against people living in rural areas. The other substantial group of people who are at a huge disadvantage in the distribution of public services are migrant workers.[10]

Why doesn't the Chinese government do more to solve these problems? The simple cynical answer is that the leaders do very well out of the existing arrangements so the incentives to change things, from their personal points of view, just don't exist. Another more technical systemic answer can be found in the banking system. Despite everything that has changed, China is still a poor country. On average Chinese people can only afford three-quarters of the average for the world, less than people in Kazakhstan and only a fifth of the UK.[11] Nonetheless, faced with all these anxieties, poor people have no alternative but to save as much as they can. Between 1995 and 2005 the average urban household savings rate in China rose by 7 per cent to a quarter of disposable income.[12] Returns on these savings are low. Because the retail financial services market is not well developed, there is little competition in savings products. There are also few efficient financial instruments for borrowing against future earnings and limited opportunities for portfolio diversification. Conventional economic theory would suggest that the lack of flexible financial products would reduce people's propensity to save, but not in contemporary China. The emotional incentives to save as a hedge against fear and anxiety are too strong.

This high proportion of income saved is not only the result of Chinese habits and culture, as is sometimes argued. The pattern of who saves the most, and during what stage of their life, is unusual by international standards and it reveals people's true motives for savings. In other countries young adults save less because they expect their incomes to rise in the future. Similarly, older people save less in most places because, so long as there is a welfare system, fewer calls are made on savings in the later years. By contrast in Chinese households young adults and old people save the highest proportion of their incomes. 'These patterns are best explained by the rising private burden of expenditures on housing, education and health care.'[13] Housing has been massively privatised and the now widespread home ownership motivation has contributed greatly to increased savings. In 1990 only 17 per cent of households owned their own home. By 2005 that had risen to an amazing 86 per cent. The rising cost of education has also encouraged people to save in the early years of adulthood, soon after becoming parents. At the other end of the age spectrum, savings in old age are almost entirely explained by health fears. As Farrel *et al.* noted in 2006, 'given the importance of health care to Chinese families, the country's rapidly ageing population and the challenges facing the public health care system, we project that private health expenditures by urban consumers will grow at a rate of more than 11 per cent annually over the next two decades.'[14] In other words health care costs will consume ever larger proportions of income even if the economy continues to grow rapidly.

These high savings suppress domestic consumer demand for the vast surplus of China's manufactured goods. In the absence of domestic demand, export demand must be sustained if the economy is to keep up its rate of growth. As is widely reported, the need for exports to fuel job creation and economic growth has led the Chinese government to buy vast quantities of dollar-based assets, keeping down the value of the *renminbi* and delivering a massive trade surplus. To put it another way, inadequate social protection in China and the incentives and pressures it creates to save rather than spend is distorting the entire system of global trade.

These distortions created by the unusually high levels of savings are mirrored in the banking system. The heart of the Chinese banking system is just four state-owned banks: Bank of China, China Construction Bank, Agricultural Bank of China and, the biggest, Industrial and Commercial Bank China. These four banks control 43 per cent of China's total financial assets.[15] Since bond markets are controlled by the banks and equity markets are so volatile they can seem like casinos, 'in China, the banks are the financial system, nearly all financial risk is concentrated on their balance sheets.'[16] The short history of these banks has been characterised by regular crises and requirement for recapitalisation at the end of the 1970s, 1980s and 1990s caused by dramatic government-sponsored over-lending. At the end of 1999 Standard & Poor's, the rating agency, suggested that non-performing loans could be as high as 70 per cent of bank lending. Deutsche Bank estimated the figure at 50 per cent. The banks were bust. The recapitalisation in 2000 injected US$157 billion, reducing, according to Deutsche Bank, the proportion of non-performing loans to about 30 per cent.[17] As a consequence China's financial institutions carry a huge over-hang of non-performing loans on their balance sheets, the poor and irre-deemable quality of which is rarely fully disclosed or written down. Instead they are distributed by various instruments across the entire financial system. Since all these financial institutions are state-owned, both those selling and those buying, they constitute a de facto sovereign debt that is rarely disclosed as such. Even in normal years, before the gigantic fiscal stimulus of 2009, the big four banks increased their lending by 20 per cent a year with predictable consequences. 'Today in 2010, in every provincial capital across the country, exactly the same kind of real-estate boom has developed and for the same reasons: Party-driven bank lending,' note two seasoned observers of the Chinese financial scene, Walter and Howie.[18]

Between 1978 and 2005 the proportion of deposits made by ordinary households, 'retail deposits', has more than doubled, rising from 27.2 per cent to 55.8 per cent. Over the same period government deposits dropped from 40.3 per cent to 9.9 per cent, while the proportion of deposits from enterprises remained roughly static, 32.4 per cent in 1978 to 29.5 per cent in 2005.[19] Total deposits have obviously greatly increased over the same period from RMB113 billion to more than RMB18 trillion. So much of the money being recklessly lent by these banks is money deposited by ordinary citizens. If the loans made with their deposits turn out to be non-performing, either they will lose their deposits or a massive bailout will be needed; unless, as has happened before, non-performing loans are simply recycled elsewhere through the creation of new financial instruments. This of course only hides and postpones the problem and leaves the risk amplified and ineradicably in place. Furthermore, without retail deposits continuing at these levels, lending to state-owned enterprises and local and central government will have to be dramatically curtailed, bringing to an end the rapid upgrading of infrastructure and the construction boom. In other words the high propensity to save among ordinary Chinese is essential to China's current growth model. If ordinary consumers were to feel, as they do in the US, that they can spend now on credit and repay later, that would pose a serious problem. Similarly, if ordinary citizens were to feel that the need to maintain such high levels of savings was obviated by universal social welfare provisions, as they do in many European countries, that too would be a problem. The absence of a social welfare system and its effect on savings and consumer behaviour is therefore an essential component of China's economic policy framework. Some investments will be made in welfare, but never so much as to lead citizens to conclude that the financial risks of the future costs of their well-being have been, like bank debt, safely lodged with the state and they are free to go on a spending spree.

Some of these deposits have also been used in a clever series of transactions to strengthen the banks' own capital position. In 1998 when the banks had to be recapitalised after the disclosure of massive bad debts, they needed RMB270 billion to raise their capital adequacy ratios back to 8 per cent of total assets in line with the Basle agreements on international banking standards. This was a huge sum, equivalent to a year's worth of government bond issuance or 25 per cent of China's famed foreign exchange reserves. 'To do this the Ministry of Finance nationalised savings deposits largely belonging to Chinese people. . . . This washing of RMB270 billion through the Ministry of Finance made the banks' depositors – both consumer and corporate – de facto shareholders, but without their knowledge or attribution of rights.'[20] Such a sequence of events could all too easily recur:

> if risk classifications based on international standards are applied consistently, a repeat of the 1990s experience is in the making [in 2010], with huge volumes of unpaid loans and the banks again in need of massive recapitalisation. Already, the tsunami of lending and high dividend payouts have stretched bank capital adequacy ratios and forced the need for more capital, which comes largely from the state itself.[21]

One of the most dangerous sources of potential non-performing loans is municipalities. After much soul-searching the Party permitted municipalities to run fiscal deficits in 2008. This was enthusiastically embraced by local authorities which, with the help of the Ministry of Finance, created a variety of borrowing vehicles secured on their assets. According to official statistics these local borrowings amounted to 14 per cent of total lending in 2009 and, for some banks, as much as 40 per cent of total new credit issued. Beijing was 'publicly admitting to RMB7.8 trillion of outstanding local government debt, more than US$1 trillion'.[22] This is the equivalent of 23 per cent of China's GDP. By 2012 these debts had risen to RMB10.7 trillion.[23] The government's plan is simply to roll these loans over, allowing their value to diminish by inflation and as a proportion of growing GDP – a risky one-way bet on future growth with inflation helping to devalue the cost of loans.

Walter and Howie note: 'today's financial system is almost wholly reliant on the heroic savings rates of Chinese people; they are the only source of non-state money in the game . . . From this viewpoint a profusion of new investments and consumer lending products appears unlikely. Similarly this view suggests that full funding for social security is a reform whose time will not come'.[24] The Party leaders do not, in other words, introduce beneficial social policies because they can't. That would run the risk of turning their long economic boom into a collapsed house of cards. Ordinary people's dreams of security have in part been mortgaged and buried in the arcane interstices of a wildly overstretched and hugely risky banking system.[25]

CHAPTER 12

Trauma without Recovery

Saving more, banding closer together with family and friends, reasserting Confucian values and rekindling old religious beliefs while simultaneously espousing newer mystical prophets are all understandable, more or less rational ways for people to respond to anxieties. There are, however, negative ways of responding too. Self-destructiveness is an irrational reaction that turns anxiety into trauma and leads to perverse, incomprehensible behaviour. Self-destruction is, of course, rarely distant from the destruction of others.

In April 2010 an unemployed 47-year-old man entered a kindergarten in Jiangsu province and stabbed 28 children, two teachers and a security guard. The next morning a 45-year-old farmer broke down the gates of a school in Shandong province with a motorcycle. He hit several students with a hammer, grabbed two and set fire to himself. The farmer died and five students were injured. Two days later, in the afternoon of 12 April, a man in the Guangxi region stabbed seven people with a vegetable knife near a school, killing a student and an 81-year-old woman. He had been treated for mental illness in 2005 and 2008, and family members wanted to send him to hospital for further treatment. The following week a 33-year-old man attacked a primary school in Guangdong province. He slashed 15 students and a teacher before he was surrounded by teachers and arrested by police. He was a teacher at another nearby school, but had been on sick leave since 2006. In the same month a 42-year-old surgeon was executed for a bloody assault on an elementary school in Fujian province. In a few minutes he stabbed eight students to death and seriously injured five others waiting to enter the school. The court, announcing his death sentence, said he acted out of anger because he had been repeatedly frustrated in his romantic life.[1] Imitation played a part in these tragedies in quick succession. Poverty and social exclusion have also contributed. Untreated mental illness has been at work in all these attacks.

Rates of mental illness are high in China. According to research, in 2009 17.5 per cent of the population suffer from at least one mental disorder.[2] Mood and anxiety disorders were the most common in women, whereas alcohol use disorders were much more prevalent in men. The overall rate of alcohol abuse in China has risen nearly tenfold from 660 cases per 100,000 people in 1990 to 5,813 per 100,000 in 2009. People in rural areas had a higher prevalence of mental disorders than city dwellers. This difference was more marked for depression and alcohol dependence. Mental disorders are less common in younger adults (aged 18 to 39) in comparison to middle-aged (40 to 54) or older adults (over 55). Middle-aged individuals were significantly more likely to have substance use disorders, especially alcohol, than other age groups. Whereas 70 per cent of those with psychotic disorders – illnesses such as schizophrenia where a sense of reality is distorted or lost – received professional help, less than 12 per cent of those with non-psychotic disorders received such help. External factors such as financial worries and family conflict are significant contributors to non-psychotic mental illnesses. China does not have any national system of mental health law even after many efforts to establish one. Despite the high rates of mental illness in China, just 2.35 per cent of the health budget is spent on mental health. In 2004, less than 15 per cent of the population had health insurance that covered psychiatric conditions. There are only 20,000 psychiatrists in China, which equates to 1.5 for every 100,000 people. Rural areas have a poorer service than urban areas and the last remaining psychiatrist in Tibet has left.[3] In other words, people use alcohol to numb the pain, but it doesn't work. All too many are simply overwhelmed by depression for which no professional help is given, even if it could make any difference.

As well as mental illness, drug use, prostitution, gambling and, most terribly of all, suicide are all on the rise. Towards the end of the 1980s, the 'China Channel', along the borders of the Golden Triangle of Burma, Laos and Thailand, earned notoriety as the drug trafficking pathway for Asia. The Golden Triangle was the biggest opiate-producing zone in the world.

Largely drug free by the 1970s, China was a huge potential market for the unscrupulous and well-organised international drugs trade. Dropping drugs off in China was easy, a way station en route to feeding the insatiable Western habit. Drugs were brought first to Yunnan, later to Sichuan and Guangzhou as well as Hong Kong and Macau. Close to the Golden Triangle, Guangzhou, one of China's most booming cities, is the capital for drug trafficking both into and out of the country.[4] In 1990, 70,000 drug users were registered. By 2006 that rose to 1.16 million, rising at 122 per cent on average a year. There are many more unregistered drug users, perhaps as many as 3.5 million. Drug abuse has also spread from urban to rural areas, becoming widespread once more. Nearly 72.7 per cent of counties report drug problems.[5] The escalating usage of drugs has depressingly familiar consequences. Heroin users sharing needles sparked a big rise in HIV infection. Drug users account for over 60 per cent of the HIV cases. An estimated one million people in China are living with HIV.[6]

The government has implemented a law that forces users into detoxification programmes when drugs are detected. If users relapse they are required to spend between three months and a year at a detoxification camp.[7] There are currently around 700 compulsory detoxification settings, about 300 camps and about 200 voluntary detox clinics. The biggest can treat 3,000 patients and the smallest about 100. Patients have to pay for their detoxification treatment, but not if they undertake the treatment in camps for 're-education through labour', China's miserable gulags. In 2002, a cumulative total of 252,500 drug abusers who have been through detoxification several times undertook compulsory detoxification and 76,000 were 'rehabilitated' in camps for re-education through labour.[8]

The age demographic of drug users has changed since the 1980s. Previously most drug users were mature people; however, recently 17- to 35-year-olds account for approximately 74 per cent of users. Drug usage is associated with minimal education and a lack of job prospects.[9] A 2010 study of 730 club drug users in Shanghai in 2006 found that drug usage was significantly higher among currently unemployed men with less than a high school education; the 'bare branches' taking their frustrations out on themselves. While opium-based heroin is the drug of choice, the club drugs such as methamphetamine, ketamine, and Ecstasy are replacing opiates to become the most prevalent drugs among the 'slacker' generation:

young people from newly wealthy families who have quickly developed sybaritic and work-shy lifestyles.[10] They are to be seen fashionably dressed and fiddling distractedly with their cell phones in basement bars all over Chinese cities, while shaking and quivering on the way up or down from taking drugs.

Gambling is another old Chinese vice the authorities tried to crush in Mao's days, but which is now making a comeback. Apartments are used as secret gambling dens where people play cards and other games for money. The lottery, which several respondents to the Wish Tree wanted to win, is the only legal form of gambling. Set up in 1987, it already raises *RMB*100 billion a year in revenue for Beijing. It is owned and run by the state, to which the profits accrue. Since its inception playing the lottery has become a national obsession. But the *RMB*100 billion spent on the lottery is dwarfed by money wagered illicitly. In 2009 some 600,000 people were arrested for gambling. Anyone who admits they need help may be confined to a mental hospital. Therefore many gambling addicts choose to stay in 'a private hell of debt and despair'.[11] Internet gaming sites have opened up a vast new range of temptations for gamblers and the better-off can travel to Macao which, since being rejoined to China, rivals Las Vegas as a gambling mecca complete with familiar vulgarities.

The recent history of prostitution follows a similarly miserable trajectory. After a long, decadent history of concubinage and, in effect, polygamy, the Communists thought they could stamp it out so 'they monitored people's houses, hairstyles and make-up'. Prostitution, however, was never stamped out in Mao's China (or anywhere else), but 'there was no open prostitution 25 years ago', according to Jing Jun, a sociology and AIDS policy professor at Tsinghua University interviewed in 2007 by Maureen Fan of the *Washington Post*. 'Fifteen years ago, you didn't find sex workers in remote areas and cities. But now it's prevalent in every city, every county.'[12] In many communities sex workers are open and trusted members of the community. A poll in 2009 showed that they are trusted more than Party officials.[13]

Some suggest the rise in prostitution can be attributed to the decline of socially conservative values, perceived as part of a wider crisis in values the doctrines of the harmonious society seek to address. They cite, for example, the rise of fashionable and provocative clothing for girls. In fact, many prostitutes are young women who have migrated to economic hotspots like Guangzhou and Shenzhen in pursuit of legitimate employment, but supply exceeds demand in the highly fluid and sensitive labour market for young female factory workers. Without unemployment or social security benefits, these girls have no alternative but prostitution. They still have to support themselves and send money back to their families in the countryside, sometimes as much as half their earnings. 'Among government officials, Chinese social scientists and health professionals, they are coming around to see prostitution is not fundamentally connected to a lack of values but a lack of jobs, choices, opportunities and education,' according to Jing.[14] Nobody knows how many prostitutes there are in China. Ten million would be a conservative estimate. No one doubts the numbers are rising, in part with official collusion in payoffs and backhanders from organised criminal handlers to police and local government officials. This is an embarrassment to officialdom, and there are regular crackdowns on the prostitutes and their protectors, often high-up officials in the Party and the army. One such was Bo Xilai's high-profile campaign in Chongqing in 2009; however, the many vested interests prevent sustained effective action.

The ever-growing supply of prostitutes has rapidly reduced the price of sex. Prostitutes are ubiquitous, so it is difficult for girls new to the game to find a patch. The usual brothels, bars and clubs are available in every town and city, as well as telephone services for hotel guests. Prostitutes are also on streets and in car parks, even in supermarkets (which sell the normal range of goods as well). In the evening some barber shops turn into brothels. Sex can be bought for *RMB*10 under a bridge or flyover in Sichuan. Increasingly fierce competition among prostitutes gives ignorant and exploitative customers growing leverage. Prostitution is becoming less an organised business and more an exercise in individual entrepreneurship. Mid-level sex workers with a few years of experience are striking out on their own in leafy residential compounds, renting apartments and finding their own customers without the rapacious middlemen and far from the prying eyes, crackdowns and corrupt protection rackets of local police. The health consequences are depressingly predictable. Syphilis and other sexually transmitted diseases are rife. Services for people with sexually transmitted diseases, like all public health services, are inadequate and poorly co-ordinated. Many sufferers rely on underground doctors to avoid embarrassment or disclosure and so reliable numbers are hard to come by.

Worse than all this unhappiness is the most tragic and extreme manifestation of China's dystopia, the suicide rate, which is one of the highest in the world. An estimated 287,000 Chinese kill themselves each year, a rate of 23 people per 100,000, more than double the US rate, according to a study by the Beijing Suicide Research and Prevention Centre.[15] The rate has remained high and relatively stable for years. In most countries the bulk of people who commit suicide are male, living in cities and 95 per cent have mental health problems. In China, by contrast, the proportion of suicides who are mentally ill is considerably lower, at 65 per cent.[16] For the remainder, unexpected life events and pressures, not mental illnesses, cause them to kill themselves. In Western countries, men are at least twice as likely and sometimes four times as likely as women to commit suicide. In China, again, the opposite is true. The suicide rate for women is 25 per cent higher than for men. A distinct peak of attempted suicides is reached among women between 25 and 34 years old living in rural areas, and rural suicide rates are higher than urban rates across all age groups.[17] The global trend is for more women to attempt suicide, but more men kill themselves. In China, by contrast, the number of completed suicides is greater for women. Some commentators ascribe this to the readily available and lethal pesticides in general use in rural areas, but the psycho-social factors of economic uncertainty, family control and patriarchal brutality are likely to be the biggest factors. In other words, China's experience flies in the face of international norms. Poor rural women living lives of oppression, conflict and loss are the ones most likely to commit suicide in China. In the rest of the world it is mentally ill men living in cities.

The women who commit suicide in the countryside are almost exclusively poor, ill-educated and wholly unequipped for social and economic change. In 2002, the Suicide Prevention Centre found young women who attempted to kill themselves had on average only five years of schooling and lived in households with a median per capita income of far less than a dollar a day. Most reported being unhappily married; more than 42 per cent mentioned financial problems and more than 38 per cent said their husbands beat them.[18] Student suicide is another marked feature of the social landscape regularly reported in newspapers. More than a quarter of students think about committing suicide and, though exact numbers are neither collected nor reported, according to the *China Daily*, 2009 was the worst year on record.[19]

Drug abuse, prostitution, mental illness and suicide are pervasive problems affecting millions of people in China. Regardless of the research approach, findings about the causes of these self-destructive behaviours are strikingly similar: poverty, particularly in rural areas; family conflict and collapse; unemployment and financial insecurity and lack of education. These were also the concerns highlighted on the Wish Tree by people whose lives had not gone quite so catastrophically wrong, but who still had many problems. Whichever way Chinese society is examined, the same problems are revealed: fear of the upheavals of economic transformation and consequential personal uncertainty. People who have had a range of distressing experiences simply don't know what is going to happen to them. Their dreams have become nightmares of unheralded, unwanted surprises and anxieties. The authorities minimise and deny the deep well of human misery created by hardship, leaving the people 'eating bitterness.'[20] Instead the Party sees and responds to the threat to itself.

Psychological and emotional reactions to disturbing or traumatic experiences always have a dilemma at their heart: the urge to forget painful memories competes with the sometimes unwanted inevitability of remembering, in emotional as well as intellectual ways. Flashbacks, memories, neuroses, repetitive destructive patterns of behaviour are all said to spring from irrepressible remembering. At their worst these involuntary reactions in thoughts, feelings and behaviour become omnipresent traumas. This seems to be true whether a trauma has been experienced individually, as a group, or across a whole society. China is a case study of unwanted bad memories surviving the passage of time. The idea of unquiet memories has entered the weft and warp of Chinese tradition. Nowhere more than in China is folk wisdom and mythology stocked with tales of ghosts who refuse to rest in their graves until their story is told. *Qingming*, the festival of propitiation of hungry ghosts, and the ardour with which it is observed across Chinese society is testament to that. Unhappy memories become unquiet ghosts.

The literature on trauma and in particular on post-traumatic stress disorder has grown enormously. According to Judith Lewis Herman:

> Recovery requires remembrance and mourning. It has become clear from the experience of newly democratic countries in Latin America, Eastern Europe and Africa that restoring a sense of social community requires a public forum where victims can speak their truth and their suffering can be formally acknowledged. In addition, establishing any lasting peace requires an organised effort to hold individual perpetrators accountable for their crimes. At the least, those responsible for the worst atrocities must be brought before the law. If there is no hope of justice, the helpless rage of victimised groups can fester, impervious to the passage of time.[21]

Recovery, according to Herman, unfolds in three stages: the establishment of safety; remembrance and mourning, and connection with ordinary life.[22] In their determination either to bury the past or to impose their own narrative and interpretation the Communist authorities certainly don't recognise any obligation to help people through these stages of recovery. There are some therapeutic projects and charities for individual victims; however, a process of 'remembrance and mourning' for groups, much less for society as a whole, is inconceivably threatening to the Party, particularly the requirement to bring those responsible to legal account. Nonetheless, even the Communist Party recognises that the past has at least to be acknowledged. From a practical point of view, each generation of leaders wants to distance itself from the mistakes of its predecessors. Also Party leaders realise that sudden switchbacks in policy or denunciations of people who were formerly lauded is bound to create confusion and cynicism among the citizenry. They are all too aware of public disdain for the leadership's current abstention from high-minded ideological commitments and the impression readily created that, in the absence of philosophy or belief, they and their families are simply in it for themselves. This leads to the wider possibility that the entire political and economic system is skewed towards maximum benefits for greedy and warring vested interests and away from the interests of ordinary people. Such thoughts are obviously dangerous, hence the focus by leaders like Hu Jintao and Bo Xilai on moral as well as economic strengthening. The problem, of course, is that the greatest moral weakness is not in the lovable and impressionable masses, whom the leaders continue to invoke. The absolute moral collapse is in the Party itself.

Both the importance and the sensitivity of the debate about when and in what terms to acknowledge the mistakes of the past were never illustrated in higher relief than in the Party's revisions of its attitude to the Great Leap Forward and the Cultural Revolution. The Party addressed both these undoubted traumas, and their national casualties, in a resolution adopted by the Central Committee. After going through numerous drafts it was eventually published in 1987. The long wait for the publication of the resolution points to the endless internal wrangling that preceded its release. On the Great Leap Forward the resolution had this to say:

> 'Left' errors characterised by excessive targets, the issuing of arbitrary directions, boastfulness and the stirring up of a 'communist wind' spread unchecked through the country. This was due to our lack of experience in socialist construction and inadequate understanding of the laws of economic development and of the basic economic conditions in China. More important it was due to the fact that Comrade Mao Zedong and many leading comrades both in the centre and in the localities, had become smug about their successes, were impatient for quick results and overestimated the role of man's subjective will and effort . . . From the end of 1958 to the early stage of the Lushan meeting in July 1959 Comrade Mao Zedong and the Central Committee led the whole Party in energetically rectifying the errors which had already been recognised . . . [It was due to] 'Right opportunism' together with a succession of natural calamities and the perfidious scrapping of contracts by the Soviet government that our economy encountered certain difficulties between 1959 and 1961, which caused serious losses to our country and people.[23].

This is highly coded, euphemistic and a considerable dilution both of the mistakes made and the consequences for ordinary people, notably the famine that killed 40 million people.[24] Nor is there much suggestion of regret or remorse, just the playing out of an internal set of loyalties, rivalries and balances which in the end do more to obscure rather than reveal the truth, as those people who suffered first hand will know. Limitations will also have been placed on honesty because some of the leaders still around in 1978, including Deng Xiaoping, were implicated in the Great Leap Forward.

The condemnation of the Cultural Revolution in the same resolution is rather less equivocal. Deng was banished and played little part in the Cultural Revolution. The widespread extent of denunciation and rehabilitation at the time means that most senior people can claim that they were denounced during the Cultural Revolution and were not therefore the principal perpetrators:

> On no account should the theories and methods of the 'Cultural Revolution' have been applied. Under socialist conditions there is no economic or political basis for carrying out a great political revolution in which 'one class overthrows another'. It decidedly could not come up with any constructive programme, but could only bring grave disorder, damage and retrogression in its train. History has shown that 'the Cultural Revolution' initiated by a leader labouring under a misapprehension and capitalised on by counterrevolutionary cliques, led to domestic turmoil and brought catastrophe to the Party, the state, and the whole people.[25]

Some Party leaders, like the notably outspoken, reform-minded and influential Li Ruihuan who was a member of the Politburo Standing Commitee (the most powerful cabal at the top of all China's political structures) have stressed the need for a greater willingness to acknowledge mistakes. Four years before his death in 2003, he said:

> We had the courage to conclude that the Cultural Revolution was a disaster, so we should have the same courage to face and learn from other mistakes and harm that we have brought to the people in fifty years of rule. We should admit our mistakes to the people and to history.[26]

But even Li, with his reputation for plain speaking and humility (no princeling, he began his working life as a carpenter), was unwilling to comment on the mistakes of suppressing the Tiananmen uprising, the most egregious recent trauma of them all. In recent times Premier Wen

Jiabao appears to have learnt the wisdom of not appearing arrogant and indifferent to people's suffering and has issued many apologies without going through the rigmarole of Party resolutions. The 24-hour news cycle, even in China's controlled media, does not wait for the mighty Communist Party. The crash of the bullet train in Wenzhou in July 2011 led to a flurry of criticism on the internet. People were understandably furious when the railway authorities decided to end the search and rescue operation after six hours, and then proceeded to bury the train before any investigation had taken place into the cause of the crash. Visiting the scene of the crash Wen laid a bouquet of flowers at a makeshift memorial, met the families of victims and visited the injured in hospital. In ways that would have been utter anathema to the former generations of Communist leaders, he was using media management techniques now familiar to all political leaders and enhancing his reputation for empathy with ordinary people. He said:

> Our investigation has to answer to the people . . . There will be a thor-
> ough probe into the accident, including all relevant aspects from equip-
> ment failures, management problems to manufacturing issues . . . If
> corruption is found during the investigation, we will take it seriously and
> punish those responsible to the fullest extent of the law. The key to the
> handling of the accident is whether we let people know the truth . . .
> during the process, we should release information to the public timely
> and accurately.[27]

Whether there will in fact be a transparent inquiry and report into the crash remains extremely unlikely.[28] That would certainly be a decisive break with the past. Many commitments have been made to transparency during the years of the Hu-Wen leadership, but in practice little has been achieved. The causes and consequences of the scandal over the contamination of baby milk in 2008 remain unresolved. The true reasons why so many school buildings collapsed in the Sichuan earthquake while Party buildings and others remained standing have never been set out. In the immediate aftermath of disasters the effect of dissembling, half-truths and denials, however much empathy accompanies them, is to incense the populace. The internet, particularly the micro-blogging sphere, has given voice to that anger and greatly speeded up its dissemination and amplification.

The Party has yet to find ways of dealing with that phenomenon effectively. Turning off the internet, as they did for months at a time in Xinjiang after the riots in 2008, is not really a credible possibility in a business environment like Beijing or Shanghai. But once the immediate anger passes, the citizens affected are left with their sad memories while those more distant remain frustrated and confused, their cynicism fuelled. The absence of a legitimate open space for reflection and recollection means that the process of recovery from trauma of the sort that Judith Herman describes is impossible. People must bear the pain and their memories, attenuated and undermined as they are, with whatever fortitude they can muster. In an effort to sacramentalise their memories they build impromptu and humble memorials from stones in fields and on roadsides. Recovery from trauma across society as a whole is however off the agenda because of the huge threat that the public playing out of memory would bring to the leadership. Events after the death of Zhou Enlai and Hu Yaobang left the leaders in no doubt about that.

Art is, however, one notable space for memory. The artist Ai Weiwei is renowned internationally for his political criticisms of the Communist Party and his more overt acts of rebellion, but his best work is a subtle meditation on the destruction of memory and its close cousin, tradition. He has taken the destruction of tradition and the wilful indifference on the part of the authorities to remember as one of his key themes. It is not just that they seek to cover up things that go wrong, but they destroy tradition itself. In not wanting people to remember, memory itself – along with its healing power – is expunged. One of the conceptual artworks that first brought him to international attention was 'Dropping a Han Dynasty Urn', a series of photographs showing the artist doing just that, symbolising the casual destruction of the past. In other works he has dipped ancient pottery in industrial paint covering the pots with lurid, kitsch colours, another metaphor for the banal destructiveness of contemporary Chinese society. He filled Tate Modern's Turbine Hall in London with sunflower seeds made of porcelain, as a reminder that peasants in the famine caused by the Great Leap Forward had resorted to eating these seeds when nothing else was left. In 2009 he covered the Haus der Kunst in Munich with 9,000 children's backpacks. When Ai visited the scene of the Sichuan earthquake all that remained of the collapsed, substandard schools were these plastic rucksacks strewn around. On the rucksacks, which covered the Haus der Kunst in giant Chinese characters, was the sentence, 'She lived happily for seven years in this world', a quote from the mother of one of the dead schoolchildren. Ai Weiwei's call to arms is a call for memory, without which there will be madness:

> Feel sad! Suffer! Feel it in the recesses of your heart, in the unpeopled night, in all those places without light . . . The emptiness of collective memory, this distortion of public morality drives people crazy. Who exactly died in that even bigger earthquake of 30 years ago? Those wrongly accused in the political struggles of recent history, those labourers trapped in the coalmines, those denied medical treatment for their grave illnesses – who are they? What pain did they endure while alive, what grief do they provoke now dead . . . The true misfortune of the dead lies in the unconsciousness and apathy of the living, in the ignorance of the value of life by those who simply float through it.[29]

CHAPTER 13

The Power of the Powerless

The myth of infinite inscrutable Chinese fatalism is challenged by the spread of social problems like mental illness, drugs, prostitution and suicide. Stoical acceptance by Chinese people of political authoritarianism is another fallacy. People do not accept everything that happens in the name of reform as being for the best in the best of all possible worlds. They do not take dissatisfaction with their lot lying down. Instead, they protest continuously and despite the authorities' best efforts at suppression. The government does not seek to hide either the spreading of protests or their improved organisation. In 2005 the Public Security Minister Zhou Yongkang said: 'Mass incidents have become a major problem for social stability. The number is on the increase and their scale is constantly expanding . . . the trend towards greater organisation is clear.'[1]

According to China's police the number of 'mass incidents' (defined as more than 100 people involved) has surged tenfold in 12 years: from 8,700 in 1993 to approximately 10,000 in 1994; 32,000 in 1999; 58,000 in 2003; 74,000 in 2004; and 87,000 in 2005.[2] About 40 per cent take place in the countryside. The vast majority of protests are a reaction to the abuse of power by local cadres; ad hoc fees, taxes and levies on peasants and arbitrary land seizures by local authorities and companies.[3] The government noted in 2005 the emergence of a 'small number of individuals who organise, lead and instigate the masses'. Protest leaders initially shape individual grievances into collective claims. Then they recruit activists and mobilise the public, devising and orchestrating collective action. These new leaders spread the disputes to several villages or towns.[4] Although protest is still atomised, the Party leadership fears these protests could rapidly spread, assisted by cellphones and the internet, and amalgamate into a more coherent and potentially unstoppable resistance movement. Leaders and citizens have a mutual mistrust and fear.

The size of protests varies widely – from a dozen people to 60,000 farmers in Huaxi in Zhejiang province, who turned against government indifference to the pollution caused by two chemical plants.[5] Protests are often resolved peacefully, normally through cash payment to the protesters; which does nothing to resolve the root causes or rectify the failure of administration that is generally the trigger. Protests can turn violent and lead to fatalities, usually at the hands of the much-expanded People's Armed Police. In December 2005 for example, in Dongzhou, Guangdong the security forces opened fire, killing 20 rural people protesting at the construction of a power plant.[6]

The 'new' working classes of migrant workers in factories, even though most are young women living sequestered and surreal lives in dormitories, have staged walkouts, protesting against working or living conditions and job insecurity. The working conditions in factories, many run by firms that have benefited from overseas investment, are 'appalling: low pay, long working hours, despotic management and unsafe environments'.[7] One authoritative analysis by a Berkeley academic has noted three major types of workplace grievance that often lead to labour arbitration, litigation and protests: first, unpaid wages, illegal wage reductions or substandard wage rates; second, disciplinary violence, harassment or attacks on workers' dignity; and third, industrial injuries and lack of compensation.[8] But the proximate cause of a strike or a protest is generally an immediate griev-ance. The wider structural aspects of the problem come to the fore when the provocation proves intractable. Protests are often organised by locality or gender, as the workers are generally grouped with others from their region. Their overseer is usually from the same region, speaking the same dialect and judged better able to keep the factory workers in line because of local knowledge. There is also some evidence of hidden labour organ-isers, though these people are running great personal risks.

Many of the causes of the discontents are deeply embedded within the business models of the factories and therefore local managers can do little about them, although they are often in the front line against the workers' anger and sometimes violence. Not only directed at the management, violence is also used as a tool to oblige other workers to join the strike. Once a grievance turns into a strike, copycat strikes in nearby factories are common. The concerns are similar and the word spreads through regional and friendship networks. The workers' demands have also grown more radical. In the early 1990s workers could be bought off by increasing food allowances, improving accommodation, or by minimal increases in non-contractual payments. Over time demands for minimum wages and improved legal protection have spread. A Labour Contract Law was introduced in 2007 and the minimum wage was dramatically increased after a wave of strikes in 2004 and 2005. Strikers have also grown more willing to take their battles to the public streets, no longer confining their anger behind the factory gates.[9]

Even in service sectors like retail and catering protests about wages or managerial behaviour are common. Construction workers also often lay down their tools or paint big red characters on walls to protest about unpaid wages. According to a 2002 study of migrant workers in Beijing a quarter could not collect their pay or had it held back. Almost 40 per cent of these migrant workers found themselves penniless at one time or another. More than 60 per cent worked more than ten hours a day. A third of these worked more than 12 hours a day, and some worked more than 16 hours a day. More than 40 per cent of migrants have been sick at some time and none had received any help with healthcare costs.[10] No wonder they protest.

Nor have the 'old' working classes of the *danweis* and the state-owned enterprises taken wholesale industrial restructuring passively and without complaint. Since the 1990s, lay-offs have been accompanied by waves of protests. The protesters call in aid old Maoist slogans and traditions, particularly the 'iron rice bowl'. China's north-eastern rust belt, especially Liaoning province, is most troubled by large-scale labour unrest. The biggest protest since Tiananmen Square in 1989 occurred there in 2002, when between 20,000 and 50,000 laid-off workers from the Daqing oilfield demonstrated for over two weeks to demand better severance terms.[11] A further estimated 30,000 workers from ten other factories in nearby cities followed suit during the next fortnight. Many shouted old Maoist slogans, sang the Internationale, 'The East is Red' *(Dongfang hong)* and the national anthem. One of the protesters in the city of Liaoyang said, 'The older workers are not afraid. They see no difference between starving to death and being killed.'[12]

In Liaoyang 60 to 80 per cent of the workers are unemployed.[13] For this group, the current generation of Communist leaders has become as greedy and corrupt as the Nationalist leaders that Mao and the first generation of Communist leaders replaced. The future is far from bright and memory is playing nostalgic tricks: the worst excesses of the past have faded. Their eyes are sometimes not on a better tomorrow, but a mythical better yesterday.

People whose land or property has been confiscated and redeveloped at vast profit are also frequent protesters. During the Olympics two elderly women – who were among the 1.5 million Beijing residents whose homes disappeared to make way for Olympics buildings – applied five times for permission to protest in one of the tightly controlled, officially designated protest areas. They were threatened with a year of 're-education through labour' if they did not follow government orders.[14] Out of 77 applications to protest, 74 were 'withdrawn', two were suspended and one was vetoed as contrary to the laws of China.[15]

Rural communities are another source of disquiet. There are three common types of grievance that result in protest. First, compensation for those farmers who lose their land to urban development is often inadequate, not paid at all, not paid in full or paid only after much delay and complaint. Second, unfair and arbitrary taxation is levied on the farmers to support a burgeoning, self-serving local bureaucracy and its ever more comfortable lifestyle. Beijing has made several pronouncements that the tax burden on peasants should be reduced, but proportionately it remains much higher than the taxes paid by city dwellers.[16] This does not include the many illegal ways of extorting money that local Party cadres visit on local people for their own benefit. Failing to pay these simply results in you and your family being denied the minimal public services available by way of retribution. Third is the bullying and corruption of local officials, who not only extort money and often live the high life off the backs of the peasants but also use bullying and violence against the recalcritant payers or the perceived troublemakers.

Although news is routinely suppressed, it is widely suspected there have been many violent confrontations – some involving fatal shootings by police or security forces. Typically, a dispute flares up locally and one of the better-educated members of the local community will seek to master the rules and take on the authorities. That person does not generally get very far, because most protests are against the behaviour of the people who are enforcing the rules! Instead, the instinct of the local officials, once complaints are to hand, is either to buy off the complainants with a payment or a gift of a television or some other such trivia, or to seek ways to cover up the complaint and, most important, to prevent it coming to the notice of their superiors. A tenacious group of local people with a knowledgeable and determined spokesperson can seek to pursue their grievance up the many levels of the hierarchy. This is a 'long road'. Even if their complaint reaches the middle ranks, the response is likely to be that middle-ranking officials tell the junior officials whose behaviour is the source of complaint that they must work harder to suppress – not redress – the complaints and the protests. Infrequently, as a result of journalistic investigations reported privately to senior cadres, action is taken against the offending group, but the action is tokenistic and rarely rounds up all the culprits. Because this process is so frustrating and there are few alternative ways for protesters to get their voices heard, at any stage in this long process tempers can flare and protests can gather force and run out of control.[17]

One tenacious couple was not to be thwarted and harnessed the power of the international media to their cause, a rare event indeed. Pictures of this protest travelled around the world in March and April 2007. This couple in Chongqing had resolutely refused to leave their home and accept the inadequate compensation. They remained even after the bulldozers arrived, defying the developers to demolish the house with them in it. The developers excavated all around the house leaving it standing on a small, high plateau roughly the dimensions of the house. This image of the 'nail house' appeared in newspapers across the globe. The developers had blinked and not demolished. The battle of brinkmanship was won by the couple who owned the house. They got their increased compensation, but that has not led to increased levels of compensation for others. Their experience has contributed to an already growing appetite for protest, hold-outs and sit-ins. As Bill Emmott observes, 'the spirit of resistance – and successful negotiation – shown by the Chongqing couple was evidently inspiring'.[18]

The new middle-class suburbs can also be awakened from their somnolent political lethargy. In January 2008, for example, the local authorities in Shanghai announced plans to extend the city's maglev line (ultra-high-speed trains that use magnetic forces to levitate the train off the railway lines, increasing the speed to an astonishing 430 kilometres per hour). Organisers started resistance on the internet and thousands of suburban residents gathered in the centre of Shanghai's People's Square, for a *sanbu*, a 'walk' since protest marches are illegal. Another group went for a spontaneous 'shop' on the city's main retail streets shouting anti-maglev slogans. These protests had been organised using text messages and YouTube and copied similar protests in Xiamen, which had ended plans to build a chemical factory.[19]

Zheng Enchong, a Shanghai lawyer, took up many residents' complaints and was arrested and re-arrested many time for his troubles. Eventually in 2007 he wrote an open letter to Hu Jintao denouncing Shanghai's political leaders:

> People have been driven from one corner to another corner of the city. Many among us also have to endure illegal surveillance, home searches, forced repatriation, detention, re-education through labour, being locked in psychiatric asylums, phone-tapping, harassment and other ways of suppression.[20]

Environmental protests are also on the rise. According to China's top environmental official, Zhou Shengxian, in 2005 there were 51,000 pollution-related protests, in some of which more than 10,000 people participated.[21] In November 2009 more than a thousand well-to-do people protested outside Guangzhou's municipal offices against the creation of a giant incinerator for burning rubbish. There had been similar protests in Chengdu in 2008 against an ethylene plant, but the Guangzhou protest was different first, because the middle-class residents in an expensive neighbourhood started the protests and second, because Twitter and social media sites were used to organise them.[22] The government likes to think they have banned social networking websites, but people have found ways round these bans, such as using proxy servers.

Another widely held, abiding myth, along with the fallacy of Chinese stoicism, asserts that Chinese culture is a uniform, unbroken tradition going back 5,000 years. For all that time the Chinese way of thinking and living is said to have reigned serenely unchallenged over the fixed territory of the Middle Kingdom. Contrary to this view Chinese history has in fact been as convulsive as that of any other region of the world, inevitably bringing about large shifts in culture and identity. Borders have changed. Foreign invaders have taken charge, becoming warlords in the countryside and emperors in the capital. Empires have come and gone with ruling dynasties from Mongolia and Manchuria. The last Imperial dynasty, the Qing, with their Manchu origins went to great pains to distinguish between the elite Manchus from the north and ethnic Han Chinese, including making Han men wear a long thin plait, the *queue*. Buddhist religious influences have been absorbed from India and Tibet. Confucius has held sway in Korea and Japan as in China. The idea that democracy is not a Confucian or Chinese tradition is belied by South Korea's and Taiwan's peaceful shifts to democratic rule brought about by people's protests. Religions have come and gone. A short survey of Chinese poetry or porcelain will quickly reveal that many influences and traditions have waxed and waned.

Ethnic diversity is the legacy of that history, far greater than conventional wisdom or the authorities allow. After the Communists took power some 400 minorities answered an invitation to identify themselves, rather more than the authorities had bargained for or intended to tolerate, so social scientists whittled this down to about 50. Ever since, the official wisdom has been that China contains around 50 ethnicities, with the Han Chinese an overwhelming majority.[23] Contrary to that neat official version ethnic and cultural diversity is evident everywhere. People's physiognomy and stature are visibly different, reflecting, for example, Manchu, Mongolian or Tibetan heritage. One of the joys of Chinese cuisine remains its regional diversity. Travellers encounter great varieties of dialect, even though standard Mandarin has been vigorously imposed through the education system. Many so-called regional dialects are in fact different languages, incomprehensible to the ears of people living less than a hundred kilometres apart. Notwithstanding all the kitsch displays of ethnic harmony in Tiananmen Square and during the opening ceremony of the 2008 Olympics, these local, regional and ethnic identities are strengthening at the expense of the nationally imposed narrative, nowhere more so than in Taiwan, where since the 1990s rock singers have taken to singing in Taiwanese and incorporating traditional Taiwanese instruments.[24]

Because China has historically had such difficulties in maintaining its borders, Mao never had any doubt that ethnic nationalism or federal structures (like those in the Soviet Union) were off the agenda. The borders and the territory have been successfully defended by the Communists, unlike previous dynasties, but ethnic tension and suppression in Tibet, Xinjiang and Mongolia has been the result. Although Tibetan Buddhists believe they are the spiritual teachers of Chinese emperors in a priest–patron relationship, not their colonised vassals, the Chinese authorities are in no doubt as to who is in charge.[25]

Buddhist monasteries in Tibet are tightly controlled. The incarnation of the next Dalai Lama is certain to foment a dispute between Beijing and the Tibetan religious leaders trusted by the people. During the appointment of the last Panchen Lama in 1995 the Chinese authorities were sufficiently agitated to take the Dalai Lama's choice of Panchen Lama into custody, where he has remained. The government restricts the number of monks, and official approvals are required at every turn.

In April 2008 a group of 500 monks from Drepung monastery called for the release of their imprisoned colleagues and reductions of religious constraints. A few days later the monks of Ramoche temple marched through Lhasa, the Tibetan capital. The police tried to stop them, provoking laypeople to attack the police. The protests turned to riots and, to the unprecedented horror of the authorities, Tibetans vented their anger on Han Chinese inhabitants of Lhasa, many relatively recent incomers. Shops were smashed up and set on fire and 18 Han Chinese people are reported to have died. Protests and riots began to break out in the Tibetan parts of China, in the monasteries and villages of Kham and Amdo. Some turned violent. The protesters in some places occupied official buildings and took down the Chinese flag, replacing it with the Tibetan flag.[26] In Sichuan, police fired at a crowd after the rioters had burned down public buildings, including a police station, and destroyed police cars and other vehicles. Police officers had even been stabbed with swords and protesters had tried to wrest their firearms from them. The internal security services and the army were soon deployed to bring the spreading chaos under control. Foreign journalists were locked out of Tibet and the other restive regions. International television coverage was censored.

I was in China during the protests led by monks in the spring of 2008. International television news channels went blank for hours and Chinese state TV transmitted long broadcasts of official statements led by Wen Jiabao criticising and cursing the rebels, instantaneously shedding his carefully cultivated avuncular image. Token Tibetans were paraded on TV criticising the protesters and supporting the government. The Dalai Lama said afterwards that more than 400 Tibetans had been killed and thousands imprisoned. Protests, including self-immolation, have continued ever since.

In Xinjiang, the Turkic Uighurs face west and do not relate to Han culture. They were inspired by Tibetan protests to mount protests of their own, provoking a heavy-handed response from the authorities. On 5 July 2009 young Uighurs rioted in Urumqi, the regional capital, after the police blocked off a protest about the death of two Uighurs in a factory brawl in Guangdong. As in Tibet during 2008, the rioters attacked Han Chinese people. Two days after the riot, thousands of Han gathered to carry out revenge attacks. The riot police kept the mob away from the Uighur quarter of the city, preventing another bloodbath. Some Uighurs were seriously beaten, and some may have been killed, that day. This orgy of violence left nearly 200 dead and more than 1,600 injured.[27] Tensions continue to run high and sporadic protests turn violent regularly in Urumqi. The Beijing authorities have publicly aired suspicions about Islamic fundamentalists in Xinjiang in order to garner international and domestic support for the repression. Mongolians similarly seek to maintain their separate identity, having suffered terrible repression during the Cultural Revolution. The migration of millions of Han settlers to these areas has evidently only increased tension. The incomers prosper, traducing traditional ways of life, inevitably angering the locals.

Religion too is a resurgent and recalcitrant marker of diverse identities, with the powerful psychological grip of being a badge of resistance. The government has, within strict limits, become less hostile to religious traditions and old-fashioned ways of thinking and behaving. The state recognises five official religions: Buddhism, Daoism, Islam, Catholicism and Protestantism. Other faiths are still illegal. Religious organisations must register with state-sanctioned patriotic religious associations supervised by the State Administration for Religious Affairs. Groups which fail to affiliate are denied legal protection. Christian worship requires official permission. I know from my own experience that meetings about religious affairs will often take place at the local Party headquarters. Party officials take the lead in discussion and negotiations. Religious leaders are often passive bystanders in debates about their own role and future. Despite all these restrictions, according to the Council for Foreign Relations in the USA, 31.4 per cent of adults are religious, three times the government estimate. In 2007, two professors of East China Normal University polled 4,500 people about their religious beliefs. Their findings showed that the five official religions account for 67.4 per cent of religious adherents, leaving nearly a third outside the recognised groupings.[28]

Many of the unregistered believers were said to worship legendary figures like the Dragon King or God of Fortune. Peter Hessler reported in *Country Driving* that the wife of the family he had befriended in the village of Sancha, outside Beijing and near the Great Wall, had rekindled her beliefs in traditional animistic spirituality, of the sort that long predates Buddhism, Communism, Falun Gong and all contemporary religious manifestations. The family ran a canteen in which she cooked the food, an activity that filled her with guilt. Fish and chicken can turn into hungry ghosts too:

> If I have to kill a fish or a chicken I pray for them. They're innocent; they had a good life, but I killed them. So I pray for their souls to be released from purgatory. If I don't pray for them to be released, then I'm afraid they will come back to punish me.

The villagers spoke of snake spirits, fox spirits, rabbit spirits and weasel spirits that can inhabit your home and turn it good or bad. Some people are believed to have the gift of understanding; they are clairvoyants, seers (*mingbairen*). A famous clairvoyant used to live in the village of Sancha and attracted many devotees, keen to gain his elucidation of the animal spirits that affected their well-being. By holding their wrist and feeling their pulse he could apparently speak in detail about the spirits within. He conducted complex rituals, which were observed devoutly by the followers. The Cultural Revolution put paid to all that. But the times have turned more tolerant and the clairvoyants have reappeared in force above ground, advising people on the particular animal spirit that is affecting them and recommending shrines to dispel the ill effects.[29]

Among the official religions about 20 million Muslims are members of ten predominantly Muslim ethnic groups. The largest is the Hui, an ethnic group closely related to the majority Han, but religiously distinct. Ranking after the Hui in numbers are the Uighurs, who live primarily in Xinjiang. There are also five million Tibetan Buddhists, not just in Tibet but in parts of Sichuan, Qinghai, Gansu and Yunnan provinces in the west of China.[30] The traditional cultural heartland of Tibetan Buddhism extends beyond Tibet's contemporary boundaries.

Since the 1980s Christianity has grown significantly throughout China but many choose not to register with the state, because the state-sanctioned form of Christianity is considered too liberal by many socially conservative country people. Some Catholics practise off the record because the state forbids them from pledging allegiance to any foreign figure, including the Pope. The government has a long-running dispute with the Vatican about who has the final authority to appoint Roman Catholic bishops. An uneasy balance had been struck whereby the government would submit its chosen candidates for papal approval, but Chinese authorities broke this pattern with the appointment of Guo Jincai as a bishop in Chengde in 2010.[31] The number of people who can join each church is limited, so some Christians who want to join a state-sanctioned church find they are excluded simply on grounds of numbers, regardless of beliefs. The Pew Research Centre reports that between 50 and 70 million people practise Christianity in unregistered groups. Many hold services in 'house churches', private religious forums in their own homes.[32] One respondent to the Wish Tree was keen to talk about her Christian faith, very different to traditional Chinese ways of thinking about life after death: 'I have faith in Jesus. [My greatest worry is to] go against the will and plans of God. [I wish] to be together with God when I am dead.' Although written without subversion in mind, this response highlights Party concerns about religion. A belief in a higher power and the promise of an eternal afterlife can endow people with a separate moral code used to judge actions of the Party and, in some cases, the inner strength to actively defy the power of the Party.

Arbitrary denial of permission and suppression of religious groups are both routine and unpredictable; a particularly difficult combination.

According to a report from the China Aid Association, in at least 60 cases in 2007 officials harassed house churches, resulting in 788 arrests and 693 detentions.

On New Year's Day 2007 in an unnecessary demonstration of over-whelming force 100 police broke up a meeting of 50 Christians being held in the little-used auditorium of the Hebei Party School in Baoding. The vice-principal of the Party School and Professor of Philosophy Geng Sude, who had organised the meeting, was fired and stripped of her Party membership; a perplexing over-reaction in her view. She thought she was doing the right thing:

> It never occurred to me that the authorities would regard this seriously. I did not break the law. I did not say anything anti-government. The Bible study session was aimed at helping to build a harmonious society, the Party should ease not create contradictions. Class struggle is no longer the Party culture – the Party should be more forgiving and tolerant.[33]

In all innocence she had put her finger on one of the Party's biggest difficulties. Class struggle may no longer be the Party's culture, but what is? The 'harmonious society' is vague and technocratic, certainly not likely to grip people's hearts, minds and imagination. In any case, the harmonious society is a fake, as she found out. Authoritarianism is still the name of the game. John Gray has an explanation for this religious resurgence, which expands on Professor Geng's point: 'the secular ideologies of the past century, such as communism and belief in the free market, have become museum pieces. There are few who now believe in any project of political salvation, and partly for this reason religion has revived.'[34] Nowhere is this truer than China because of the fervour with which the former ideology of Mao's statism was prosecuted and, then, the bewildering speed with which it has been abandoned for 'socialism with Chinese characteristics' and the 'harmonious society'.

The most determined religious suppression has been reserved for Falun Gong. During the 1980s a curious set of cults and beliefs began to grow up, often with the support and blessing of senior Communist officials, including Qian Xuesen, the father of the Chinese atom bomb. The founder of Falun

Gong, Li Hongzhi, taught that the world was divided into three levels. The top level is the gatekeeper, Li Hongzhi himself. The second level belongs to spirits of unusual virtue – the Christian God, Buddha and so on. Ordinary people live at the third level. The belief system has five sets of meditation exercises and seeks to develop practitioners' heart and character according to the principles of truthfulness, compassion and forbearance. The roots of these beliefs can be traced to a much older tradition of 'cultivation practice', *qigong*, which is not suppressed by the authorities. The teachings of Li Hongzhi claim to unite science with *qigong*, to promote moral renewal and, most incomprehensibly to a non-believer, endow followers with supernatural powers in their own lifetime. Established as recently as the 1990s Falun Gong was estimated by the government to have around 100 million followers in China by 1999.[35]

A Falun-Gong-inspired protest in April 1999 spooked the authorities and they concluded that the movement must be suppressed at all costs. Ten thousand (some say 15,000) Falun Gong members protested peacefully outside Zhongnanhai in Beijing. One Sunday morning, as if from nowhere, Falun Gong followers surrounded the high red walls. They sat down on newspapers, praying and reading. They were protesting against beatings of followers in Tianjin. After 12 hours, as quickly and quietly as they had gathered, they dispersed and disappeared. The government leaders, as ever, were paralysed by indecision and division. The forthright and popular Premier Zhu Rongji reportedly went out to meet the demonstrators and told them Falun Gong would not be banned. President Jiang Zemin took a much more hostile view. Following the protest he arranged for Falun Gong to be declared an illegal cult and banned. He wanted Interpol to arrest Li Hongzhi in New York. Interpol did not share the view that the Supreme Being was an international criminal and a threat to public security. They took no action.

Falun Gong followers were undeterred. They staged surprise demonstrations, all entirely peaceful, repeatedly in Tiananmen Square. When the riot police came to clear and arrest them they submitted passively and were taken away. Thousands have been detained; some died, but many of those who survived detention simply returned to the square upon being released. Then, to the utter consternation of the authorities, they took to setting themselves alight in Tiananmen Square (a tactic now also deployed by Tibetan Buddhist protestors) to flee once and for all this mortal coil. 'One man sat on the ground, doused himself in gasoline and set himself on fire. Four women walked along their bodies aflame, holding their hands up in a classic Falun Gong meditation pose.'[36] Security forces 'saved' four of the protesters. One of the women died. The Chinese authorities, as in the Middle East, had discovered that those who would die for their beliefs are not readily intimidated. Whether Falun Gong had – or still has – political ambitions is a matter of endless speculation.

One winter evening, on a casual stroll with friends through Tiananmen Square, I got a sense of the authorities' sensitivity to Falun Gong. The merest hint of one of Falun Gong's spontaneous peaceful protests brought about a complete evacuation and lockdown of the enormous square, reputed to be big enough for a million people. The few gates in the low perimeter fence and the subway entrances were closed. Everyone in the vast square was expelled. An eerie and empty silence instantly descended with an unconcealed air of menace.

The rise of millenarian cults as a critical response to rapid social change is not new or unique to China. Marc Bloch has noted that this tradition is both continuous and deeply rooted, even though the cults may seem dormant or even extinct to historians and anthropologists. Writing about 'peasants' revolts' in France from 821 through to the revolution in 1789, he says:

> The forms these rebellions took (and they were nearly always the same) were . . . traditional: mystical fantasies; a powerful preoccupation with the primitive egalitarianism of the Gospels, which took hold of humble minds well before the Reformation.[37]

The anthropologist James C. Scott notes similar phenomena in Buddhist and Islamic regions of South East Asia as well as in the largely Christian Philippines: 'It goes without saying that these religious traditions in South East Asia have also formed the ideological basis for countless rebellions.'[38] He goes on to note:

> The paradox of millennial beliefs is of course that they typically envision the most radical change in the distribution of power, status and wealth – not to mention human nature – while at the same time being very much

leadership-centred. At the centre of virtually all such movements is a leader, a prophet, a just king, a saviour who will set things right.[39]

China has one of the richest traditions of religious insurgencies of any culture in history. The two most famous are the reign of the Taiping and the Boxer uprising.

Hong Xiuquan was the fourth of five children from a hard-working rural family. His parents made great sacrifices for their son to succeed in the examinations system and win a place in the local elite. But the degree exams defeated him. After a third examination failure in 1837 a strange dream showed him how to slay evil spirits and convinced him he was the younger son of Jesus Christ. He began to preach his message, baptise converts and destroy Confucian and ancestral shrines. He established his base in remote Guangxi. His movement spread rapidly, attracting 10,000 followers by 1849. Emboldened, Hong was now committed to his variant of Christian religion and, audaciously, the destruction of the Manchus who led the Qing dynasty. His powerful rhetoric, falling on fertile ground of social discontent, an ineffective Imperial power and warring local gangs and militias, drew an ever-growing following and the movement turned into a paramilitary force that could enforce instructions against corruption, sensuality and opium taking. All communal money was pooled and kept in a central treasury and the men cut off their *queues*, the long plaits that Manchu leaders insisted on as a distinguishing mark of Han heritage.

In December 1850 Qing forces sent to deal with this new threat were soundly defeated and their Manchu commander killed. Emboldened once more, Hong declared himself Heavenly King of *Taiping Tianguo*, 'Heavenly Kingdom of Great Peace'. By 1851 his forces had captured the city of Yongan and had more than 60,000 followers and over time they advanced to Nanjing, bloodily evicted the Manchus, and ruled their heavenly kingdom for 11 years, instituting an ascetic lifestyle, land reform, shared finances, military discipline and utopian notions of governance. In July 1864, after Hong's death, Qing forces finally got the better of the Taiping in Nanjing. The leader of the Qing forces, Zeng Guofan, noted their unflagging commitment. 'Not one of the 100,000 rebels in Nanjing surrendered themselves when the city was taken but in many cases gathered together and burned themselves and passed away without repentance. Such a formidable band of rebels has been rarely known from ancient times to the present.'[40] Perhaps they were an inspiration to Falun Gong devotees.

Later on the Dowager Empress Cixi aided and abetted the Boxer Rebellion against the foreign legations stationed all over China at the end of the nineteenth century. The Boxers were a sect that subscribed to a range of exotic, superstitious beliefs about destructive magic powers held by foreigners. They emerged in 1898 after the Catholic Church had sought to suppress their mix of entrenched rural beliefs and traditions, some based on operatic dramas performed at country fairs featuring ancient gods and heroes, boxing and martial arts. Charms were written on pieces of cloth and, if he repeated them for three nights, the believer could withstand swords – and even firearms if the chanting and the concentration had been strong enough. Their superstitions and beliefs were combined with a rigorous moral code. Their attacks on foreign legations, in which hundreds of foreigners died in fairly bloodthirsty ways, were stopped when foreign troops eventually arrived. Twenty thousand foreign troops were sent to quell a rebellion in which 230 foreigners had died.

Spiritual belief in China is rooted in tradition and ritual, not religious authority. Because of this commitment to ritual and the way things are done through the life cycle rather than a belief in a single godhead, a sacred text or deference to a specific human religious authority, spirituality and religious belief can be experienced as a powerful antidote to political authoritarianism. It is another more fluid, inclusive way of seeing the world which seems to take in reactions and insights that the rigidities of political orthodoxies and Party slogans inevitably exclude. The latter always empha-sise order and control. This unstructured approach makes it relatively easier to evolve new spiritual commitments, either mutated and absorbed from other religions or simply devised for oneself. The limitations on accepting new thoughts and ideas are the extent to which they fit into the 'practice or rituals' of religion and the social structures these practices helped to sponsor.[41] Confucian philosophy makes clear that moral and spiritual beliefs are intertwined with the rituals of practice as well as with family and social structures. They all come together in the great harmony. Within this epistemology all sorts of new spiritual beliefs can take root and grow in an amorphous, organic way without replacing their antecedents as a rapidly changing society continues to throw up new challenges to the traditional rituals and the accepted social hierarchies. Some sort of sense, however mystical or seemingly irrational, must be made of change.

As well as all the reasons for and types of protests adumbrated here, there are countless everyday forms of resistance that are not conceived as group solidarity or shared identity, much less building blocks in larger movements for political change: foot-dragging, malingering, dishonesty, pilfering, cheating, non-compliance, minimal compliance, the pretence of compliance, silent disobedience, absenteeism, slander, sabotage, arson and many others beside can all be deployed to undermine unwanted, unaccepted authority. The anthropologist James C. Scott notes that these forms of resistance are tremendous irritants to the powerful in part because of their lack of structure. Suppression needs something to get hold of. These methods on the other hand, 'require little or no co-ordination or planning; they make use of implicit understandings and informal networks; they often represent a form of individual self-help, they typically avoid any direct symbolic confrontation with authority.'[42] Regardless of China's political future these forms of resistance will be unending. The suppression of memory, combined with the contests of the present between the leaders and the led, guarantees continuing argument about history, symbols, meaning and identity.

The responses to the Wish Tree contained unvarnished criticism of government policy and local administrative practice expressed in the main in terms of the negative effects on the individual. These answers can themselves be seen as an act of resistance, even rebellion. Given the open-ended nature of the questions, people could have given bland and evasive responses if they were frightened of the official response or they could have chosen to write exclusively about private matters. They chose not to do either and that choice was made openly in the presence not just of officialdom, but of foreigners. This was not an act of rebellion designed to lead anywhere specific or linked to any political plan, but such acts are not performed with rebellion in mind. People take the opportunities presented to make their voices heard. The Wish Tree responses conform to the archetype of the 'weapons of the weak', as described by James C. Scott.

The complaints that can turn into protests are rooted firmly in homely, practical concerns with direct, immediate consequences. The ambitions are not abstract notions of progress and the enemies are not historical forces. The resisters defend traditional values *because* they are traditional and familiar. They use their familiar norms of behaviour and community relations as the crucible for anger and resistance. Ordinary people can often seem conservative and resistant to change, as they seek to use what they know to resist what seems to be unwelcome deleterious change. The tried and tested techniques are disinterred and activated once more. The goals are generally modest: reversing their losses and achieving incremental improvements in the day-to-day conditions of their lives. The methods deployed are not hot-headed or foolhardy. They are prudent and realistic. Flight, if practicable, is a rational option for resistance. If that is closed off, a vast vista of tiny possibilities, both symbolic and practical, can be deployed with infinite and adept creativity to leave no doubt that their answer to whatever has happened to them is no.[43]

The Party authorities can never wholly win out over this. Their ideological and propaganda tools are undermined every day by a thousand spontaneous events, both trivial and significant, that fatally contradict the official line and never fool those who experience them. Ideologies, however sophisticated in their analysis and careful in their preparation, are inevitably simplified in the handing down and retelling. In those simplifications, the limitations are revealed. All around are contradictions and paradoxes which fall outside the ideological propaganda. Each one undermines the credibility of imposed orthodoxy and the authorities that promote it and creates a little store of resentment readily turned, in anger, to resistance. Part of that practical awareness among ordinary people is the knowledge that some unwelcome, unjust restraints or coercions will just have to be tolerated, because there is no ready alternative to hand, but toleration is not acceptance; it is not victory for the authorities.[44]

These machinations of the angry and dispossessed are often disguised in respectful but misleading supplications and petitions. However, the officials accused of corruption or maladministration had better remain on the lookout; revenge is best served cold. Worse still, the faraway big bosses may get to hear of the misdemeanours of the local officials. Obloquy from above will descend to take its unwelcome place alongside detestation from below. Power corrupts, but the corrupted, once corrupted, can look forward to a lifetime spent nervously looking above their heads and over their shoulders. The current generation of national Chinese leaders are past masters at blaming all government failures on local – not national – officials. Highly structured, inflexible, formal, hierarchical channels seek to block the flow of dissident or dissonant counter-currents, keeping everyone on the safe, straight and narrow. In Communist China checks and balances (such as an independent legal system, a free media, civil society or unrestricted access to the internet) are disdained and the doctrine of separation of powers, so dear to Western liberal political thinkers, is simply political heresy. But keeping everyone in line, whatever the authorities say or like to think, is of course impossible. Dissent, dispute and disappointment must find a channel. The more rigid a society, the more gossip, intrigue and conspiracy it inevitably creates. These are all forms of resistance, but not revolution. They are practical not apocalyptic, but they are resistance nonetheless.

CHAPTER 14

Plutocrats in the Leviathan

The Chinese elite – political, business and military – ignore all the subtleties of symbolism and meaning so richly encountered by ordinary people. The leaders have a vision of modernity that places themselves at the centre, legitimating despotism as well as market reforms. Financial capital is valued over natural wealth, traditions or community and family life. They do, however, bow to one tradition: a self-serving one. In line with ancient Chinese thought leaders take to themselves a special moral and cleansing role.[1] They promulgate the notion of transition and benign progress and advocate themselves as benign, wise guides. If everything is in transition all contemporary problems, however trying, are removable over time. No problem is perceived as permanent. The Party seeks to build hope on these intellectually shaky foundations, knowing that its old Marxist-Leninist rhetoric, with its combination of bellicosity and idealism, rings entirely hollow and unconvincing. Within this idea of transition there is no acknowledgement that gross inequality, lack of social protection and rapid environmental degradation may, in fact, be unavoidable parts of the contemporary condition in a market society. The history of economic reform since the 1980s shows that these problems will not be eradicated any time soon; probably never. The rise of modernity has caused the decline of tradition and community and the great harmony has been once more postponed indefinitely.

Though foreseen and regretted by traditional Chinese thinkers, this seems to be inevitable. Modernity, as promoted in consumer societies, can never be contained in neat, determinist, unemotive officially sponsored certainties of 'development' and 'progress'.[2] Other versions of modernity, as essential as science and capital, inexorably start to infect everyday ways of living, social relations and public attitudes. Modernity is perceived as 'Western' culture but it is as much the manifestation of a rebel spirit in the young, who seek something simpler and more authentic and reject the barnacles of habit that have attached themselves to social relations at the hands of tradition or authority which no longer seem relevant. So modernity makes other counter-cultural, unofficial ways of thinking popular. 'Modernism, the avant-garde, decadence, kitsch and post-modernism',[3] complete with irony, scepticism and detachment, acquire their advocates in the search for modernity. All of those subaltern ways of thinking have taken hold in contemporary Chinese culture regardless of the Communist dead hand. Beijing, Shanghai and Shenzhen with their evident power and money have also acquired a heady, racy quality that surprises and often impresses many first-time visitors. With images of the Soviet Union and Mao's China in their mind's eye foreigners expect something more down at heel and dour. In China modernity has created all sorts of counter-currents and instabilities which run against the officially sponsored positivist narrative of moving smoothly towards becoming a moderately well off society.

But some certainties remain. None of these moves towards greater economic and social freedom should be taken as diminishing the Party leadership's commitment to authoritarianism, with the Party itself overarching all other institutions. Despite the introduction of village-level elections, which are rarely contested and almost never won by opposition candidates, serious moves towards democracy are out of the question. Although the Party's appetite to control information has not been diminished, the Chinese media scene is no longer simply a state-controlled propaganda machine. Commercialisation, globalisation, technology, public sophistication and cynicism have combined to multiply the sources of information open to people and to complicate the task of controlling their access. Nevertheless, censorship is ubiquitous and journalists remain wary, knowing that some of their colleagues have been arrested and imprisoned. They know that departing too openly and critically from the Party line may lead to their arrest but is more likely simply to mean that the article will be cut by the censors, who are embedded in media outlets reading everything before publication. So they stick to accepted codes, deploying irony, sarcasm and understatement as ways of evading the literalism of censors.

Some criticism is officially encouraged, such as critical comment on the failings of local officials, the hegemonic ambitions of the United States, Japan's heartless contempt for China's suffering during the Second World War, or the deceitful, manipulative behaviour of the 'Dalai-clique'. But these criticisms, assisted by the spreading capacity of the internet, can all too easily run out of control. Criticism of local officials, for example over the collapse of school buildings in the Sichuan earthquake, turned to criticism of the Party when commentators started to note that Party buildings proved the most robust in the face of the earthquake or when anti-Japanese feelings threatened to turn into rabid nationalistic fervour.

In 2005 anti-Japanese protests grew over several weeks, after Japan allowed schools to use a textbook allegedly 'whitewashing' its role in the Second World War. The protests, once they started to get out of hand, were officially discouraged and curtailed with detentions.[4] Anti-Japanese sentiments were again stirred in 2010 following a collision between a Japanese coastguard boat and a Chinese fishing boat. The government quickly brought a strong police presence into cities around the country to stop protests early. Many commentators suggested that the strength of nationalist rhetoric during the 2005 protests left the leadership unable to stomach a second round.[5]

These episodes highlight the complicated relationship the Party has with nationalist sentiment. It is often encouraged, and manipulated, now that Marxism-Leninism looks unconvincing as a cohesive force, but public emotion can quickly turn it into a tiger, with the Party left clinging helplessly to its tail. Party leaders are hyper-sensitive to the role that the press might play should things turn ugly. Many senior journalists working for state-owned outlets, like the *People's Daily*, are themselves ideologues of some standing with strong and sometimes threatening views on the Party's shortcomings. They too must be watched carefully: 'The daily shadow boxing among propaganda authorities, media producers, public consumers and commercial interests is intense in China today.'[6]

The internet has become a new battleground between Party control and citizens' free expression. Nothing symbolises the Communist Party's contemporary dilemma better than the technological explosion created by the web and its offshoot activities and mindsets. Economists can plainly see the potential of the internet for value and wealth creation; after all, it was technology like this that partly saved the US economy from the last 'Asian invasion' in the 1970s by Japanese and Korean companies. They know also that the full benefits of globalised capital are simply not available to countries which haven't built their house close to the information superhighway where capital markets now reside. But political rather than economic analyses suggest that the internet's capacity to destroy space and time as barriers to information transfer are unprecedented. In their time sociologists and economists may have recorded the capacity of telephones, cars and aeroplanes to shorten distance and delay, but the instantaneous capacities of the internet and the network society it has spawned are, in social as well as scientific terms, a quantum leap. Party leaders are constantly reminded of the importance of instantaneous news management. Disturbances in Tibet, environmental or food safety scares, news of train crashes – failure to take charge of the communication of these events simply means that all kinds of stories get out, some of them inevitably politically subversive to a regime so unsure of its own legitimacy. Party leaders enjoin officials to use the internet for their own purposes, while controlling its capacity to spread free information. As Hu Jintao has said, 'Whether we can cope with the internet is a matter that affects the development of socialist culture, the security of information and the stability of the state'.[7] The results of these contradictory wishes to gain access to technological innovation and simultaneously control what it is used for have so far proved almost incompatible. Countless political and administrative bodies, technological word and image filtering tools and human monitors are charged with controlling internet content and identifying and punishing subversive online influences. Internet service providers are held responsible for the behaviour of their customers, leaving businesses with little choice but to proactively censor material being published, doing the authorities' work for them.

Efforts to build the 'Great Firewall', which is intended to give the authorities absolute control over what citizens can see and read on the internet, have prevented ordinary people from accessing information about Tibet or Taiwan, for example, but the 'Great Firewall' has also been circumvented by proxy servers and other technological devices. Political blogs, bulletin boards, instant messaging and microbloggers can attract a vast audience before they are closed down. There were 420 million internet users in China by June 2010, according to the government's network information centre.[8] They are disproportionately young, well-educated and urban. The leadership's sensitivity to information on the web is not confined to overt political challenges. It extends to information about senior officials that is deemed sensitive, including, for example, their expensive watches. After the train crash in Wenzhou in July 2011 Daniel Wu, a watch buff, noticed in a news photograph that the Railways Minister, Sheng Guangzu, appeared to be wearing a Rolex Oyster Perpetual, which retails for *RMB*70,000. A simple web search on pictures of Sheng revealed that the Minister possessed many expensive watches. Mr Wu is knowledgeable enough to be able to tell whether the watches are genuine or fake. He started writing about high-ups' expensive watches on his blog devoted entirely to watches. At first the offending posts were removed but before long the whole blog was removed by censors; subversion is perceived in unlikely corners of cyberspace.[9]

In 2011, the internet carried calls for a Jasmine Revolution to follow the example of the Arab Spring. The authorities were spooked and fielded a blanket police presence in Beijing and Shanghai. No protesters appeared.[10] Contemporary dissidents have learnt from one of Mao's most important tutorials in the art of guerrilla war: never appear when or where the enemy is expecting you. The netizens are fighting a cyber-guerrilla war with information both as the ammunition and the prize. The weapons of resistance being deployed against the vast but uncertain power of official censorship are characteristic of the 'weapons of the weak'. A modicum of power and freedom are being grabbed back online 'in the form of political satire, jokes, songs, popular poetry, code words, mockery and euphemisms'.[11]

This unending commitment to authoritarianism has not, however, made the Party secure and confident in its ability to infuse every power structure in Chinese society. Since 1949 the Party has several times teetered on the verge of collapse. Mao's destabilising campaigns often left the Party bewildered and demoralised. Tiananmen provoked much soul-searching, but the event which sapped the confidence of the Chinese Communist Party more than anything else by far was the collapse of the Soviet Union and its aftermath in Russia. In my experience, all academics, journalists and politicians even in casual conversation point to the collapse of the Soviet Union and how Russia developed afterwards as a clinching argument against rapid, radical political reform in China. The demise of the Soviet Union was extensively studied by the Chinese Communist Party at the time and has been continually since. In a speech given on 30 August 1991, less than a fortnight after the failed coup in the Soviet Union Gao Di, editor of the *People's Daily* (a noted ideologue himself) drew six lessons for the Party in China, almost certainly with the active support of Party leaders – all pointing in the direction of continued authoritarianism. The leadership of the Party should prevail and any suggestions of a multi-party system should be eschewed. The Party (not the government) should maintain control over the military and not countenance any suggestion that the armed forces should be seen as at all independent. 'Bourgeois democratic freedoms', presumably including press freedom and human rights, are permanently off the agenda. Marxism should not give way to ideological pluralism. Efforts should instead be concentrated on further reform and opening. Lastly, public ownership under Party control must continue; privatisation is beyond the pale. Notwithstanding market reforms, the Party has followed the lines laid down in Gao's speech ever since.[12] According to the best estimates, as much as 80 per cent of the economy is still state or Party controlled. High-profile entrepreneurs and billionaires are still, and will remain, minority stakeholders in corporate China.[13]

One of the most important means of maintaining political control is through appointments and promotion. Because of the Party's ubiquity and its embedding within the market as well as the government, achieving personal and professional ambition in any sector still requires Party membership. Almost all senior appointments, including military appointments, are handled in the Party's Organisation Department, where enormous power is concentrated. The Organisation Department maintains lists of many millions of jobs as well as lists of all Party committees. The rules and criteria for appointments are set out at length. Performance of officials is measured and documented against outcomes like economic growth, investment, air and water quality, public order and so on.[14] All of this creates the impression of a model modern meritocracy, but in truth there are numerous loopholes and opportunities for influence-peddling. The Party still operates the *nomenklatura* system inherited from the Soviet Union, by which all senior appointments, not just in government but also crucially in state-owned enterprises, are effectively decided by the Central Committee, including for example senior figures in state-owned banks. As a result, leaders of banks sometimes have a great deal of political clout but no banking experience. Despite this pervasive system, the Party has struggled to adapt to a new role in a market-based society and an interdependent globalised economy. Its traditional methods of propaganda, coercion and public mobilisation learnt from the Jiangxi Soviet in 1931 onwards are much less effective now the Party no longer controls industry, employment, housing, health, pensions and every other aspect of people's lives. Greater openness to ideas from abroad along with technology's capacity to instantly disseminate even the most ephemeral propositions are also eroding the Party's hegemony. Party leaders know that their current set of policies promotes development, not revolution. Revolutionary rhetoric has inevitably taken on a tinny, hollow sound and the people return an uninterested silence.

The years of development have seen seen well-advertised economic successes and a modicum of liberalising individual freedom, but development has also brought its own problems. Economic growth in coastal areas has vastly outstripped the west of China. The core of cities developed while the peripheries didn't; social stratification, once anathema to Maoist China, emerged as a highly visible feature of Chinese life. Profiteering and exploitation by the newly endowed property-owning classes has become widespread, as have the attendant and rapidly acquired meritocratic emotions of smugness and denigration of the strugglers and stragglers. These feelings are matched in equal measure by the anger and resentment of those left behind. Corruption is endemic. Always a problem in China long before the Communists came to power, bribery and graft is seen by many as a legitimate use of *guanxi* connections and an equally acceptable way of benefiting your nearest and dearest. The hapless citizenry are faced with little choice but to go along with it. It may be the only way of getting things done. It is the source of great resentment, however, and places a considerable corrosive strain on social trust already much attenuated by Mao's attempts to tear down China's traditional social fabric in the name of progress. Several Wish Tree respondents expressed open and direct criticism of corruption.

Corruption of the government cadres [changed my life]. (*Man, 39*)

[I wish to] punish corrupt officials.

Confiscation of, and inadequate compensation for land is the thing most likely to make people angry. This displaced farmer now living in Hemu Lu said:

> I'm a citizen at the bottom of society. My life can only be changed by my work. We worry that the central government policy will not be executed well. We would like to punish those who have taken away our land. (*Man, 60*)

People can express frustration and anger, but not with much effect. As little is done by way of punishment of officials found guilty of corruption, it is still a relatively low-risk activity. Most officials act illegally with impunity. Only two small groups of people get seriously punished, those whose greed, dishonesty and exploitation are so extreme and meretricious that they simply cannot be ignored and those whose denigration for corruption is a devious proxy for settling scores in a long-running factional fight. Even of the relatively few who are disciplined, about 80 per cent get off with a warning. Only 6 per cent are criminally prosecuted and of them, just 3 per cent are imprisoned, making the odds for going to jail for corruption very low indeed.[15] The famously authoritarian Chinese Communist Party turns out, in this respect, to be remarkably tolerant and forgiving.

Local government carries enormous financial obligations and debts as well as vast – and growing – responsibilities for public services, including education and welfare. Municipal authorities and their Party shadows lack competence, organisation and financial resources and have acquired a monstrous, unsustainable debt burden. They have become predatory, taking land and other assets from the poor or the powerless or asset-stripping formerly state-owned enterprises and selling them on to the emergent private sector for municipal aggrandisement, and often for private benefit too. Investment often goes to favoured, sometimes hubristic white elephants. As relationships, favours and cross-deals become more complex, law enforcement activity, which in the one-Party system has to be done through the same municipal channels, finds its way barred by vested interests that have quickly embedded themselves throughout institutional life.[16] The attenuated legitimacy of local leaders is further undermined by their failure to act against the known exploiters and criminals.

The problems of the Party-state are daunting according to David Shambaugh, including, 'declining Party legitimacy, eroding Party organisation, increasing noncompliance with Party directives, a hollow Party ideology, a moral vacuum in society, rampant corruption, parasitic officials who engage in rent seeking and other predatory practices'.[17] Richard McGregor has compared Party pronouncements to 'a radio left on in the background, a constant presence, but for the most part easily tuned out and forgotten'.[18] Yan Xuetong – one of the most influential intellectuals in China, a scholar of ancient Chinese thought and specialist in international relations who has espoused a hawkish attitude on repatriating Taiwan to China – is highly sceptical about China's capacity to be a global hegemon. His analysis is telling:

> The Party leaders realise they don't have a dominant ideology they can use to run the country anymore. For them, there is no core social value. At this moment, the sole dominant ideology shared by government and its people is money worship ... Our military budget is 1.6 times that of the Russians but we cannot build the same military. Our education spending is much larger than India's, but we cannot have one single person win a Nobel Prize. They already have ten. We have more rich people than Japan and we have more first-ranked companies but we can't build world-class products. We have more foreign reserves than anyone in the world but we cannot build a financial centre even in Hong Kong.[19]

Some of the Party's problems flow from the developmental model they have pursued and the society that economic reform has created: sharpened social stratification, growing demand for social welfare and public services, corruption, a more worldly, better-educated, technologically savvy generation seeking public accountability. But some of the Party's problems are of its own making. The campaigns, upheavals, contradictions and switchbacks in Communist Party ideology and policy give even the most loyal Party supporters a vertiginous identity crisis. Party pronouncements often seem contradictory, sometimes schizophrenic and detached from reality. The political compass is regularly and without warning sent spinning by leadership pronouncements. This confusion has unsurprisingly led the public to be cynical about politics and, in particular, about politicians.

Party officials, local and national, are widely seen as venal and self-interested, often as downright corrupt. The Party is generally perceived to be devoid either of a message or of the legitimacy to get its views heard, much less accepted. Cosmopolitan young people simply shrug at the stupidities and deceits they hear and see and press on with their opportunistic rush for success. So long as they stay out of trouble they can simply ignore ideology, even if it cannot be challenged. The poor have no alternative but to suffer stoically, but not in silence.

The Party leaders know what they need to do to rejuvenate the Party's structures and popular influence. They adopted a manifesto for Party reform in 2004. This included placing priority on economic development; making ideology flexible and adaptable; combating corruption and strengthening party discipline; rotating, retiring and changing leading personnel; promoting democracy (but only within the Party; outside the Party, the rubric was more consultation, not representative democracy); reforming and reinvigorating local Party branches; improving cadre competence and recruitment into the Party; combating Western attempts at subversion and 'peaceful evolution' of the sort that supposedly had profoundly undermined the Communist regimes of Eastern Europe; paying attention to the problem of social development; pursuing a foreign policy of openness and integration into the international community.[20] This is a massive, complex wish list. Good intentions are easier to enunciate than to implement. All these desired changes run up against deep and embedded vested interests, particularly among currently secure local Party officials who are obviously not keen to step off the gravy train. That said, internal reform of the Party is not inconceivable. It will require compelling leadership authority; force of personality, not just brute force. Assuming that the market is an intimation of the Party's mortality is a democrat's wishful thinking; much predicted, perhaps never realised.[21]

This analysis views the Party's problems through a technocratic, institutional lens. There is another more controversial, incisive and less visible way of looking at what is going on in the Party. China's superficially shiny corporate world gives some clues. The structure of reform in the 1980s was to contain new enterprises in the 'birdcages' of the SEZs. Most of the export-driven recent economic activity is still confined to the well-known growth hotspots in Guangdong as well as in Shanghai and its neighbouring areas in the south of Jiangsu province. The impact of privately owned businesses in places like Chongqing, where state-owned enterprises still dominate, has been limited. Although these new companies, their factories and the vast exports they have generated are much discussed in the West, they remain a far smaller proportion of the overall economy than the state-owned sector, which has been restructured and refinanced. The foreign and privately owned companies are important because they create jobs, crucial to the prospects for social stability. They incubate much-needed technological innovation and they accumulate China's vast foreign exchange reserves but, above all, they fuel domestic savings without which the state-owned banks would struggle to continue to finance the state-owned sector.

Most of China's largest companies, such as China Mobile and Sinopec, as well as the big four banks, are of course state-owned. They have been created by amalgamating and consolidating a ragbag of under-performing, under-funded, often loss-making assets owned by bits of the sprawling state apparatus into viable commercial companies, which benefit from professional management and economies of scale. Above all, these vast new entities can access the capital markets and attract billions of dollars of investment, crucially without unacceptably diluting the ownership of these enterprises by the Party and its associates, many of whom are the 'princelings', family members of Party leaders. State-owned enterprises, from 1993 onwards, have been the only Chinese companies permitted to list shares. These listings, although attracting huge amounts of cash, never reduced the state's stake in the enterprises below 70 per cent. The benefits of all this flowed to state officials and the state's coffers, but not to the wider society. In the decade from 1997, the period of extremely rapid economic growth, the share of workers' wages in national income fell dramatically from 53 per cent to 40 per cent of GDP, meaning they were not keeping pace with the country's economic growth. As Richard McGregor notes, 'the preferential policies meted out to government companies, of cheap land, resources and energy, ensured that the profits of China's boom were captured and kept by the state, at the expense of the population at large.'[22] Western observers imagine that rampant free market capitalism is the order of the day in China, but not according to seasoned operators in China's financial markets, Walter and Howie. They are cynical about the 'harmonious society'. They are lucid and scathing about the true motives for economic consolidation, as well as who the main beneficiaries are:

> What moves this structure is not a market economy and its laws of supply and demand, but a carefully balanced social mechanism built around the particular interests of the revolutionary families who constitute the political elite. China is a family-run business. When ruling groups change, there will be an inevitable change in the balance of interests; but these families have one shared interest above all others; the stability of the system. Social stability allows their pursuit of special interests. This is what is meant by calls for a 'harmonious society' . . . The occasional lurid 'corruption' scandal provides a critical insight into what is, in fact, the mainstream privatisation process; the struggle between competing factions for incremental economic and political advantage, nominally 'owned by the whole people', is being carved up by China's rulers, their families, relations and retainers, who are all in business for themselves and only themselves.[23]

From 1998 onwards former ministry officials in the Soviet-style government system moved across into the new consolidated state-owned enterprises, becoming executives rather than civil servants. But they made sure that they retained their place in the *nomenklatura*. The chairmen and CEOs rank on a par in the Party hierarchy with provincial governors and ministers on the state council. Many even sit on the Central Committee, so they not only have access to the highest Party powers, they *are* the Party's highest powers. Created by the Party, state-owned enterprises have executed a brilliant reverse takeover of the Party. The outlines of the Chinese elites still include the old centres of power, the government and the military, but a new group has invaded the pantheon: business people. Over all of these rules the Party, which infiltrates all arms of the state and now business as well. Jiang Zemin brought business people into the Party, meaning that not only has the Party infiltrated all aspects of power, but most of the centres of power have infiltrated the Party. The effect is that the boundary between the Party, the state and the market is so blurred that it has almost disappeared. It is no longer clear who is in charge of whom.[24]

The nature and extent of influence goes far beyond high-level connections, nepotism in seeking jobs and favours for relatives or receiving bribes. The princelings at the top of the state-owned enterprises have access to huge cash flows, broad patronage systems and significant international networks, acquired from education and working abroad themselves. Beyond the obvious financial benefits, these higher-level tools of influence mean that the princelings can have a broad say in economic policy and even in setting the policy agenda from the outset.[25] 'The state is involved at every stage of the market as the regulator, the policymaker, the investor, the parent company, the listed company, the broker, the bank and the banker.'[26] Inside each of these institutional structures are to be found 'friends and family'. This process of consolidation of the state's assets and the revenues they generate has quickly created a fabulously wealthy elite, small in number but enormous in power and with boundless financial resources.

Some of the new wealthy have humble backgrounds as farmers; one was a bicycle repairman. But the majority of the super-rich did not start from nothing; far from it. A *People's Daily* survey found that 91 per cent of their respondents believed that high-level connections were essential for making money.[27] China is not truly a meritocracy. Talent and effort are essential but real success also requires contacts to ease your path through the maze of official permissions, contradictory regulations and corrupt officials seeking graft. Yu Jianrong has noted the emergence of an elitist alliance since 1992. This alliance comprises three strands: political elites, economic elites and intellectual elites. Members of these groups shift easily from one domain to another through a 'revolving door.' The Communist Party wants to raise the standards of government and so greater emphasis has been placed on academic attainment clearing the way for intellectuals to enter the higher ranks of government. Simultaneously political elites and their families have set up businesses by quitting government and 'jumping into the sea' (*xiahai*) of enterprise or in many cases starting businesses while continuing to hold political office (*guanshang*). A great spiderweb of mutual obligations and as yet unreturned favours has spread across these groups and that web has taken institutional form in the Communist Party. A common interest binds the three groups together to create a relatively stable Chinese ruling class with a broad base of interests.[28]

It seems that the more senior the leader the bigger the fortunes their children have amassed. Their activities are rarely covered by the Chinese media. Former President Jiang Zemin's children have made fortunes in telecommunications. The daughter of former premier Li Peng is Chairman of China Power International Development, an electricity monopoly. Several of the children of another former premier, the blunt, irascible reformer Zhu Rongji, have achieved meretricious success in investment banking. Some of the Western-educated children of the current generation of Chinese Communist leaders are eschewing careers in traditional investment banking, opting instead for quicker, richer pickings in private equity. Winston Wen, the son of Premier Wen Jiabao, is the co-founder of New Horizon Capital managing a US$500 million fund backed by Temasek Holdings, Singapore's sovereign wealth fund, and a Japanese bank. Jeffrey Li, the son of former Politburo member, the candid Li Ruihuan, and Liu Lefei, the son of another Politburo member, Liu Yunshan, are also in private equity.[29] Foreign investors can readily see that returns will be improved by well-connected local representatives operating in Beijing and Shanghai.

Deng Xiaoping said 'Let some people get rich first'.[30] One of the early adherents of this view was Deng's own daughter, Deng Rong. Along with her husband He Ping, she founded the state-owned Poly Group in February 1993.[31] This started as a 'military business', before they moved on to real estate and minerals. It has become an enormous conglomerate with interests in defence, coal mining, iron ore, oil, real estate and, last but not least, culture. In Chongqing where the municipality has built a huge new opera house at the confluence of the two rivers, the management of this opera house, along with many other similarly large new cultural centres in big cities around China, has been subcontracted to the Poly Group. The new opera house has given itself an air of cosmopolitanism by eschewing acrobats, folklore and Peking and Sichuan Opera. Instead it has staged reworkings of Kung Fu classics in contemporary dance vernaculars. Their most successful show so far has been *Cats* with an international cast. The tickets can cost up to US$75, so this is not popular entertainment for the masses but bland middlebrow international entertainment for the bland middlebrow new middle classes. No wonder Bo Xilai felt the need to reinstate free performances of revolutionary opera in Chongqing.

The army is also in on the act. The People's Liberation Army is much more than an army. It is a conglomerate. Since its inception, recognising the unreliability of the Communist production system, the army has grown its own food, raised its own animals and engaged in local construction activities and sideline businesses. But since the 1990s the PLA's reach into business and commerce has grown exponentially, assisted by preferential rates of taxation and easy credit. It has obviously grown in weapons procurement and other directly defence-related industries, such as satellites, electrics and telecommunications. PLA commercial activities have expanded in other sectors too. The armed forces have initiated numerous lucrative joint ventures with foreign companies. They own some of China's prime real estate commanding premium rents. Many local airlines are managed by PLA front companies. They have construction, metals and minerals businesses. Army hospitals admit and treat paying civilians.

This is all semi-legitimate, but the PLA is also involved in many shady business activities, including brothels, karaoke bars and saunas. It has stakes in criminal prostitution and smuggling rings too. These activities are not centrally controlled by the army high command. They are made up of numerous small and large enterprises controlled by whichever part of the military system originated them. The vast majority of the earnings stay where the money is made, used, at best to defray local costs and to support central allocations of funds, which are woefully short for the objectives that have been set.[32] At worst, of course, a substantial proportion of the funds simply disappear in graft. Alongside tensions between professional and military priorities is the competition between military and commercial priorities contained within the PLA behemoth. Since 1993 the Party and the government have sought to curb the excesses of military commercial activities, particularly illicit activities – with limited success. In May 2010, after reports of prostitution in the private rooms, the enormous army-owned sauna in Chaoyang, Beijing's 'international residential district', was closed in a fanfare of publicity. A few weeks later it reopened without comment in the press.

These gains for the few have not gone unnoticed by the many. The infamous 'Ten Thousand Character Manifesto', which appeared anonymously as early as 1997, was widely circulated. Apparently written under the auspices of the leftist critic Deng Liqun, the exact provenance of the manifesto is not known, but its authenticity is undoubted. It has been widely reproduced by the BBC and in academic journals:

> In the course of such change effected in the ownership structure there has been a drain of over 500 billion yuan of state funds since 1982, an average of over 50 billion yuan a year and over a 100 million yuan a day. These state assets which have been turned from public to private are the main source of the primitive accumulation of the new bourgeoisie. We can say that the new bourgeoisie are fed with the toil and sweat of the whole country over the past 40 years.
>
> Some people who have suddenly become rich through means other than labour vie with one another in eating, drinking, visiting prostitutes and gambling, which strongly stimulates the masses and sets examples. Luxurious hotels and shops, nightclubs, golf courses, saunas, massage parlours and brothels, specially designed for tycoons, have been set up in the prosperous economic regions. Money not only is the condition for material comfort but also has become the criteria for the media to judge a man's social value and career. Ultra-egoism, hedonism and money worship have become the main theme of life and creed pursued by an increasing number of people . . . Rational incomes obtained through hard labour are no longer regarded as the norm in life and making money through specu-lation has become the ideal of an increasing number of people.[33]

But wealth has not made the plutocrats secure. The Tiananmen demon-strations and the collapse of the Soviet Union and the Warsaw Pact still haunt the Party leaders. They know that, despite their determined efforts to eliminate political opposition, disagreements and protests are wide-spread and could boil over at any time into street protests that might spread rapidly. They also noted the contribution that technology made to the spreading of civil unrest during the Arab Spring. They fear that, as so often before, the internal security services and the police may again prove unequal to an emergent threat, which would by definition be unpredictable and uncoordinated. In those circumstances the Party would once more have to turn to the army. If the military were at that moment to follow what Gennady Gerasimov, an urbane Soviet Foreign Ministry spokesman, called the Sinatra Doctrine at the beginning of the rebellions in Warsaw Pact countries in 1989 and announce that the demonstrators could do it their way, the Party would instantly be in deep trouble, brought quickly to the point of imminent extinction. Chinese Party leaders anxiously noted also that the Soviet military were not willing to step in during the 1991 coup in Moscow. When the military were called into Tiananmen Square on 4 June 1989, though they did the job of suppression, alarming and profound questions were raised about the loyalty of some senior officers, who didn't want to proceed with the military intervention. At least one senior officer, General Xu Qinxian, disobeyed orders and was stripped of his command.[34] Young soldiers may not have bought the Party's ideological message or may just have been terrified. As a consequence they deserted or shot at demonstrators without orders.[35]

Reasserting firm political control over the PLA as well as drastically improving the competence of the police and the internal security services were obvious lessons for the Party. Within the army political priorities were strengthened inevitably at the expense of independent military concerns. Since the middle 1990s there has been a tripartite struggle between the army, the government and the Party. The army faces great challenges in modernising its capability. To the consternation of the PLA, its analysis of every new military engagement by the USA and its Western allies confirms that military technology, hardware and strategy in the West continue to develop apace. All the recent US and NATO engagements abroad have shown that the PLA has a lot of catching up to do. Keeping up with strategic thinking, technological innovation, human resources competence and, of course, financial resources is an enormous struggle that is never complete. Modernisation requires reconfiguring the structure of the forces, personnel and recruitment (insisting on absolute loyalty as well as professional competence), military education, approaches to military training, hardware needs, research and development, weapons procurement and operational strategy.[36] These changes respond to a constantly revised understanding of the world and the global pressures on China. The current doctrine is that it may have to engage in 'limited war under high technology conditions'.[37] The PLA knows as well as any defence strategist that armies should be judged not by intentions, but by capabilities. The biggest challenge it faces in meeting that challenge is in weapons technology.[38]

Many senior military people conclude that these great challenges require greater independence in strategic decision-making, at least in relation to future planning. Their urge for greater professional independence springs in part from the absence of military experience among the Hu-Wen era leaders and their successors. Meanwhile, the Party and the government jockey with each other, as well as with the military top brass, for more influence over military affairs. This has had an inevitable drag effect on reform. According to David Shambaugh, 'no radical restructuring of Party–army relations has been undertaken. To do so would call into question the very legitimacy and sustenance of the Chinese Communist Party.'[39]

Yet despite the need to change, the revised doctrine and an emerging degree of political independence, the on-the-ground deployment of the PLA has not changed since the end of the Cold War. In the light of this failure to move forces around substantially, Shambaugh has concluded that the PLA is still deployed to meet long-standing state priorities: to cover the borders, particularly the populous and wealthy eastern parts of China closest to the Taiwan hotspot and to defend internal transport links. Lastly and most significantly, the military remain deployed in the places where the government and the Party believe the biggest threats to internal security arise.[40]

There has been a massive demobilisation of those who were unsuitable for high-technology war: some 1.6 million military personnel have been stood down since 1985. Many, however, have gone into the vastly expanded internal security services to enhance capacity there and in recognition of the different organisational and strategic requirements for internal security rather than international security. The internal security forces, principally the People's Armed Police, are regularly deployed against protesters, farmers, miners and secessionists in Tibet and Xinjiang. The citizenry are implacably hostile to their interventions, as they are to the local government law enforcers, the *chengguan*. The internal security services have also been trained to respond to hijackings and terrorist threats.[41] Members of these services accompanied the Olympic flag around the world to protect it from protests about Chinese control of Tibet in the lead up to the Beijing Olympics. Their uniforms of light blue tracksuits and wraparound sunglasses did not conceal the fact they were not athletes but riot police.

The military recognises the supremacy of the Party and also knows that it has an internal security brief should the riot police once more be about to fail. On current reckoning they will fulfil their obligations, but in the minds of Party leaders the fear of insubordination remains potent, regardless of protestations of loyalty. In essence the military's current stance is pragmatic. They know they must respect and support the Party because that is where their resources and legitimacy ultimately come from, but they also seek greater independence in order to become a modern, professional military force.[42]

Some have predicted a scenario in which central political control is much weakened over time by protracted leadership infighting. The infighting will be, as it already is, partly ideological, but also the arguments of a plutocratic elite over the division of the spoils. But the divided factions will have to hold together, for fear of social chaos and the re-emergence of the old ghosts of foreign domination; even the break-up of the country, starting with incipient nationalist movements in Tibet and Xinjiang. In these circumstances the wealthy cities of the east will see themselves more as city-states, distant from the failing countryside and the restive reaches of the west. They may increasingly feel like going it alone.[43] The military will be placed once more in the position of power brokers, keeping factional fighting from descending into chaos. The economy, with islands of Western-friendly economic progress, will retain pockets of continuing development existing alongside areas of growing deprivation. Each, with its different pressures, will be controlled by local political machines. These will be concerned to protect their status and privileges, together with their money-making wheezes. They will not see the need to challenge Beijing's authority; ignoring it should be sufficient. Doctrinal control from Beijing will weaken further and stop–start economic progress will continue alongside economic stagnation in many sectors and geographies. 'The only interest that can possibly bridge these differences is the commitment of the military, as an institution to the maintenance of order in China.'[44]

China is a modern-day, fractious Leviathan, in which the Communist Party, the institutions of government, business and international relations have effectively fused, not just intertwined. The competing interests of economic growth, politics, social welfare and environmental sustainability are not moderated or mediated. China is controlled by an interconnected, mutually dependent but mistrustful and faction-ridden plutocracy focused on a single purpose: the creation and consolidation of wealth in their own hands. The free and fair distribution of the new-found wealth and prosperity to a 'harmonious society' is simply a rhetorical flourish to put citizens off the scent. China is no longer a party-state as Mao and his successors intended. Instead it has become a market-state of plutocrats seeking to dominate the Leviathan with money if possible, by force if necessary. The Chinese dream cultivated in the 1980s of prosperity, security, stability and even the beginning of freedom is at an end.

Afterword: What next for China?

People who claim to know something about China are routinely asked a series of contradictory questions. Can China's economy continue to grow at the current rate? Will the Communist Party collapse? Will China become a superpower? The answer to all three of these questions is no. The economy can continue to grow rapidly because the country still has much surplus labour and human ingenuity as well as a great deal of pent-up consumer demand. But the problems in China's banking system are bound to come home to roost eventually and stall economic growth. Nor is China immune to the ups and downs of the global economy and the business cycle. Indeed, because of the size of China's economy and the rate of recent growth, economic volatility is, if anything, likely to be greater than in more developed economies. Also China's economy cannot continue to grow at the current rate simply because of the logic of large numbers. Ten per cent growth on a low total GDP is 10 per cent of not very much. Two per cent growth of a high GDP is in aggregate a great deal. As China's economy gets bigger the annual percentage growth rate is bound to slow.

Again because of the logic of large numbers, China is bound to become the largest economy in the world in the future. But it will be decades before the majority of Chinese people enjoy the same prosperity as people in Europe or the USA. Possibly the majority will *never* achieve these standards of living. The current global economic system depends on an exploitation of natural and energy resources which would simply not support the whole world's population using the same level of resources as Americans or Europeans, even ignoring the imminent depletions caused by global warming and climate change.

The Communist Party, so long as it has the support of the People's Liberation Army, can continue to control China using, as necessary, authoritarian means. Ideological friction among the leaders, frozen decision-making and the inevitable confusions brought about by the one-party state, such as widespread corruption, the absence of human rights or independent redress for the citizenry and a controlled media, will all continue to disfigure China's internal governance and its international reputation. Nothing about the Communist Party's behaviour however suggests that they will cultivate an appetite for freedom. Quite the opposite, in fact.

The fact that the Communist Party can stay in control does not mean they will have the support of the people. People will continue to be traumatised by memory, anxiety and a frightening sense of having no control over their future. Chinese society will continue to be beset by protests, uprisings and upheavals. The 'weapons of the weak', the hidden narratives, the ridicule and contempt for the Party can only grow. Strands of protest may coalesce into a serious and violent challenge to the Party involving millions of people, perhaps even a national uprising. It has happened unexpectedly in so many other countries, why should China's citizens be different? But extensive preparations have been made for these possibilities and the Party believes it can prevail over most challenges.

China is a long way behind the USA in any potential arms race. It is surrounded by America's allies, in Taiwan, Japan and South Korea. It is strategically encircled, the very outcome that traditional Chinese thinking about military strategy most fears.[1] Though it will seek to assert its influence within the Asia-Pacific region and particularly over Taiwan, much to its chagrin, it is hard to see how China could break out of the USA's potential military stranglehold on any realistic timescale.

When I tell them about the Wish Tree, some of my Chinese friends say I have become a fortune teller. They must be joking. Prediction obviously runs the risk of instant ridicule. Recent history is full of examples of unheralded turns of event. When I was studying South African twentieth-century history as an undergraduate in the late 1970s my ANC-supporting tutors explained to the students, with the use of convincing maps and historical documents, why the apartheid system had taken social and

political control to a new level of authoritarianism and built an unprecedented security state. The people could not possibly peaceably overthrow
the regime. This was the ANC view at the time. My tutors were wonderfully wrong. With the possible exception of Zbigniew Brzezinski no
commentator or expert predicted the collapse of the Soviet Union and the
Warsaw Pact in 1989.[2] Certainly no one in China saw it coming. I travelled
extensively in Egypt, Lebanon, Syria and the Palestinian territories between
2006 and 2010. I met hundreds of academics, government officials and
people working for NGOs. To a woman and a man they told me that there
would be no progress on democracy in Middle Eastern countries without
an independent Palestine and until the forces of fundamentalism, most
vividly represented by Al-Qaeda, had been contained. As it turned out, the
Arab Spring in early 2011 saw dictators dumped from Egypt, Tunisia and
Libya and uprisings in Yemen, Bahrain and Syria.

South Africa is now a vibrant democracy, the Soviet Union has collapsed,
former Warsaw Pact countries are now democratic and dictators have been
given their marching orders in several countries in the Middle East. In all
these cases the experts were proved wrong by the citizenry. Several countries in Latin America have also gone from dictatorship to democracy.[3] On
the other hand in North Korea and Zimbabwe, among others, economic
and social collapse have not so far presaged the downfall of dictators. The
past is evidently a poor guide to the future and one country's experience is
rarely replicated in another. But, political systems in many uncompro-
mising and unpromising nations, with much suffering and bolstered by
irrepressible optimism, change for the better mostly at the hands of their
own citizens.

Notes

Chinese names begin with family names followed by given names, often of two syllables. These are given without commas. Western names or Chinese people who have adopted Western given names are stated as surname, given name.

CHAPTER 1: GETTING NOWHERE IN CHINA

1. Henry Kissinger reports on many such encounters between Mao Zedong and Zhou Enlai, himself and President Richard Nixon in the 1970s. Mao's main point often came right at the end of the meeting in an elliptical reference to an ancient Chinese saying. The discussions during the rest of the meeting were neither here nor there. Kissinger (2011: 258–262). Prime Minister Margaret Thatcher was similarly discomfited by Deng Xiaoping, who punctuated their meetings with frequent use of his spittoon.
2. The Chinese word *nongmin* is made up of the characters for 'rural' and 'people'. Its usage in China is usually best translated as 'farmer', or 'peasant' in English. Both translations will be used in this book.
3. See Wilson (1996).
4. See Young and Lemos (1997).
5. I was for a while involved with a non-governmental organisation called Homeless International which, among other activities, promoted what they called 'people's dialogue'.
6. See He (2008: 227).
7. *Guanxi* can be translated directly into English as *relationships*. In Mandarin it generally has a wider meaning of influential connections and the benefits derived from them.
8. See Chetham (2002: 184).
9. *RMB* stands for *renminbi* (people's currency) and is generally the term used within China to denote the Chinese Yuan (¥). In September 2011 £1 = *RMB*10.1 and $1 = *RMB*6.4.
10. See Chen and Wu (2006) for numerous examples of egregious banqueting by local officials at peasants' expense.

CHAPTER 2: CHONGQING

1. In spoken Mandarin *kuai* usually replaces *yuan* or *renminbi* when referring to Chinese currency.
2. Sang (2006: 33).
3. See Dunlop (2008: 133–134).
4. 'Golf courses increasingly in the rough', *China Daily*, 20 September 2011.
5. See Aiyar (2008: 117).
6. In 2007 I attended several academic conferences at different universities in Chongqing and listened to many presentations by econometrists showing the exponential possibilities for economic growth in the west of China. They all assumed movements of

population on an epic, biblical scale, enormous levels of investment and massive urban growth. I am not an economist, but it was clear even to me that no one seemed to have factored in risks of shortages of capital, inflation, a collapse in demand or a banking crisis – all of which have subsequently come to pass.

7. Leonard (2008: 69).
8. See Nathan and Gilley (eds) (2003: 127–130).
9. Jacobs, Andrew, 'Chinese trial reveals vast web of corruption', *New York Times*, 3 November 2009.
10. 'Texting in China: well red', *The Economist*, 18 February 2010.
11. An Baijie, 'Farmers in Chongqing say "no thanks" to hu kou', *Global Times*, 29 September 2010.
12. Xinhua news agency, 'Public rental housing eases distress in Chongqing', *China Daily*, 14 February 2011.
13. Lam (2010).
14. A brief summary of Bo Guagua's educational history is given in Foster, Peter, 'Photos leaked online fuel rumours of romance between China's "red royals"', *The Telegraph*, 21 February 2011.

CHAPTER 3: CHAOS, REFORM AND INEQUALITY

1. Fukuyama (2011: 92).
2. Quoted in Meisner (2007: 162).
3. Quoted in Kissinger (2011: 93–94).
4. See Chang Jung (1991: 378).
5. See Wang (2009: 9).
6. See Cheng Nien (1995).
7. See Chang Jung (1986: 24–25).
8. My friend Zhou Xun of Hong Kong University has had these violent attacks recounted to her for her collection of oral reminiscences.
9. Yan (2011: 1).
10. Nathan and Gilley (eds) (2003: 122–123).
11. Zheng Yi. 1996. *Scarlet Memorial: Tales of Cannibalism in Modern China.* (trans.) Sym, T.P. Boulder, CO: Westview. Quoted in Mitter (2004: 225).
12. Kissinger (2011: 195).
13. Wood (2007: 150).
14. Confucius is the Latinised version of Kong Zi, the Chinese social philosopher of the Spring and Autumn Period traditionally said to have lived 551–479 BC. Mencius is the Latinised form of Meng Zi a later Chinese philosopher and the principal interpreter of Confucian thought. He probably lived around 372–289 BC.
15. Wood (2007: 143).
16. Wood (2007: 144) writes 'we have buried 460,000 scholars', but elsewhere the number 46,000 is given, which would make the assertion of 'a hundredfold' correct.
17. Kissinger (2011: 302–303).
18. Palmer (2012: 114).
19. Castells (1999: 308).
20. Ge (1999).
21. All Chinese official statistics should be treated sceptically; even now they tend to exaggerate the positive and minimise the negative. Egregious lies are not so common these days, mostly because no one believed them anyway. Cover-up however is an oft-deployed tactic. Accurate, up-to-date statistics are also inherently difficult to collect in a country of 1.3 billion people and because of the pace of change in China, they don't remain up to date for long. They are quoted in this book as reasonable evidence of trends rather than precise calculations.
22. World Bank (1996).

23. http://faostat.fao.org/2011
24. See Xinran (2007: 18–19) Zhang and Sang (1987: 3–8).
25. See Chang, Leslie (2010: 56–57) Harney (2009: 59).
26. See Dikköter (2010: 209).
27. Schell and Shambaugh (eds) (1999: 159).
28. Schell and Shambaugh (eds) (1999: 159).
29. Obrist (2011: 78–79).
30. Mitter (2004: 19); Spence (1991: 271–272).
31. Spence (1990: 318).
32. *People's Daily* quoted in Schell and Shambaugh (eds) (1999: 160).
33. Buruma (2002: 59–68).
34. Nathan and Link (eds) (2002: 29).
35. Nathan and Link (eds) (2002: 44).
36. Nathan and Link (eds) (2002: 115).
37. Zhao (2009: 5).
38. Nathan and Link (eds) (2002: 116).
39. Nathan and Link (eds) (2002: 110).
40. Nathan and Link (eds) (2002: 574).
41. Shambaugh (2005: 22).
42. Leonard (2008: 32).
43. Nathan and Link (eds) (2002: 58).
44. Wang (2009: 44).
45. Wang (2009: 36).
46. Wang (2009: 37).
47. McGregor (2010: 42).
48. Nathan and Gilley (eds) (2003: 40).
49. Shambaugh (2008: 115).
50. Extracted from a speech delivered by Wen Jiabao at the closing ceremony of a seminar organised for leading figures at the ministerial, provincial level, 29 February 2004, quoted in UNDP (2008).
51. See Mitter (2004: 16) and Yan (2011: 35–39).
52. Analects 12, quoted in Yan (2011: 38).
53. Jacobs, Andrew, 'Confucius statue vanishes near Tiananmen Square', New York Times, 22 April 2011.
54. Ravallion and Chen (2004).
55. Author's calculations from Statistical Communiqué.
56. Huang et al. (2003).
57. Zhu et al. (2006): *mu* is a Chinese measurement of land equivalent to $666\frac{2}{3}$ m^2.
58. Author's calculation using per capita urban income in 2006.
59. Zhu and Prosterman (2007).
60. French, Howard W., 'Protesters say police in China killed up to 20', New York Times, 10 December 2005.
61. Lenin wrote *Socialism: Utopian and Scientific* in 1880.
62. From 1978 to 1985 China sent 38,000 students abroad to study, over 90 per cent of whom studied a scientific discipline.
63. For Francis Bacon's thoughts on scientific method refer to Francis Bacon, *Novum Organum*, London, 1620. Since it is no longer copyrighted many prints are available and it is freely available to read online at http://www.constitution.org/bacon/nov_org.txt.
64. Shambaugh (2008: 120).

CHAPTER 4: THE WISH TREE

1. One of the oldest of the Chinese classic texts, containing a system for divination thought to date back to c.1000 BC.

2. Long after I had completed the Wish Tree in China I discovered that Yoko Ono had been erecting wish trees as part of her artworks since the 1990s. She was inspired by wish trees she had seen in temples in Japan as a child.
3. See Hussey (1927).
4. These quotes are taken from a briefing note that we were given, which was translated later in the UK.
5. See Nathan and Perry (eds) (2002) and Chen and Wu (2006) for many examples of this arcane process at work.

CHAPTER 5: THE CHINESE DREAM

1. Spence (1991: 731).
2. UNDP (2010: 10).
3. UNDP (2010: 11).
4. Ravallion and Chen (2004). In measuring Gini coefficients a value of zero corresponds to perfect equality (where everyone has the same income) while a value of one corresponds to total inequality (where one person has all the income).
5. UNDP (2010: 12).
6. UNDP (2010: 12).
7. Where the respondent indicated these, gender and age will be provided with all quotes from the Wish Tree. Only gender or age is given if that was all that was recorded.
8. Farrel et al. (2006).
9. Whyte (2010: 169).
10. Xinran (2007: 36–37).
11. Brown (2007: 29–30, 128).
12. Zhang, Ling, 'Universities a preparation for life, not just work', *China Daily*, 25 March 2010.
13. '1.4M sit China's Civil Service exam,' *People's Daily*, 6 December 2010.
14. Walter and Howie (2011: 190).
15. Farrel et al. (2006).

CHAPTER 6: UNHAPPY FAMILIES

1. Mencius (2004: 60).
2. Yu (2009: 21).
3. Hvistendahl (2011: 35).
4. Banister and Harbaugh (1994: 23).
5. Hvistendahl (2011: 142).
6. Hvistendahl (2011: 143).
7. Spence (1991: 686).
8. Vink, Michele. 'Abortion and Birth Control in Canton China'. *Wall Street Journal*, 30 November 1981.
9. Mosher, Stephen W. 1984. *Broken Earth*. New York: The Free Press, p.225, quoted in Hvistendahl (2011: 143).
10. Nilekani (2008: 56–60).
11. Xinran (2010: 81).
12. In Li's (2009) novel, *The Vagrants*, one of the characters, Mrs Hua, rescues abandoned girl babies.
13. Waldmeir, Patti. 'Little Girl Found'. *FT Magazine*, 12 August 2011.
14. Xinran (2010: 10).
15. Xinran (2010: 178).
16. Xinran (2010: 178).
17. The statistics in this paragraph can be found in UNFPA (2006).

18. Lomborg (1998: 54–59).
19. UNFPA (2006: 6).
20. The statistics in this paragraph can be found in UNFPA (2006).
21. Hvistendahl (2011: 137).
22. Hvistendahl (2011: 5).
23. Sen, Amartya, 'More than 100 million women are missing', *New York Review of Books*, 20 December 1990.
24. Hvistendahl (2011: 21).
25. Hvistendahl (2011: 165).
26. Hvistendahl (2011: 166).
27. Hsu, Jeremy, 'There are more boys than girls in China and India', *Scientific American*, 4 August 2008.
28. Spence (1991: 185).
29. Hudson and Den Boer (2005: 23).
30. Edlund, Lena et al. 2007. 'More men, more crime: evidence from China's one-child policy', *Institute for the Study of Labour, Discussion Paper Series*. Bonn: Institute for Study of Labour. quoted in Hvistendahl (2011: 222).
31. Reported in Hsu, Jeremy, 'There are more boys than girls in China and India', *Scientific American*, 4 August 2008.

CHAPTER 7: EDUCATIONAL PRESSURE, HOPE AND DESPAIR

1. Spence (1991: 649).
2. UNDP (2008: 46).
3. Jiang Zhongyi (2007).
4. UNDP (2008: 38).
5. UNDP (2008: 45).
6. Yuan Wu, 'Parents pay too much for education', *China Daily*, 1 April 2005.
7. Sang (2006: 235–243).
8. 'Less spending on education', *China Daily*, 23 December 2004.
9. Chen and Wu (2006: 153).
10. UNDP (2008: 46).
11. Liu and Yuan (2007).
12. Mei and Wang (2006).
13. Jiang Zhongyi (2007).
14. Zhu Zhe, 'Poor students set to benefit from US$99m State grant', *China Daily*, 17 August 2006.
15. Zhang (2007).
16. Zhang (2007).
17. Wang Ying, 'Three-good student under revision', *China Daily*, 24 March 2005.
18. Though better-off parents with children who didn't make the grade in the exams can pay extra to have their child admitted to a better school.
19. 'Ants' Tribes' is the title of a book published in China by Si Lian, a Beijing university professor who interviewed 600 'ants'.
20. Chua (2011: 5, 94–95).
21. Xie Chunjiao, 'China's suicide rate among world's highest', *China Daily*, 11 September 2007. See also Jonathon Watts, 'Suicide blights China's young adults', *The Guardian*, 26 July 2005.
22. He Na, 'Too much pressure', *China Daily*, 26 May 2009.
23. Qiu Quanlin and Wang Zhuoqiong, 'All work and no play makes kids depressed', *China Daily*, 1 June 2006. And UNESCO (2009).
24. Yang Binbin et al., 'Why did so many Sichuan schools collapse?' *Caijing*, 17 June 2008.
25. Branigan, Tania, 'Suffer in silence', *The Guardian*, 26 August 2008.

26. Branigan, Tania and agencies, 'China jails investigator into Sichuan earthquake schools', *The Guardian*, 9 February 2010.
27. Yang Binbinetal 'Why did so many Siehnam schools collapse' Caijing, 17 June 2008.
28. Wong, Edward, 'Year after China quake, new births, old wounds', 5 May 2009.
29. Yang Binbin et al., 'Why did so many Sichuan schools collapse?' *Caijing*, 17 June 2008.

CHAPTER 8: FAILING HEALTH

1. Aiyar (2008: 53–61).
2. Jakes, Susan, 'Beijing's SARS attack', *Time*, 8 April 2003.
3. UNDP (2008: 50, 92).
4. Yardley, Jim, 'Chinese SARS hero urges party to admit error for '89 massacre', *New York Times*, 8 March 2004.
5. Kahn, Joseph, 'China bars US trip for doctor who exposed SARS cover-up', *New York Times*, 13 July 2007.
6. Pan, Philip P., 'The last hero of Tiananmen', *The New Republic*, 9 July 2008.
7. Wen Jiabao quoted in Rohrer, Finlo, 'China drinks its milk', *BBC News Magazine*, 7 August 2007.
8. Rohrer, Finlo, 'China drinks its milk', *BBC News Magazine*, 7 August 2007.
9. Quoted in Rohrer, Finlo, 'China drinks its milk', *BBC News Magazine*, 7 August 2007.
10. McGregor (2010: 186).
11. Yu Le, 'China milk victims may have reached 94,000', *Reuters*, 8 October 2008.
12. See 'China pledges to treat all tainted milk-affected babies', *Xinhua*, 16 September 2008. Also see '25% Beijing babies consumed tainted milk powder', *Xinhua*, 26 October 2008 and McGregor (2010: 172, 182, 186). China pledges to treat all tainted milk-affected babies. *Xinhua*. 16 September 2008.
13. Wen Jiabao quoted in *Xinhua*, 21 September 2008.
14. UNDP (2008: 50).
15. Palmer (2012: 159).
16. UNDP (2008: 51).
17. UNDP (2008).
18. UNDP (2008: 51).
19. UNDP (2008: 52).
20. UNDP (2008: 54).
21. UNDP (2008: 92).
22. UNDP (2008: 53).

CHAPTER 9: LIFELONG FINANCIAL INSECURITY

1. Francis Spufford (2010) gives a vivid account of Soviet delusions and how they spread round the Communist world during the Khrushchev era. Eric Hobsbawm (1994) shows not only how deluded the Soviet Union and Mao's Communist government were, but their propaganda also convinced some in the West that they might even outstrip capitalism's capacity for innovation and growth. Many foreign visitors to China came back with glowing reports of rapid agricultural and industrial development, see Wright (2010) for examples.
2. Kissinger (2011).
3. Dikötter (2010: 148–152).
4. Watts, Jonathon, 'Faces in a billion', *The Guardian*, 5 July 2008.
5. State Council (1999).
6. Shang and Wu (2004).
7. UNDP (2008: 56).
8. National Population and Family Planning Commission of China (2010).

9. 'China's inflation accelerates to 6.5% in July', *Xinhua*, 9 August 2011.
10. Hughes, Mark, 'Inflation putting heat on govt', *China Daily*, 7 March 2011.
11. UNDP (2008: 58).
12. UNDP (2008: 61).
13. UNDP (2008: 60).

CHAPTER 10: EXODUS FROM THE SUFFERING LAND

1. Economy (2004: 33).
2. UNDP (2010: 35).
3. Woetzel et al. (2009: 18, 366).
4. UNDP (2010: 36–37).
5. UNDP (2010: 38).
6. Watts, Jonathan, 'Invisible city', *The Guardian*, 15 March 2006.
7. http://siteresources.worldbank.org/DATASTATISTICS/Resources/table3_13.pdf, 2011.
8. UNDP (2010: 41).
9. Brown (2007: 111).
10. Wasserstrom (2010: 128).
11. UNDP (2010: 3).
12. 'Yangtze pollution irreversible'. *BBC*, 16 April 2007.
13. Economy (2004: 69).
14. UNDP (2010: 20).
15. Gray (2002: 181).
16. Fenby (2008: xl).
17. Watts (2010: 153).
18. Wasserstrom (2010: 128).
19. UNDP (2010: 3).
20. UNDP (2010: 3).
21. Economy (2004: 18) and Leonard (2008: 41).
22. Leonard (2008: 41).
23. Economy (2004: 65).
24. Economy (2004: 10).
25. UNDP (2008: 99)
26. UNDP (2008: 100)

CHAPTER 11: LOSERS AND THEIR LOSSES

1. See Wu (2003) for these iconic images.
2. Becker (2008: 43).
3. Becker (2008: 37).
4. Ai Weiwei, 'The city: Beijing', *Newsweek*, 28 August 2011.
5. McGregor (2010: 42).
6. UNDP (2008: 99).
7. UNDP (2008: 95).
8. Judt (2009: 416).
9. McGregor (2010: 199–200).
10. The priorities highlighted here are drawn from the recommendations set out in UNDP (2008).
11. Source: IMF, GDP per capita at purchasing power parity.
12. Chamon and Prasad (2008).
13. Chamon and Prasad (2008).
14. Farrel et al. (2006).
15. Walter and Howie (2011: 27), Hutton (2007: 158).

16. Walter and Howie (2011: 25).
17. Chang, Gordon G. (2002: 124).
18. Walter and Howie (2011: 35).
19. Walter and Howie (2011: 53).
20. Walter and Howie (2011: 53).
21. Walter and Howie (2011: 80)
22. Walter and Howie (2011: 126).
23. Rabinovitch, Simon, 'China acts to solve provincial debt crisis', *Financial Times*, 13 February 2012.
24. Walter and Howie (2011: 80).
25. Hutton (2007: 163).

CHAPTER 12: TRAUMA WITHOUT RECOVERY

1. Ramzy, Austin, 'China's alarming spate of school knifings', *Time*, 30 April 2010.
2. Philips, Michael R. et al. (2009).
3. Cyranoski (2010).
4. Fang et al. (2006).
5. Lu and Wang (2008).
6. Fang et al. (2006).
7. Zhao, Chengzheng et al. (2004).
8. National Narcotic Control Commission 2002 report cited in Zhao, Chengzheng et al. (2004).
9. Zhao, Chengzheng et al. (2004).
10. Yang and Xia (2010).
11. Eimer, David, 'China's secret gambling problem', *Daily Telegraph*, 9 January 2010.
12. Quoted in Fan, Maureen, 'Oldest profession flourishes in China', *Washington Post*, 5 August 2007.
13. 'Drain of credibility'. *China Daily*, 4 August 2009.
14. Quoted in Fan, Maureen, 'Oldest profession flourishes in China', *Washington Post*, 5 August 2007.
15. Reported in Fan, Maureen, 'In rural China a bitter way out', *Washington Post*, 15 May 2007.
16. Philips, Michael R., 'Foxconn and China's suicide puzzle' *http://online.wsj.com*. 1 June 2010.
17. Yip and Liu (2006).
18. Fan, Maureen, 'In rural China a bitter way out', *Washington Post*, 15 May 2007.
19. Xie Chunjiao, 'China's suicide rate among the world's highest', *China Daily*, 11 September 2007. See also He, Na, 'Too much presssure', *China Daily*, 26 May 2009.
20. *Chi hu* or 'eating bitterness' is a widely used phrase in China expressing resigned stoicism. 'Soldier on' or 'keep going' might be suitable English analogues.
21. Herman (1992: 242).
22. Herman (1992: 155).
23. Schell and Shambaugh (1999: 38–39).
24. See Frank Dikköter (2010: 324–334) for a full explanation of how this figure has been derived. This is the most recent and authoritative assessment of the numbers who died because of the famine.
25. Schell and Shambaugh (1999: 44).
26. Shambaugh (2008: 81).
27. Jiang, Steven, 'Chinese Premier visits train crash site, pledges transparent probe', *CNN*, 28 July 2011.
28. LaFraniere, Sharon, 'Anger and suspicion as survivors await Chinese crash report', *New York Times*, 20 September 2011.
29. Ai and Siemons (2009: 17).

CHAPTER 13: THE POWER OF THE POWERLESS

1. Shirk (2007: 56).
2. Information collated and table provided Keidel (2006: 3).
3. Shambaugh (2008: 117).
4. Li and O'Brien (2008).
5. Yardley, Jim, 'Thousands of Chinese villagers protest factory pollution', *New York Times*, 13 April 2005.
6. French, Howard W., 'Protesters say police in China killed up to 20', *New York Times*, 10 December 2005.
7. Chan (2007).
8. Lee (2007: 167).
9. Chan (2007).
10. Study conducted in 2002 in Beijing by sociologist Li Qiang results reported in Chen and Wu (2006: 205).
11. Pomfret, John, 'Chinese oil country simmers as workers protest cost-cutting', *Washington Post*, 17 March 2002.
12. Chang, Leslie T. (2010: xviii).
13. Chang, Leslie T. (2010: xx).
14. Cha, Ariana Eunjung, 'Protest application brings labor-camp threat, woman says', *Washington Post*, 21 August 2008.
15. Bristow, Michael, 'China "yet to approve protests"', *BBC News*, 18 August 2008.
16. Chen and Wu (2006: 151).
17. Chen Guidi and Wu Chuntao (2006) set out both the indignities visited on the peasants and their attempts to resist in their book *Will the Boat Sink the Water*. To the authors' surprise, it became a bestseller and was suppressed by the authorities, but not before it had achieved wide circulation. Since its publication the authors have been subject to more or less continuous official harassment.
18. Emmott (2008).
19. Dyer, Geoff, 'Stirrings in the suburbs', *Financial Times*, 20 July 2008.
20. McGregor (2010: 137).
21. Zissis et al, China's Environmental Crisis Council on Foreign Relations, 4 August, 2008.
22. Ramzy, Austin, 'China environmental protests gather force', *Time*, 23 November 2009.
23. Fenby (2008: 362).
24. Taipei Fine Arts Museum at the Fifty-fourth Venice Biennale (2011).
25. Van Schaik (2011: 214).
26. Van Schaik (2011: 266).
27. Ramzy, Austin, 'Tens of thousands protest in Xinjiang', *Time*, 4 September 2009.
28. Wu, Jiao, 'Religious believers thrice the estimate', *China Daily*, 7 February 2007.
29. Hessler (2010: 241).
30. Bhattacharji (2008).
31. 'China ordains bishop despite Vatican objection', *BBC*, 20 November 2010.
32. Grim, Brian, 'Religion in China on the eve of the 2008 Beijing Olympics', *Pew Research Center*, 7 May 2008.
33. Lim, Benjamin Kang, 'Civil servant purged over Bible session', *The Standard*, 2 March 2007.
34. Gray (2011: 207).
35. Fang Bay, 'An opiate of the masses', *US News*, 14 February 1999.
36. Chang, Gordon G. (2002: 18).
37. Bloch, Marc. 1970. *French Rural History: An Essay on its Basic Characteristics* (trans.) Janet Sondheimer. Berkeley, CA: University of California Press p. 169, cited in Scott (1985: 332).
38. Scott (1985: 332).
39. Scott (1985: 333).

40. Spence (1991: 178).
41. Laven (2011: 238).
42. Scott (1985: xvi).
43. Scott (1985: 347).
44. Scott (1985: 318).

CHAPTER 14: PLUTOCRATS IN THE LEVIATHAN

1. Yan (2011: 52–54).
2. Baudrillard (1996).
3. Wang (2009: 77).
4. 'China rejects calls for apology', BBC, 17 April 2005; and Watts, Jonathan, 'China stops anti-Japanese protests', The Guardian, 5 May 2005.
5. Dickie, Mure and Dyer, Geoff, 'Tensions surface after clash at sea', Financial Times, 20 September 2010.
6. Shambaugh (2008: 110).
7. Shirk (ed.) (2011: 207).
8. http://www.cnnic.net.cn/en/index/0O/index.htm, 2011.
9. Hille, Kathrin, 'China calls time on internet watchdog', Financial Times, 22 September 2011.
10. Branigan, Tania, 'China's jasmine revolution: police but no protesters line streets of Beijing', The Guardian, 27 February 2011.
11. Shirk (ed.) (2011: 210).
12. Quotes from speech provided in Shambaugh (2008: 59).
13. McGregor (2010: 199–200).
14. McGregor (2010: 81).
15. Shambaugh (2008: 133–134).
16. Shambaugh (2008: 17).
17. Shambaugh (2008: 24).
18. McGregor (2010: 27).
19. McGregor (2010: 133).
20. Shambaugh (2008: 125).
21. Chang, Gordon G. (2002).
22. McGregor (2010: 56).
23. Walter and Howie (2011: 21–22).
24. Wang (2009: 62–63).
25. Walter and Howie (2011: 174).
26. Walter and Howie (2011: 19).
27. Xie, Yu, '91% think new rich use government connections', China Daily, 9 February 2010.
28. Yu Jianrong (2007).
29. Carew, Rick, 'Private equity's new princelings', Wall Street Journal, 1 February 2010.
30. Quoted in Fan, Maureen, 'Cashing in on Communism', Washington Post, 8 February 2007.
31. Chen Jie, 'Impressario par excellence', China Daily, 8 June 2010.
32. Shambaugh (2005: 201).
33. Anon. 'The Ten Thousand Character Manifesto', Quoted in Schell and Shambaugh (eds) (1999: 119 and 127).
34. Shambaugh (2005: 24).
35. Nathan and Link (eds) (2002: 289–291, 504).
36. Shambaugh (2005: 74–78).
37. Shambaugh (2005: 60).
38. Shambaugh (2005: 70).

39. Shambaugh (2005: 12).
40. Shambaugh (2005: 153).
41. Shambaugh (2005: 170).
42. Shambaugh (2005: 17).
43. Friedman (2009: 96–99).
44. Swaine, Michael D. quoted in Schell and Shambaugh (eds) (1999: 116).

AFTERWORD: WHAT NEXT FOR CHINA?

1. Kissinger (2010: 23–25).
2. Brzezinski (1989: 232).
3. See Reid (2007) for a full description of the transitions in Latin America.

Bibliography

Ai Weiwei and Siemons, Mark. 2009. *Ai Weiwei: So Sorry*. Munich: Prestel.

Aiyar, Pallavi. 2008. *Smoke and Mirrors: An Experience of China*. Delhi: Fourth Estate.

Arendt, Hannah. 1990 [1963]. *On Revolution*. London: Penguin.

Arrighi, Giovanni. 2007. *Adam Smith in Beijing: Lineages of the Twenty-First Century*. London: Verso.

Ash, Robert, Shambaugh, David and Takagi, Seiichiro (eds) 2007. *China Watching: Perspectives from Europe, Japan and the United States*. London: Routledge.

Banister, Judith and Harbaugh, Christina Wu. 1994. 'China's Family Planning: Inputs and Outcomes'. *CIR Staff Paper* No. 73. Washington, DC: Center for International Research Bureau of the Census

Baudrillard, Jean. 1996 [1968]. *The System of Objects* (trans. Benedict, James). London: Verso.

Becker, Jasper. 1996. *Hungry Ghosts: China's Secret Famine*. London: John Murray.

—— 2008. *City of Heavenly Tranquility: Beijing in the History of China*. London: Allen Lane.

Bhattacharji, Preeti. 2008. *Religion in China: Backgrounder*. http://www.cfr.org/china/religion-china/p16272: Council on Foreign Relations, 2010

Brown, Kerry. 2007. *Struggling Giant: China in the 21st Century*. London: Anthem.

Brzezinski, Zbigniew. 1989. *The Grand Failure: The Birth and Death of Communism in the Twentieth Century*. New York: Charles Scribner.

Buruma, Ian. 2002. *Bad Elements: Chinese Rebels from Los Angeles to Beijing*. London: Weidenfeld and Nicholson.

Castells, Manuel. 1999 [1998]. *The Information Age: Economy, Society and Culture Vol. III: End of Millennium*. Oxford: Blackwell.

Chamon, Marcos and Prasad, Eswar. 2008. 'Why Are Saving Rates of Urban Households in China Rising?' *IMF Working Paper WP/08/145*. Washington, DC: International Monetary Fund.

Chan, Chris King-Chi. 2007. 'The Emerging Patterns of Workers' Protest in South China.' Paper presented at a joint seminar by the Centre for Comparative Labour Studies and Industrial Relations Research Unit: 'Class Conflict in Post-socialism?', University of Warwick, 29 November 2007.

Chang, Gordon G. 2002 [2001]. *The Coming Collapse of China*. London: Arrow.

Chang Jung. 1991. *Wild Swans: Three Daughters of China*. London: HarperCollins.

—— 2005. *Mao: The Unknown Story*. London: Jonathan Cape.

Chang Jung with Halliday, Jon. 1986. *Mme Sun Yat-Sen*. London: Penguin.

Chang, Leslie T. 2010. *Factory Girls: Voices from the Heart of Modern China*. London: Picador.

Chen Guidi and Wu Chuntao. 2006. *Will the Boat Sink the Water: The Life of China's Peasants*. London: Public Affairs.

Cheng Nien. 1995 [1987]. *Life and Death in Shanghai*. London: Flamingo.

Cheng Pei-Kai and Lestz, Michael with Spence, Jonathan D. (eds). 1999. *The Search for Modern China: A Documentary Collection*. New York: Norton.

Chetham, Deirdre. 2002. *Before the Deluge: The Vanishing World of the Yangtze's Three Gorges*. New York: Palgrave Macmillan.

Chua, Amy. 2011. *Battle Hymn of the Tiger Mother*. London: Bloomsbury.

Confucius. 1979. *The Analects* (trans. Lau, D.C.). London: Penguin Classics.

Cyranoski, David. 2010. 'China Tackles Surge in Mental Illness'. *Nature* Vol. 468 p.145.

Dikköter, Frank. 2010. *Mao's Great Famine*. London: Bloomsbury.

Dollar, David. 2007. Poverty, Inequality and Social Disparities during China's Economic Reform. *Policy Research Working Paper 4253*. Washington, DC: The World Bank.

Duckett, Jane. 2011. 'Challenging the Economic Reform Paradigm: Policy and Politics in the Early 1980s Collapse of the Rural Co-operative Medical System'. *China Quarterly* Vol. 205 pp.80–95.

Dunlop, Fuchsia. 2008. *Shark's Fin and Sichuan Pepper: A Sweet-sour Memoir of Eating in China*. London: Ebury Press.

Economy, Elizabeth C. 2004. *The River Runs Black: The Environmental Challenge to China's Future*. Ithaca, NY: Cornell University Press.

Emmott, Bill. 2008. *Rivals: How the Power Struggle between China, India and Japan Will Shape Our Next Decade*. London: Allen Lane.

Fang Yuxia et al. (2006) 'Recent Trends in Drug Abuse in China'. *Acta Pharmcalogica Sinica* Vol. 27(2) pp.140–144.

Farrel, Diana, Gersch, Ulrich A. and Stephenson, Elizabeth. 2006. 'The Value of China's Emerging Middle Class'. *McKinsey Quarterly* June pp.60–69.

Fenby, Jonathan. 2008. *The Penguin History of Modern China: The Fall and Rise of a Great Power 1850–2008*. London: Allen Lane.

Friedman, George. 2009. *The Next Hundred Years: A Forecast for the 21st Century*. New York: Doubleday.

Fukuyama, Francis. 2011. *The Origins of Political Order: From Prehuman Times to the French Revolution*. London: Profile.

Ge Wei. 1999. 'Special Economic Zones and the Opening of the Chinese Economy: Some Lessons for Economic Liberalization'. *World Development* Vol. 27(7) pp.1267–1285.

Grant, Charles with Barysch, Katinka. 2008. *Can Europe and China Shape a New World Order?* London: Centre for European Reform.

Gray, John. 2002 [1998]. *False Dawn: The Delusions of Global Capitalism*. London: Granta.

—— 2007. *Black Mass: Apocalyptic Religion and the Death of Utopia*. London: Allen Lane.

—— 2011. *The Immortalization Commission: Science and the Strange Quest to Cheat Death*. London: Allen Lane.

Hahn, Emily. 2003 [1941]. *The Soong Sisters*. New York: e-reads.

Harney, Alexandra. 2009. *The China Price: The True Cost of Chinese Competitive Advantage*. London: Penguin.

He Qinglian. 2008. *The Fog of Censorship: Media Control in China* (trans. Frank, Paul). New York: Human Rights in China.

Herman, Judith Lewis. 1992. *Trauma and Recovery: The Aftermath of Violence – From Domestic Abuse to Political Terror*. New York: Basic Books.

Hessler, Peter. 2001. *River Town*. London: John Murray.

—— 2006. *Oracle Bones: A Journey between China's Past and Present*. New York: HarperCollins.

—— 2010. *Country Driving: A Chinese Road Trip*. Edinburgh, Canongate.

Hobsbawm, E. J. 1994. *Age of Extremes: The Short Twentieth Century 1914–1991*. London: Michael Joseph.

Huang, JR-Tsang et al. 2003. 'The Inequality of Regional Economic Development in China between 1991 and 2001'. *Journal of Chinese Economic and Business Studies* Vol. 1(3) pp.273–285.

Hudson, Valerie M. and Den Boer, Andrea M. 2005. 'Missing Women and Bare Branches: Gender Balance and Conflict' *ECSP Report,* Issue 11 pp.20–24.

Hussey, Christopher. 1927. *The Picturesque: Studies in a Point of View.* London: G.P. Putnam.

Hutton, Will. 2007. *The Writing on the Wall: China and the West in the 21st Century.* London: Little, Brown.

Hvistendahl, Mara. 2011. *Unnatural Selection: Choosing Boys over Girls, and the Consequences of a World Full of Men.* New York: Public Affairs.

Jacques, Martin. 2009. *When China Rules the World: The Rise of the Middle Kingdom and the End of the Western World.* London: Allen Lane.

Jiang, Rong. 2008. *Wolf Totem* (trans. Goldblatt, Howard). London: Hamish Hamilton.

Jiang, Zhongyi. 2007. The Role of 'Two Exemptions and One Subsidy' Policy in Alleviating Poverty in Rural China'. http://conferences.ifpri.org/2020Chinaconference/pdf/014JiangZhongyi.pdf: International Food Policy Research Institute and Rural Policy Research Centre under the Ministry of Agriculture, 2010

Judt, Tony. 2009 [2008]. *Reappraisals: Recollections on the Forgotten Twentieth Century.* London: Vintage.

Karlsson, Sune et al. 2007. 'FDI and Job Creation in China'. *IFN Working Paper No. 723.* Stockholm: Research Institute of Industrial Economics.

Keidel, Albert. 2006. 'China's Social Unrest: The Story behind the Stories'. *Carnegie Endowment for International Peace Policy Brief* No. 48.

Kissinger, Henry. 2011. *On China.* London: Allen Lane.

Klotzbücher Sascha et al. 2010. 'What is New in the "New Rural Co-operative Medical System"? *China Quarterly* Vol. 201 pp.38–57.

Kochhar, Geeta. 2008. 'China's Urban Poor: An Expanding Social Stratum'. *Discussion Paper 37.* Nottingham: University of Nottingham China Policy Institute.

Kynge, James. 2006. *China Shakes the World: The Rise of a Hungry Nation.* London: Weidenfeld and Nicholson.

Lai Hongyi, Wang, Zhengxu and Tok, Sow Keat. 2007. 'China's Politics in 2006: Harmony on the Road to the 17th Party Congress. *Briefing Series – Issue 17.* Nottingham: University of Nottingham China Policy Institute.

Lam, Willy Wo-Lap. 2006. *Chinese Politics in the Hu Jintao Era: New Leaders, New Challenges.* Armonk, NY: M.E. Sharpe.

—— 2010. 'Xi Jinping's Chongqing Tour: Gang of Princelings Gains Clout'. *China Brief* Vol. 10(25).

Laven, Mary. 2011. *Mission to China: Matteo Riccci and the Jesuit Encounter with the East.* London: Faber and Faber.

Lee Ching Kwan. 2007. *Against the Law: Labor Protests in China's Rustbelt and Sunbelt.* Berkeley, CA: University of California Press.

Leisering, Lutz, Sen, Gong and Hussain, Athar. 2002. *People's Republic of China: Old-Age Pensions for the Rural Areas: From Land Reform to Globalization.* Manila: Asian Development Bank.

Leonard, Mark. 2008. *What Does China Think?* London: Fourth Estate.

Li Bingqin and Piachaud, David. 2004. 'Poverty and Inequality and Social Policy in China'. *CASEpaper* No. 87. London School of Economics Centre for Analysis of Social Exclusion.

Li Yiyun. 2009. *The Vagrants.* New York: Random House.

Li Lianjiang and O'Brien, Kevin J. 2008. 'Protest Leadership in Rural China'. *China Quarterly* Vol. 193 pp.1–23.

Liu Zeyun and Yuan Liansheng. 2007 [2006]. 'The Ratio of Public Investment in Education in China'. *Frontiers of Education in China* Vol. 2(2) pp.240–249.

Lomborg, Bjørn. 1998. *The Skeptical Environmentalist: Measuring the Real State of the World*. Cambridge: Cambridge University Press.

Lou Jiwei and Wang Shuilin (eds). 2008. *Public Finance in China: Reform and Growth for a Harmonious Society*. Washington, DC: The World Bank.

Lu Lin and Wang Xi. 2008. 'Drug Addiction in China'. *Addiction Reviews 2008, Annals of the New York Academy of Sciences* Vol. 1141 pp.304–317.

Lu Xun. 2009. *The Real Story of Ah-Q and Other Tales of Chnia: The Complete Fiction of Lu Xun* (trans. Lovell, Julia). London: Penguin.

Ma Jian. 2009. *Beijing Coma*. London: Vintage.

McGregor, Richard. 2010. *The Party: The Secret World of China's Communist Rulers*. London: Allen Lane.

Mei Hong and Wang Xiaolin. 2006. *China's Budget System and the Financing of Education and Health Services for Children* Hodges, Anthony (ed.). Beijing: United Nations Children's Fund and Office of the National Working Committee on Children and Women under the State Council.

Meisner Maurice. 2007. *Mao Zedong: A Political and Intellectual Portrait*. Cambridge: Polity.

Mencius. 2004 [1970]. *Mencius*. (trans. Lau, D.C.) London: Penguin Classics.

Micklethwaite, John and Woolridge, Adrian. *God is Back: How the Global Rise of Faith is Changing the World*. London: Penguin.

Mitter, Rana. 2004. *A Bitter Revolution: China's Struggle with the Modern World*. Oxford: Oxford University Press.

Nathan, Andrew J. and Gilley, Bruce (eds). 2003 [2002]. *China's New Rulers: The Secret Files*. London: Granta.

Nathan, Andrew J. and Link, Perry (eds) 2002. *The Tiananmen Papers*. Compiled by Zhang, Liang. London: Abacus.

National Population and Family Planning Commission of China. 2010. *China Statistical Yearbook*. Beijing: National Population and Family Planning Commission of China.

Nilekani, Nandan. 2008. *Imagining India: Ideas for the New Century*. Delhi: Allen Lane.

Obrist, Hans Ulrich. 2011. *Ai Weiwei Speaks with Hans Ulrich Obrist*. London: Penguin.

Office of the Secretary of Defense. *Annual Report to Congress: Military and Security Developments Involving the People's Republic of China 2011*. Washington, DC: Office of the Secretary of Defense.

Ownby, David. 2008. *Falun Gong and the Future of China*. Oxford: Oxford University Press.

Pakula, Hannah. 2010. *The Last Empress: Madame Chiang Kai-Shek and the Birth of Modern China*. London: Weidenfeld and Nicholson.

Palmer, James. 2012. The Death of Mao: The Tangshan Earthquake and the Birth of New China. Faber and Faber.

Pan, Philip. 2009. *Out of Mao's Shadow: The Struggle for the Soul of a New China*. London: Picador.

Pew Forum, The. 2008. *Religion in China on the Eve of the 2008 Beijing Olympics*. http://pewforum.org/Importance-of-Religion/Religion-in-China-on-the-Eve-of-the-2008-Beijing-Olympics.aspx: Pew Research Center.

Philips, Michael R. et al. 2009. 'Prevalence, Treatment, and Associated Disability of Mental Disorders in Four Provinces in China during 2001–05: An Epidemiological Survey'. *The Lancet* Vol. 373 (9680) pp.2041–2053.

Rabinovitch, Simon. 'China acts to solve provincial debt crisis', *Financial Times*, 13 February 2012.

Ravallion, Martin. 2009. 'A Comparative Perspective on Poverty Reduction in Brazil, China and India'. *Policy Research Working Paper 5080*. Washington, DC: The World Bank.

Ravallion, Martin and Chen, Shaohua. 2004. 'How Have the World's Poorest Fared since the Early 1980s'? *World Bank Research Observer*, Vol. 19(2) pp.141–169.

—— 2007. 'China's (Uneven) Progress against Poverty'. *Journal of Development Economics* Vol. 82(1) pp.1–42.

Reid, Michael. 2007. *Forgotten Continent: The Battle for Latin America's Soul*. New Haven, CT: Yale University Press.

Riley, Nancy E. 'China's Population: New Trends and Challenges'. *Population Bulletin* Vol. 59(2). Washington, DC: Population Reference Bureau.

Rozelle, Scott, Zhang Linxiu and Huang Jikun. 2000. 'China's War on Poverty'. *Working Paper* No. 60. Stanford, CA: Center for Research on Economic Development and Policy Reform.

Sang Ye. 2006. *China Candid: The People on the People's Republic*. Barthé, Geremie and Lang, Miriam (eds). Berkeley, CA: University of California Press.

Saunders, Peter. 2007. 'Comparing Poverty among Older People in Urban China Internationally'. *China Quarterly* 190, pp.451–465.

Schell, Orville and Shambaugh, David (eds). 1999. *The China Reader: The Reform Era*. New York: Vintage.

Scott, James C. 1985. *Weapons of the Weak: Everyday Forms of Resistance*. Newhaven, CT: Yale University Press.

Seagrave, Stirling. 1985. *The Soong Dynasty*. New York: Harper and Row.

Shambaugh, David. 2005. *Modernizing China's Military: Progress, Problems and Prospects*. Berkeley, CA: University of California Press.

—— 2008. *China's Communist Party: Atrophy and Adaptation*. Washington, DC: Woodrow Wilson Center Press/Berkeley, CA: University of California Press.

Shang Xiayuan and Wu Xiaoming. 2004. 'Changing Approaches of Social Protection: Social Assistance Reform in Urban China'. *Social Policy & Society* Vol. 3 pp.259–271.

Shirk, Susan L. 2007. *China Fragile Superpower: How China's Internal Politics Could Derail its Peaceful Rise*. Oxford: Oxford University Press.

Shirk, Susan L. (ed.) 2011. *Changing Media, Changing China*. Oxford: Oxford University Press.

Singh, Arvinder. 2006. 'Labor Mobility in China and India: The Role of Hukou, Caste, and Community', in *China and India: Learning From Each Other: Reforms and Policies for Sustained Growth*. Aziz, Jahangir, Dunaway, Steven and Prasad, Eswar (eds). Washington, DC: International Monetary Fund.

Spence, Jonathan D. 1991 [1990]. *The Search for Modern China*. New York: Norton.

Spufford, Francis. 2010. *Red Plenty*. London: Faber and Faber.

Spurling, Hilary. 2010. *Burying the Bones: Pearl Buck in China*. London: Profile.

State Council. 1999. 'The Regulation of Minimum Living Security for Urban Residents (3)', in *Collected Documents on Urban Minimum Living Security*. Bureau of Disaster and Social Relief (ed.). Beijing: Bureau of Disaster and Social Relief.

Stern, Nicholas. 2010. *A Blueprint for a Safer Planet: How We Can Save the World and Create Prosperity*. London: Vintage.

Taipei Fine Arts Museum at the 54th Venice Biennale. 2011. *The Heard and the Unheard – Soundscape Taiwan*. Guidebook to the Exhibition. Taipei: Taipei Fine Arts Museum.

Tooley, James. 2009. *The Beautiful Tree*. Washington, DC: Cato Institute.

Tsang, Steve. 2010. 'Consultative Leninism: China's New Political Framework?' *Discussion Paper 58*. Nottingham: University of Nottingham China Policy Institute.

UNDP (United Nations Development Program). 2008. *China Human Development Report 2007/2008: Access For All: Basic Public Services for 1.3 Billion People*. Beijing: China Translation and Publishing Corporation.

—— 2010. *Human Development Report 2010: The Real Wealth of Nations*. New York: UNDP.

UNESCO (United Nations Educational, Scientific and Cultural Organization) Institute for Statistics. 2009. *Global Education Digest: Comparing Education Statistics across the World*. Montreal: UNESCO.

UNFPA (United Nations Population Fund). 2006. *Population Ageing in China – Facts and Figures*. Beijing: UNFPA.

—— 2007. *UNFPA Annual Report 2006*. New York: UNFPA.

Van Schaik, Sam. 2011. *Tibet: A History*. New Haven, CT: Yale University Press.

Walter, Carl E. and Howie, Fraser J. T. 2011. *Red Capitalism: The Fragile Financial Foundation of China's Extraordinary Rise*. Singapore: John Wiley (Asia).

Wang Hui 1998. 'Contemporary Chinese Thought and the Question of Modernity' *Social Text* Vol. 16(2) pp.9–44.

—— 2009. *The End of the Revolution: China and the Limits of Modernity*. London: Verso.

Wasserstrom, Jeffrey N. 2010. *China in the 21st Century. What Everyone Needs to Know*. Oxford: Oxford University Press.

Watts, Jonathan. 2010. *When a Billion Chinese Jump: How China Will Save Mankind – or Destroy it*. London: Faber and Faber.

Whyte, Martin King. 2010. *Myth of the Social Volcano: Perceptions of Inequality and Disruptive Injustice in Contemporary China*. Stanford, CA: Stanford University Press.

Wilson, William Julius. 1996. *When Work Disappears: The World of the New Urban Poor*. New York: Knopf.

Wilson, Dominic and Purushothaman, Roopa. 2003. 'Dreaming with BRICs: The Path to 2050'. *Global Economics Paper* No.99. www.gs.com: Goldman Sachs.

Woetzel et al. 2009. *Preparing for China's Urban Billion*. New York: McKinsey Global Institute.

Wood, Frances. 2007. *The First Emperor of China*. London: Profile.

World Bank 1996. *World Development Report: From Plan to Market*. Oxford: Oxford University Press/The World Bank.

—— 2001. *China: Overcoming Rural Poverty*. Washington, DC: The World Bank.

Wright, Patrick. 2010. *Passport to Peking: A Very British Mission to Mao's China*. Oxford: Oxford University Press.

Wu Bin and Zheng Yongnian. 2008. 'A Long March to Improve Labour Standards in China: Chinese Debates on the New Labour Contract Law'. *Briefing Series – Issue 39*. Nottingham: University of Nottingham China Policy Institute.

Wu Hung. 2003. *Rong Rong's East Village 1993–1998*. Chicago: Art Media Resources.

Wu Yangrui, Wang Zhengxu and Luo Dan. 2009. 'China's Investment Record and its Fiscal Stimulus Package'. *Briefing Series – Issue 50*. Nottingham: Nottingham University China Policy Institute.

Xinran. 2003 [2002]. *The Good Women of China* (trans. Tyldesley, Esther). London, Vintage.

—— 2007. *Miss Chopsticks* (trans. Tyldesley, Esther). London: Chatto and Windus.

—— 2009 [2008]. *China Witness: Voices from a Silent Generation*. London: Vintage.

—— 2010. *Message from an Unknown Chinese Mother: Stories of Loss and Love*. London: Chatto and Windus.

Yan Xuetong. 2011. *Ancient Chinese Thought: Modern Chinese Power*. Bell, Daniel A. and Sun, Zhe (eds) (trans. Ryden, Edmund). Princeton: Princeton University Press.

Yang Xiushi and Xia Guomei. 2010. 'Causes and Consequences of Increasing Club Drug Use in China: A Descriptive Assessment'. *Substance Use and Misuse*. Vol. 45 1–2 pp.224–239.

Yao Shujie, Wu Bin and Su Fang. 2008. 'The Impact of Higher Education Expansion on Social Justice in China: A Spatial and Intertemporal Analysis'. *Discussion Paper 34*. Nottingham: University of Nottingham China Policy Institute.

Yip, Paul S. F. and Liu Ka Y. 2006. 'The Ecological Fallacy and the Gender Ratio of Suicide in China'. *British Journal of Psychiatry* Vol. 189 pp.465–466.

Young, Michael and Lemos, Gerard. 1997. *The Communities We Have Lost and Can Regain*. London: Lemos and Crane.

Yu Dan. 2009. *Confucius from the Heart: Ancient Wisdom for Today's World* (trans. Tyldesley, Esther). London: Pan.

Yu Jianrong. 2007. 'Social Conflict in Rural China'. *China Security* Vol. 3(2) pp.2–17. World Security Institute.

Zhang Hong. 2007. 'From Resisting to "Embracing?" the One Child Rule: Understanding New Fertility Trends in a Central China Village'. *China Quarterly* 192: 855–875.

Zhang Xinxin and Sang Ye. 1987. *Chinese Lives: An Oral History of Contemporary China.* Jenner, W.J.F. et al. (eds and trans.). New York: Pantheon.

Zhao Chengzheng et al. 2004. 'Drug Abuse in China'. *Current Status of Drug Dependence/ Abuse Studies: Cellular and Molecular Mechanisms of Drugs of Abuse and Neurotoxicity, Annals of the New York Academy of Sciences* Vol. 1025 pp.439–445.

Zhao Ziyang. 2009. *Prisoner of the State: The Secret Diary of Chinese Premier Zhao Ziyang* (trans. Bao Pu, Chiang, Renee and Ignatius, Adi). London: Simon and Schuster.

Zheng Yongnian. 2006. *Hu Jintao Firmly in Command. The Sixth Plenum of the 15th Central Committee of the Chinese Communist Party.* Nottingham: University of Nottingham China Policy Institute.

—— 2007. 'Hu Jintao's Road Map to China's Future'. *Briefing Series – Issue 28.* Nottingham: University of Nottingham China Policy Institute.

Zhu Keliang et al. 2006. 'The Rural Land Question in China: Analysis and Recommendation based on a Seventeen-Province Survey'. *Journal of International Law and Politics* Vol. 38(4) pp.761–839.

Zhu Keliang and Prosterman, Roy. 2007. 'Securing Land Rights for Chinese Farmers *A Leap Forward for Stability and Growth'. Center for Global Liberty and Prosperity Development Policy Analysis* No. 3. Washington, DC: Cato Institute.

Zissis, Carin and Bajoria, Jayshree, 'China's Environmental Crisis, 4 August 2008, Council on Foreign Relations.

INDEX